THE STATES AND THE NATION SERIES, of which this volume is a part, is designed to assist the American people in a serious look at the ideals they have espoused and the experiences they have undergone in the history of the nation. The content of every volume represents the scholarship, experience, and opinions of its author. The costs of writing and editing were met mainly by grants from the National Endowment for the Humanities, a federal agency. The project was administered by the American Association for State and Local History, a nonprofit learned society, working with an Editorial Board of distinguished editors, authors, and historians, whose names are listed below.

D1435869

Vermont

A History

Charles T. Morrissey

**With a Historical Guide
prepared by the editors of
the American Association for
State and Local History**

W. W. Norton & Company
New York · London

American Association for State and Local History
Nashville

Copyright © 1984, 1981
American Association for State and Local History
All rights reserved
Published and distributed by W. W. Norton & Company, Inc.
500 Fifth Avenue
New York, New York 10110

Library of Congress Cataloging in Publication Data
Morrissey, Charles T
  Vermont, a history.
  (The States and the Nation series)
  Bibliography: p.
  Includes index.
  1. Vermont—History. 1. Title. II. Series:
States and the Nation series.
F49.M67   1981   974.3   80-21296

ISBN: 978-0-393-30223-3

Printed in the United States of America

3 4 5 6 7 8 9 0

For Michael C. Morrissey
and Susan K. Morrissey;
Vermont is in your sinews, too
—like it or not.

Contents

Historical Guide

TO VERMONT

prepared by the editors of the
American Association for State and Local History

Introduction

The following pages offer the reader a guide to places in this state through which its history still lives.

This section lists and describes museums with collections of valuable artifacts, historic houses where prominent people once lived, and historic sites where events of importance took place. In addition, we have singled out for detailed description a few places that illustrate especially well major developments in this state's history or major themes running through it, as identified in the text that follows. The reader can visit these places to experience what life was like in earlier times and learn more about the state's rich and exciting heritage.

James B. Gardner and Timothy C. Jacobson, professional historians on the staff of the American Association for State and Local History, prepared this supplementary material, and the association's editors take sole responsibility for the selection of sites and their descriptions. Nonetheless, thanks are owed to many individuals and historical organizations, including those listed, for graciously providing information and advice. Our thanks also go to the National Endowment for the Humanities, which granted support for the writing and editing of this supplement, as it did for the main text itself.   —*The Editors*

Old Constitution House

Windsor

★ In 1791 Vermont be-
came the nation's fourteenth
state, the first to join the
original union of thirteen. The
new state's tardiness in joining the young republic did not
indicate any lack of patriotic
zeal but rather reflected the
tangle of maneuvers, threats,
and negotiations that had
complicated the would-be
state's status. Indeed, for the
fourteen years prior to
achieving statehood, Ver-
mont functioned as a separate
independent republic, refusing to yield to British allegiance but unwilling to accept its neighbors' claims to
jurisdiction. The constitution

Elijah West's tavern

of this "Free and Independent Republic of Vermont" was adopted on
July 8, 1777, at a tavern in Windsor. Now preserved as the Old Constitution House, this historic structure commemorates the struggle for
independence and identity in eigheenth-century Vermont.

Between 1750 and 1764, Benning Wentworth, the royal governor
of New Hampshire, made grants of nearly three million acres of land
in the region west of the Connecticut River and north of Massachusetts. His actions proved highly controversial and provoked decades of
dispute between the local residents and the governments of New
Hampshire, New York, and Massachusetts. The settlers who obtained
the land from Wentworth's grantees in the 1760s staunchly defended
the legality of the New Hampshire official's actions despite the questionable nature of that colony's claim to jurisdiction over the region.
In fact, New York clearly had the stronger case and attempted in the

late 1760s and early 1770s to secure control over the area that had become identified as the Hampshire Grants (or, simply, the Grants). To counter those actions, Ethan Allen organized the settlers in 1770 to protect their titles. Known as the Green Mountain Boys, this organization took the lead in pushing for the independence of the Hampshire Grants from any other colonial government.

The quarrel between the Grants and New York continued right up to the Revolution. When Allen and his men captured the British Fort Ticonderoga in 1775 shortly after Lexington and Concord, they acted less out of rebel zeal than from a desire to maintain a strong bargaining position with both the patriots and the crown. Meeting at Dorset in January 1776, representatives of the Grants decided to support the Revolution—but not at the cost of yielding autonomy to either New York or New Hampshire. So instead of joining the Continental Congress, the Grants declared its independence in a convention at Westminister on January 16, 1777 and adopted the name "New Connecticut."

On June 4, 1777, seventy-two delegates convened at Windsor to frame a constitution for the new republic. Dr. Thomas Young, a radical patriot from Philadelphia and close friend of Ethan Allen, sent the convention a copy of the Pennsylvania Constitution, apparently hoping they would follow suit and produce a truly revolutionary document. Young also suggested a different name—Vermont. The delegates were amenable to both suggestions. When they convened on July 2 at Elijah West's tavern, they framed a constitution much like that of Pennsylvania but with two unique features: the prohibition of slavery and the establishment of universal manhood suffrage. On July 8, 1777, the day after the only Revolutionary War battle on Vermont soil, the delegates adopted the new constitution and referred it to the voters for ratification. Despite some questionable aspects of the vote, the constitution was ratified the following March, and Vermont became an independent republic—a status it retained until 1791, when it was admitted to the United States.

Elijah West's tavern was still relatively new when the constitutional convention met there in July 1777. The two-story clapboard structure was erected apparently around 1775 for use as a tavern and continued as such until about 1848. After that it housed retail shops and small manufacturing and in 1870 was converted into tenement housing. By

1914 it was used as a warehouse. In that year, William M. Evarts and
the Old Constitution House Association rescued the historic structure
and moved it to its present site. The Association restored the building
and operated it until 1960, when the property was deeded to the State
of Vermont. Collections on exhibit include eighteenth- and nineteenth-
century furniture, American paintings and prints, and Vermontiana.

Now known as the Old Constitution House, Elijah West's tavern
was once the scene of one of the most significant meetings in Vermont
history. Truly this site merits the cherished nickname ''Birthplace of
Vermont.''

Shelburne Museum

Shelburne

★ The Shelburne Museum
in the northwestern part of
Vermont brings together an
amazing array of objects and
structures that reflect the variety of the state's historical
experience. Electra Have-
meyer Webb, who founded
the museum in 1947 with her

Dorset House

husband J. Watson Webb, wrote that she hoped the museum ''would
depict the manner of living in Vermont . . . during the early days and
that the buildings and the collections housed therein would show the
fine craftsmanship and ingenuity of our forefathers.'' The museum's
thirty-five historic structures and ''collection of collections'' ably ful-
fill Mrs. Webb's expectations and provide the visitor with an extraordinary opportunity to learn about the culture and society of the Green
Mountain State.

The Webbs reportedly decided to establish the Shelburne Museum
in order to preserve a Webb family carriage collection, but equally
important was Mrs. Webb's interest in opening to the public her own
extensive collections of art and Americana. Regardless of which initially motivated the project, the two needs led to a common solution—

a museum. The couple purchased an eight-acre lot in the Burlington-Shelburne area, where the Webb family country estate was located. Weed House, a two-story brick structure standing on the property, became the museum's first gallery. Then a new structure, a great horseshoe-shaped barn, was erected to house the carriage collection. The first year, the Webbs also moved to the property a one-room schoolhouse, erected in 1830 at Vergennes, Vermont. Badly deteriorated when they found it, the structure was rebuilt and restored to its nineteenth-century appearance. Although not the original intention of the couple, the preservation and restoration of other similarly endangered historic structures became one of the museum's central missions in the decade that followed.

The Shelburne Museum complex now encompasses thirty-five structures in a forty-five-acre parklike setting. They range in age and style from an eighteenth-century Massachusetts saltbox to the Greek Revival-style Electra Havemeyer Webb Memorial Building, opened in 1967. Within the restored and reconstructed buildings, visitors can view one of the most important collections of American folk art in the world. Collections include quilts and textiles, hunting decoys, advertising signs and figures, weathervanes, hand tools, toys and dolls, as well as fine furniture and art from all over the world. Of particular interest are the structures and objects with Vermont origins, for they provide invaluable insight into how Vermonters lived in the past.

The majority of Shelburne's historic structures were relocated there from elsewhere in Vermont. The oldest residence is the Dutton House, a saltbox erected in 1782 in Cavendish. When discovered in 1949, it had survived almost unaltered. Now reconstructed and restored, it houses a collection of furniture typical of that accumulated by a family over successive generations. In contrast, the Vermont House, erected at nearby Shelburne in 1790, contains period rooms furnished with fine American Queen Anne and Chippendale furniture, as would have been typical of a retired sea captain's home. A third and quite different example of Vermont housing is the Sawyer's Cabin, a crude structure built about 1800 with square-hewn logs, typical of early settlers' dwellings in the northwestern timber region. The Little Stone Cottage was only a bare stone shell when discovered in South Burlington in 1947, but it has been skilfully reconstructed and furnished as a typical farm family home in mid-nineteenth-century Vermont. A final example of a Vermont residence is the Dorset House, a Greek Revival frame structure built in 1840 in East Dorset and now housing the museum's exceptional decoy collection.

The Shelburne Museum complex includes a variety of nonresidential structures as well. Typical of small-town Vermont are the Vergennes School; the Charlotte Meeting House, a Methodist church erected at Charlotte in 1840; the Stagecoach Inn, also from Charlotte and dating from 1783; the Tuckaway General Store and Apothecary Shop, erected in 1840 and now standing only a quarter-mile from its original site; the Castleton Jail, a slate and brick structure dating from 1890; and the Up and Down Sawmill, originally constructed at South Royalton in 1787. Particularly intriguing are the structures and collections associated with transportation. The museum was founded to preserve a carriage collection, and thus it is fitting that the complex includes a blacksmith and wheelwright shop complete with a forge, tools, shoeing frame, and wagon patterns just as it had in 1800 when it was erected at nearby Shelburne. Visitors to this structure can see artisans demonstrating nineteenth-century blacksmithing. Another structure associated with travel is a covered bridge originally constructed in 1845 across the Lamoille River at Cambridge. Shelburne acquired it in 1949 when the state Department of Highways decided to replace it, and it now provides a picturesque entrance to the museum.

More modern technological advances have not been neglected either. One of the museum's most popular structures is the *S.S. Ticonderoga,* the last remaining example of a vertical-beam side-paddle steamboat. Designed for the luxury tourist trade, the *Ti* was built in 1906 at the Shelburne Shipyard and traveled Lake Champlain for forty-seven years before its retirement and restoration at the museum in the mid-1950s. Near the historic steamboat stands the Colchester Reef Lighthouse, a substantial frame structure that stood guard in Lake Champlain for eighty-one years before the museum acquired it in 1952. And of course, there is the railroad. Visitors can tour the Shelburne Depot, built in 1890 by Webb's father, Dr. W. Seward Webb, then president of the Rutland Railroad. Under a nearby shed stands the *Grand Isle,* a luxurious private railroad car built about 1890 by the Wagner Palace Car Company (of which Dr. Webb was also president) and presented to Edward C. Smith, the governor of Vermont at that time.

Many of the collections also contain objects with Vermont origins, including quilts, hooked rugs, weathervanes, folk sculpture, painted furniture, paintings, and farming and homemaking implements. These collections and the historic structures together depict the folk culture of early Vermont.

In addition to tours the Shelburne sponsors public lectures, school field trips, and a variety of other programs. Open from mid-May through mid-October, the museum brings together the varieties of the Vermont experience.

Calvin Coolidge Homestead

Plymouth Notch

★ The peaceful, orderly transfer of political power—a rare process at many times and in many places—fortunately is a well-established habit in the United States. Ever since Thomas Jefferson succeeded John Adams as president in 1801, political parties and presidential aspirants have cycled in and out of office in obedience to the will of the electorate. In America the opposition has been a loyal opposition; only once, in 1860 and 1861, did a significant number of Americans conclude that the price of loyalty was too high.

Coolidge Homestead

The office of vice president was provided to protect against disruption in the executive branch. Elected at the same time (and since 1804 on the same party ticket) as the president, the vice president stands ready to serve in the event of the sudden death or incapacity of the president. Provision for such an office was a wise precaution, and over the history of the Republic several vice presidents have thus constitutionally inherited the presidency. John Tyler was the first, when William Henry Harrison died just a month after taking office in 1841.

More famously, Andrew Johnson succeeded the murdered Abraham Lincoln in 1865; likewise Lyndon Johnson followed John Kennedy nearly a century later. In between, there were others. Assassins' bullets also made presidents of Chester A. Arthur in 1881 and Theodore Roosevelt in 1901. In 1945, when a cerebral hemorrhage claimed the life of Franklin D. Roosevelt, Harry Truman stood in line for the job. In 1923, when Warren G. Harding died suddenly in San Francisco, Vermont's Calvin Coolidge was that man.

"Vermont is a state I love," Coolidge wrote near the end of his presidency, expressing in typically few words one of his abiding feelings. It is appropriate therefore that his own small part of Vermont has been preserved today. Plymouth Notch Historic District is an excellent example of a late-nineteenth- and early-twentieth-century rural village. Coolidge's boyhood home, however, made it famous. While the boyhood homes of many other presidents have also been preserved, only at Coolidge's did the boyhood and the presidency so dramatically come together. In this white clapboard house, where his family had moved in 1876, Vice President Coolidge became President Coolidge forty-seven years later.

John Coolidge, Calvin's father, bought the house with several acres and the blacksmith shop across the street for $375. ("He was a good trader," Calvin later remarked.) The elder Coolidge was something of a model versatile Vermonter—selectman, road commissioner, school teacher, deputy sheriff, justice of the peace, legislator, agent for Dun and Bradstreet, among other things—and was much admired by his son. He was also long-lived, and he lived the balance of his eighty-one years in this house. Calvin also remembered his mother with great affection, perhaps in part because he lost her when he was a boy of twelve. Just five years later, in 1889, his young sister Abigail died in the same room, a victim of appendicitis. But grief, like other emotions, was something that the quiet Vermonter kept locked tightly within himself. He also was to lose one of his own sons, Calvin, Jr., while in the White House.

The house was an excellent place to spend a boyhood and later a vacation, but unlike his father Calvin Coolidge sought his future and fortune in the larger world beyond Vermont. In this, he was joining the long line of people who for years were Vermont's chief export. As New England's agricultural prosperity declined and as cities and industries grew up elsewhere, thousands of young and not-so-young Vermonters left their native state in search of a better life elsewhere. Diligent and hard-working folk, many of them found it. In the process, they educated other Americans in steady Vermont virtues. From a stern faith and a hard land they had learned that from self-control and self-reliance comes self-respect. Of such virtues there was no better representative than Calvin Coolidge.

He went to school at Amherst College, one of the country's finest, and in the late 1890s practiced law in Northampton, Massachusetts. But then this reticent man took to the public life. Joining the Republican party, he served in the Massachusetts General Court (legislature) in 1907 and 1908, was mayor of Northampton in 1910 and 1911, and was state senator from 1912 to 1915. His political fortunes rose steadily; by 1916 he was lieutenant governor of Massachusetts, by 1919 governor. In that office Coolidge first gained national attention by his firm handling of the Boston police strike in 1919. In 1920 the Republican national convention chose him as Warren G. Harding's running mate.

The theme of Harding's front porch campaign that year was "return to normalcy," and the voters, weary from the great domestic and foreign crusades of the Wilson years, responded with an overwhelming mandate. As the "roaring twenties" began, the Republicans were swept into office, Calvin Coolidge with them. But though its beginning was propitious, the Harding administration was a sad one. Some of Harding's cabinet appointments were excellent (Herbert Hoover as Secretary of Commerce; Charles Evans Hughes as Secretary of State), but others were disastrous. His attorney general, Harry M. Daugherty, and his secretary of the interior, Albert B. Fall, involved the administration in major scandals involving violation of the prohibition statutes and the lease of naval oil reserves to private interests. The president was probably innocent of any direct complicity, but the burden of his friends' misdeeds fell heavily on him. When he died suddenly in August 1923, he was a sad and tragic figure.

Vice President Calvin Coolidge was his successor. Never close to Harding's "Ohio Gang," Coolidge was untouched by scandal. Indeed, his reputation for probity helped put the country and the government on a new and steadier path. He was elected in his own right in 1924, a year that found the Democratic opposition in disarray and a major third-party campaign mounted by Robert La Follette's Progressives. Running on a platform of lower taxes and reduced government expenditure, Coolidge and the Republicans won handily. The balmy days of the "Coolidge Prosperity" followed, with the quiet man from Plymouth Notch quietly presiding over a country contentedly at peace abroad and contentedly pursing its own business at home.

Neither Coolidge nor anybody else knew that it would not last, but happily for him the blame for the dark times ahead fell on others. Though it was generally assumed that he would seek a second full term, Coolidge surprised the nation over a year before the election with this terse and famous announcement: "I do not choose to run for President in 1928." Publicly that was all he ever said, but what he said he truly meant. His reasons, this shy and private man kept safely hidden away. The sudden death of his son, Calvin, Jr., may have had something to do with it; perhaps too he simply had decided that his duty was done and it was time for others to take their turn. In retrospect, his timing was good. The unenviable title of "depression president" fell not on him but on his unfortunate successor, Herbert Hoover. Coolidge died in January 1933, two months before Franklin D. Roosevelt (who as a Democrat also had run for vice president in 1920) took office.

Coolidge was not unlike many Vermonters who left their native state for a larger life elsewhere. But he is the only Vermonter ever to have reached the White House. The presidency came to him in part by accident, and it came fittingly while he was in Vermont. When Harding died in August 1923, Coolidge was vacationing at the family homestead at Plymouth Notch. In the small hours of the morning of August 3, his father brought him the telegram with the news of the president's death. Legally, the peaceful succession had already taken place. But it was shortly confirmed when at 2:47 A.M., by lamplight, Coolidge took the presidential oath of office administered by his father, who among other things was a notary public. The next day he left by private train for Washington. The simple wooden house and the quiet little village that he left behind suddenly were different from all the others in Vermont. Coolidge always said that this was where he had come from and was the place he would return to. Ten years later he joined earlier generations of Coolidges in the Plymouth Cemetery just down the road.

Other Places of Interest

*The following suggest other places of
historical interest to visit. We recommend that
you check hours of operation in advance.*

AMERICAN PRECISION MUSEUM, *Windsor.* An industrial museum displaying machines from the period when New England produced the highest quality guns and other items in the country.

BENNINGTON BATTLE MONUMENT, *off U.S. 7 at Monument Circle, Bennington.* A 306-foot stone monolith and a diorama; commemorates the 1777 victory of Americans over the British.

BENNINGTON MUSEUM, *W. Main Street, Bennington.* Exhibits and art on Vermont and New England history, including "oldest Stars and Stripes," Bennington pottery, early American glass, Grandma Moses paintings and mementoes.

BRATTLEBORO MUSEUM AND ART CENTER, *Old Railroad Station, Brattleboro.* Photos, art, and Estey organs in a 1915 railroad station.

BROOKFIELD VILLAGE HISTORIC DISTRICT, *Brookfield.* Churches, houses, and commercial buildings from the 1800s, and an unusual floating pontoon bridge.

DISCOVERY MUSEUM, *51 Park Street, Essex Junction.* A children's museum, including natural history, in an 1850 school.

ETHAN ALLEN BURIAL PLACE, *Colchester Avenue, Burlington.* Cemetery and marble statue of the Revolutionary War hero.

EUREKA SCHOOLHOUSE, *Springfield.* A 1785 school, a covered bridge, and items from the period.

FAIRBANKS MUSEUM AND PLANETARIUM, *Main and Prospect streets, St. Johnsbury.* General museum, largely on natural history but with ethnological artifacts and toys, tools, furniture, and other material made in the region.

FARRAR-MANSUR HOUSE, *the Common, Weston.* House built about 1797 with museum of antiques, dolls, portraits.

FRANKLIN COUNTY MUSEUM, *St. Albans.* Local history items including maple exhibit and material on the Civil War raid on St. Albans, in a nineteenth-century school.

GENERAL JOHN STRONG MANSION, *state 17, Addison*. Elegant 1795 brick house with many period furnishings.

HILDENE, *Manchester*. Robert Todd Lincoln home, with items from the family of Abraham Lincoln.

HUBBARDTON BATTLEFIELD, *Castleton-Hubbardton Road and Old Military Road, Hubbardton*. Where Americans, including the Green Mountain Boys, fought a rear-guard action against the British in 1777; museum with an electronic re-creation of the battle.

JOSEPH SMITH MONUMENT, *state 14 east of Royalton*. Where the Mormon founder was born; museum and granite monument.

KENT TAVERN MUSEUM, *County Road, Calais*. Brick 1817 stage stop with attached country store in preserved rural setting; with Vermont furnishings, decorative arts, tools, and spinning and weaving rooms.

MATTESON TAVERN MUSEUM, *East Road, Shaftsbury*. Farmhouse and tavern built in the late 1700s, containing period furniture and agricultural and woodworking equipment.

MORRILL HOMESTEAD, *Strafford*. Seven outbuildings and Gothic Revival homestead of Justin Smith Morrill, congressman and senator who wrote the act establishing land-grant colleges; with original furnishings.

MOUNT INDEPENDENCE, *six miles west of Orwell off state 73-A*. Remains of Revolutionary War fortifications, including stockade, blockhouses, gun batteries, and hospital.

OLD STONE HOUSE, *Brownington*. Antique furniture, farm equipment, and household items in a large 1836 stone academy building.

PARK-McCULLOUGH HOUSE, *North Bennington*. General history museum in large Victorian house built in 1865; home of two governors.

ROKEBY, *U.S. 7, Ferrisburgh*. The home of author Rowland Robinson and a station on the underground railroad, built about 1784.

ROUND CHURCH, *Bridge Street and Cochran Road, Richmond*. Sixteen-sided clapboard church built 1812–1813, serving as community church and town meeting center.

RUTLAND HISTORICAL SOCIETY, *101 Center Street, Rutland*. Located in old bank building; changing exhibits on the development of the Rutland area.

ST. JOHNSBURY ATHENAEUM, *30 Main Street, St. Johnsbury*. Public library and art gallery with nineteenth-century works, predominately from the United States, in original nineteenth-century building.

SCOTT COVERED BRIDGE, *West River, state 30, Townsend*. Built in 1870, 165.7 feet long; called the longest single-span bridge of its type in the world.

SHELDON MUSEUM, *1 Park Street, Middlebury.* Nineteenth-century furnishings in an 1829 house.

VERMONT HISTORICAL SOCIETY, *Pavilion Building, Montpelier.* General Vermont history museum with pewter, furniture, glass, Indian artifacts, and other items; historical library.

VERMONT STATE HOUSE, *State Street, Montpelier.* Granite state capitol erected in 1859; contains paintings, portraits, and original furnishings, as well as a brass cannon captured from Hessians during the American Revolution.

WILLARD HOUSE, *Middlebury College campus, Middlebury.* House now the admissions office for Middlebury College; where Emma Willard opened a school with an innovative curriculum for women, 1814.

WOODSTOCK HISTORICAL MUSEUM, *26 Elm Street, Woodstock.* General museum in an 1807 house; with period furnishings, material on naturalist George Perkins Marsh, sculptor Hiram Powers, and United States Senator Jacob Collamer.

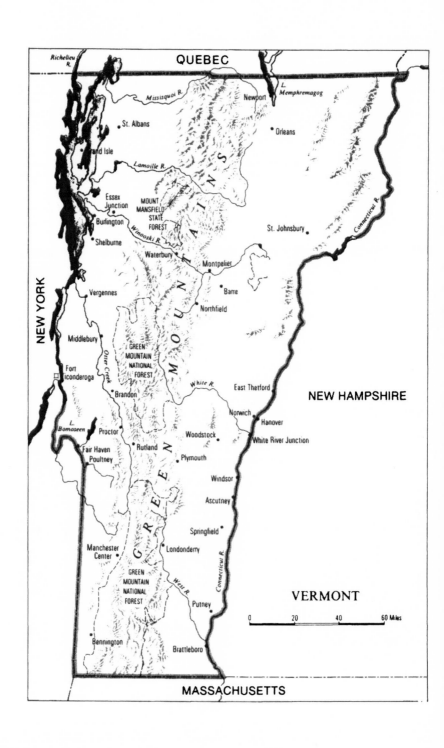

QUEBEC

Richelieu R.

Missisquoi R.

Newport

L. Memphremagog

St. Albans

Orleans

and Isle

Lamoille R.

Essex Junction

MOUNT MANSFIELD STATE FOREST

Burlington

Winooski R.

St. Johnsbury

Connecticut R.

Shelburne

Waterbury

Montpelier

Barre

NEW YORK

Vergennes

Northfield

M O U N T A I N S

Middlebury

GREEN MOUNTAIN NATIONAL FOREST

Otter Creek

Fort Ticonderoga

White R.

East Thetford

NEW HAMPSHIRE

Brandon

Norwich

Hanover

L. Bomoseen

Proctor

Woodstock

White River Junction

Fair Haven

Rutland

Plymouth

Poultney

Windsor

Ascutney

Springfield

Manchester Center

Londonderry

G R E E N

GREEN MOUNTAIN NATIONAL FOREST

West R.

Connecticut R.

Putney

VERMONT

0   20   40   60 Miles

Bennington

Brattleboro

MASSACHUSETTS

Invitation to the Reader

IN 1807, former President John Adams argued that a complete history of the American Revolution could not be written until the history of change in each state was known, because the principles of the Revolution were as various as the states that went through it. Two hundred years after the Declaration of Independence, the American nation has spread over a continent and beyond. The states have grown in number from thirteen to fifty. And democratic principles have been interpreted differently in every one of them.

We therefore invite you to consider that the history of your state may have more to do with the bicentennial review of the American Revolution than does the story of Bunker Hill or Valley Forge. The Revolution has continued as Americans extended liberty and democracy over a vast territory. John Adams was right: the states are part of that story, and the story is incomplete without an account of their diversity.

The Declaration of Independence stressed life, liberty, and the pursuit of happiness; accordingly, it shattered the notion of holding new territories in the subordinate status of colonies. The Northwest Ordinance of 1787 set forth a procedure for new states to enter the Union on an equal footing with the old. The Federal Constitution shortly confirmed this novel means of building a nation out of equal states. The step-by-step process through which territories have achieved self-government and national representation is among the most important of the Founding Fathers' legacies.

The method of state-making reconciled the ancient conflict between liberty and empire, resulting in what Thomas Jefferson called an empire for liberty. The system has worked and remains unaltered, despite enormous changes that have taken

place in the nation. The country's extent and variety now sur-
pass anything the patriots of '76 could likely have imagined.
The United States has changed from an agrarian republic into a
highly industrial and urban democracy, from a fledgling nation
into a major world power. As Oliver Wendell Holmes remarked
in 1920, the creators of the nation could not have seen completely how it and its constitution and its states would develop.
Any meaningful review in the bicentennial era must consider
what the country has become, as well as what it was.

The new nation of equal states took as its motto *E Pluribus
Unum*—"out of many, one." But just as many peoples have
become Americans without complete loss of ethnic and cultural
identities, so have the states retained differences of character.
Some have been superficial, expressed in stereotyped images—
big, boastful Texas, "sophisticated" New York, "hillbilly"
Arkansas. Other differences have been more real, sometimes instructively, sometimes amusingly; democracy has embraced
Huey Long's Louisiana, bilingual New Mexico, unicameral Ne-
braska, and a Texas that once taxed fortunetellers and spawned
politicians called "Woodpecker Republicans" and "Skunk
Democrats." Some differences have been profound, as when
South Carolina secessionists led other states out of the Union in
opposition to abolitionists in Massachusetts and Ohio. The result was a bitter Civil War.

The Revolution's first shots may have sounded in Lexington
and Concord; but fights over what democracy should mean and
who should have independence have erupted from Pennsylvania's Gettysburg to the "Bleeding Kansas" of John Brown,
from the Alamo in Texas to the Indian battles at Montana's
Little Bighorn. Utah Mormons have known the strain of isolation; Hawaiians at Pearl Harbor, the terror of attack; Georgians
during Sherman's march, the sadness of defeat and devastation.
Each state's experience differs instructively; each adds understanding to the whole.

The purpose of this series of books is to make that kind of understanding accessible, in a way that will last in value far
beyond the bicentennial fireworks. The series offers a volume
on every state, plus the District of Columbia—fifty-one, in all.

Each book contains, besides the text, a view of the state through eyes other than the author's—a "photographer's essay," in which a skilled photographer presents his own personal perceptions of the state's contemporary flavor. We have asked authors not for comprehensive chronicles, nor for research monographs or new data for scholars. Bibliographies and footnotes are minimal. We have asked each author for a summing up—interpretive, sensitive, thoughtful, individual, even personal—of what seems significant about his or her state's history. What distinguishes it? What has mattered about it, to its own people and to the rest of the nation? What has it come to now?

To interpret the states in all their variety, we have sought a variety of backgrounds in authors themselves and have encouraged variety in the approaches they take. They have in common only these things: historical knowledge, writing skill, and strong personal feelings about a particular state. Each has wide latitude for the use of the short space. And if each succeeds, it will be by offering you, in your capacity as a *citizen* of a state *and* of a nation, stimulating insights to test against your own.

James Morton Smith
General Editor

Preface

VERMONT is contrary country, and this book may be contrary to what many readers expect to find in it. First of all, in keeping with James Morton Smith's statement in his "Invitation to the Reader," this is not a comprehensive chronicle of Vermont's history, although I have tried to give historical explanations for the major features of life in Vermont into 1980. Nor is this a textbook in the conventional mode, nor a research monograph, nor a book solely for scholars. Instead, as one of fifty-one volumes in "The States and the Nation Series," I have tried to provide what Mr. Smith asked of each author—"a summing-up—interpretive, sensitive, thoughtful, individual, even personal—of what seems significant about his or her state's history." Some of the adjectives he uses are evident in this summing-up: this book is clearly "interpretive," "individual," and "even personal." To say it is "sensitive" and "thoughtful" may prompt guffaws from some readers, and they may justifiably volunteer other adjectives to describe it—like "disjointed" and "discursive."

I confess that this book is an ambling tour through Vermont's past and present, with digressions when the mountain vistas are appealing and asides where the details, like a secluded tuft of wildflowers, invite us to pause. As a tour guide I ramble as I amble. I also route readers past scenes and episodes which contrast with each other in order to juxtapose Vermont and its history against other places and their pasts, and also to emphasize how Vermont's present situation is a departure, in significant ways, from its heritage. The script is like Vermont itself—rocky and rolling, with many outcroppings—and at times we'll be bending through the underbrush in the valleys to get to the scenic mountaintops.

xxvii

Vermont has been a major part of my personal life for many years, as well as part of my professional life as a historian, writer, editor, teacher, and director of the Vermont Historical Society. Thus, when authors were approached to write volumes in this series, I was most attracted by the generosity of the proposal. "You are invited," read a statement circulated among us entitled "Some Guidelines For Authors," "to give your explanation in the form of an interpretive, even personal, essay, with all the freedom of selection that implies, with feeling for spirit and character as well as knowledge of fact and event, and with room for the anecdote that makes the point and the detail that gives the picture." That was like an invitation to go swimming in a cool Vermont pond on the hottest afternoon in summer. In responding to it I have drawn on my personal life and my professional life, and probably told anecdotes which obscure the points they were intended to make, and given details which overwhelm the picture I have tried to draw.

The main theme of this book is that Vermont is different from other states. To present this theme I have divided the narrative into four sections. Part One is a portrait of contemporary Vermont, emphasizing the characteristics which make this state a distinctive place in which to live. Part Two shows how today's Vermont is a product of its historical experiences, especially of the confused and complicated events which caused Vermont to become an independent republic two hundred years ago, and then brought it into the Union as the first state after the original thirteen. This section also emphasizes the differences between Vermont's historical development and the main trends of American history. Part Three is about the Vermont heritage as it was shaped during two hundred years of history, and how that heritage survives today. Part Four is a reckoning of Vermont's prospects for the future.

The major interpretation allied with this theme is that Vermonters are not adequately aware of their distinctiveness. This is partly because they don't know their own history and how it relates to the American story, and partly because, as residents of a bucolic and sparsely settled oasis in an urbanized and industrial nation, they don't realize that much of the rest of the

United States is different from Vermont. This means Vermonters live in a peculiar state (pun intended); in one sense their outlook and values prepare them well to deal with some of the deceits of the modern world; conversely, their heritage makes them innocent and vulnerable in dealing with the ugly features of American life which other states didn't—or couldn't—restrain.

This book is also about perceptions and historical consciousness, and this focus probably reflects my graduate training in American intellectual history under Henry F. May at the University of California at Berkeley, and my teaching of historiography at Berkeley and elsewhere. To understand how Vermonters have perceived themselves and the world beyond the Green Mountains, and how the world has perceived Vermont, can be as informative (if not more so) than a recounting of the chronological facts and events of Vermont's history. Similarly, to gauge how Vermonters have been conscious of their distinctive past is another way to sense their views of themselves and the worlds they live in.

All this is complicated by the fact that I have entwined Vermont's past and present with my personal perceptions of both, and this subjectivity will disappoint some people who would prefer a different kind of book. But this is the book I had churning in me, and this is the book I have written. It comes from a native New Englander; I'm not the first to say he was "born in Massachusetts, educated in New Hampshire, and found peace and contentment in Vermont." And I am one acquainted with Vermont: trying to understand this state has been my avocation as well as one of my vocations for twenty-seven years. But as an oral history consultant I have had the good fortune to travel widely in the United States, visiting forty-five other states in the last eight years. This travel has provided a view of Vermont from beyond its borders as well as within them. The result is a mood picture of Vermont—written by a moody observer.

Many people have helped enormously while I was trying to get this book out of my psyche, but none should be held accountable for what spills forth. The trustees of the Vermont Historical Society allowed me for six months to reduce my duties as director of the Vermont Historical Society to the less onerous task of editing *Vermont History,* its quarterly magazine, so I could give time to research for this volume, and for their assistance I am grateful. Characteristically, Laura ("Peggy") Abbott and her staff at the Library of the Vermont Historical Society in Montpelier have been invaluable, as has Vivian Bryan in the Vermont Department of Libraries next door. Librarians elsewhere have been helpful because I have used the Baker Library at Dartmouth College, the Bailey-Howe Library at the University of Vermont, the Bancroft Library of the University of California at Berkeley, and the Kellogg-Hubbard Library in Montpelier. Dale Kyle, Dee Thomas, Leslie Goodman-Malamuth, Carol Ellingwood, and Elizabeth Dodge typed the manuscript at different stages with expertness and promptness.

Several friends offered space and sustenance, and much of this book was composed while ambling their fields and using their kitchen tables as writing desks. To mention some runs the risk of omitting others, but special thanks go to Jean Brownell of Chittenden, Vermont; Jonathan Brownell of Norwich, Vermont; Margaret Howard of Hardwick, Vermont; Edward Howard of Winooski, Vermont; Brian and Nancy Vachon of Montpelier; Lettie Penland of Manhattan Beach, California; Amelia Roberts Fry of Washington, D.C.; and my parents, Leonard Eugene and Margaret McCarthy Morrissey of Hanover, New Hampshire. For other assistance I am grateful to Peter Herman, Richard J. Rushmore, Jr., and David M. Otis, all of Montpelier; and to the late Ruth O'Donnell of Newton, Massachusetts, and the late Alexander Laing of Norwich, Vermont. Barbara W. Morrissey of Montpelier deserves the most thanks of all.

Charles T. Morrissey

Montpelier, Vermont
August 20, 1980

Vermont

A History

Part I
Portrait

1

Green Mountains and Mystic Chords

ERMONT is an experience to live as well as a state to live in. Its hills and valleys furnish scenery as picturesque as any in the nation. "If it is not the most beautiful state in the union," Bernard DeVoto asked in 1954, "which is?" [1] He was not the first nor last to view this remote corner of northern New England as a place apart, a "special world." Some who have let Vermont into their lives explain unabashedly that it evokes a warm affection and infuses the soul with joy and tranquillity. Sarah Cleghorn expressed this feeling as keenly as anybody ever has: "In Vermont, wherever you turn, you drink up beauty like rich milk, and feel its wholesome strength seep into your sinews." [2]

Vermont is aptly called the Green Mountain State because 420 named peaks rise within its land area of 9,608 square miles. The Green Mountains are part of the Appalachian chain which runs from the Gaspé Peninsula in Canada to northern Alabama, and they provide Vermont with a sturdy backbone which varies from twenty to thirty-six miles in width. Parallel ridges also dominate most of the state; only 15 percent of Vermont is clas-

1. Quoted by Charles T. Morrissey, "Wanted: An Oral History of Vermont During the Prohibition Era (1920–1933)," *Vermont History: The Proceedings of the Vermont Historical Society* 43 (1975): 320.

2. Sarah N. Cleghorn, *Threescore: The Autobiography of Sarah N. Cleghorn* (New York: Harrison Smith and Robert Haas, 1936), p. 107.

sified as flat and fertile. Admittedly, these elevations are not spectacular like the Rocky Mountains or the Sierra Nevada in California; the Green Mountains are older, geologically, and more rounded than their western counterparts. But eons ago the Green Mountains soared 15,000 feet and higher into the sky—almost like the mighty Himalayas. Then occurred the earth-shaping action of a mile-high sheet of ice, advancing and retreating across Vermont at the rate of a few inches each year, planing the summits and gouging lakes and ponds. It redirected the flow of water between the rock-hard hills, and scattered glacial debris all over the terrain. The consequence of that geologic action is evident everywhere in today's Vermont: boulders in the fields, scratches on exposed rock surfaces, even the oldest coral reef in the world on Isle La Motte in Lake Champlain. People who love Vermont aren't annoyed by westerners who exult in the soaring majesty of the Rockies and the Sierra; they would rather smile than argue the matter. But if piqued (and be warned that Vermont humor includes a lot of punning) they might remark that a mountain, like a woman, can express her beauty more by her personality than by her measurements. When the ice sheet receded to Greenland about 100,000 years ago it left only eighty peaks in the Green Mountains rising 3,000 feet or more above sea level, and only seven higher than 4,000 feet. Those aren't impressive statistics, but nevertheless the Green Mountain state exudes its own distinctive charm.

This is because the Vermont landscape seems almost everywhere to be rolling. Roads rise and dip and meander with the contours of the countryside. Water is the most abundant natural resource—narrow brooks tumbling down hillsides, shallow streams moving swiftly over rocky creekbeds, ponds and lakes filling from the brooks or emptying into rivers, many of which flow to the Connecticut River along Vermont's eastern border with New Hampshire or discharge into Lake Champlain bordering New York on the west. Except for the hills of view the horizons in Vermont are usually marked by ridges or bends in the road; Vermont is not Big Sky country. Other geologic actions caused this state to fold and compress its surface, forming hard granite and marble in the process. Vermont is bent, forked, and wrinkled: "it takes trigonometry, solid geometry, and calculus to get at Vermont," wrote one of its historians, Charles Edward Crane.[3] Rocky fields and angled visions have caused Vermonters to think with a hillside mentality. Their world is tilted in ways they take for granted:

"Senator, how did you get your start in life?" asked the reporter. "I was born on a hillside farm in Vermont," said the eminent statesman, "and at an early age I rolled down."[4]

Even today my neighbors in Montpelier say they are going "down-street" when they are going to the store, and "up to Barre" when they mean they are going to Barre, seven miles to the southeast. But an outlook on life which encompasses stony fields and sharp proclivities is not a disadvantage in dealing with life. "Problems are like a large rock in a farmer's field," said George D. Aiken, Vermont's former governor and senator. "He may hire a derrick to have it removed only to find two larger ones underneath. But, after all, problems are what make life worth living."[5] The folds of the land have also caused many Vermonters to compress their emotions about what they see and feel. "Our manners and deportment partake of the austere Mountains among which we live," wrote Edward Arthur Rockwood. "We have none of that affluence of the Frenchman and the Italian, and none of the openheartedness of the Southerner and Westerner. Our hearts are never carried on our sleeves."[6]

The hillside mentality was a natural development in Vermont. The early settlers first cleared the upper slopes because morning fog tended to envelop the valleys in white cocoons while the uplands were basking in sunlight. After heavy storms, the val-

3. Charles E. Crane, *Let Me Show You Vermont* (New York: Alfred A. Knopf, 1946), p. 7.
4. Quoted from the *Chicago Tribune* in *Expansion: Vermont's Industrial Magazine* 3 (1905): 3.
5. Jack Anderson, "Sen. George Aiken: The Outspoken Sage of the Senate," *Parade*, June 2, 1968 (copy in Aiken Papers, Crate 79, Box 3, University of Vermont, Burlington).
6. Edward Arthur Rockwood, "On Being Vermontish," *The Vermont Review* 2 (1928): 103.

leys were more likely to be flooded, and in hot spells which
spawned mosquitoes the danger of sickness seemed greater. In
the winters the valleys often were colder than the hilltops because, as every Vermonter knows, cold air is heavier than warm
air and can bring frosts to the lowlands while the highlands are
spared. Vermont farmers often built their barns to fit the contours of their hillsides; different entrances at different levels
meant that hay could be stored on upper floors and raked
through trap doors to cattle on lower floors. But a wise farmer
never built a barn above his house site because spring water
flowing downward on a gravity course would be contaminated
by his stock if it flowed through the barnyard to the house. Hillside living instills an awareness of such constraints and the need
to comply with the natural shape of things.

This mentality also makes Vermont an aesthetic pleasure to
enjoy because its countryside seems in harmony with the lives
of the people who nurtured this land. As Robert Frost put it,
Vermont is "a state in a natural state." Stone walls along the
roadsides were erected with rocks carried from the fields where
the glacier had spewed them. Where a road crosses a stream a
covered bridge may still be standing and used by automobiles
although built originally for horse-drawn vehicles. In 1980 Vermont has 114 of these structures still in daily use. An iron or
cement bridge is most likely a successor to a covered bridge
because once there were hundreds of these structures in Vermont before floods and modern "improvements" caused them
to be replaced as outmoded. Planks and beams for a covered
bridge were probably cut from trees which once blanketed the
nearby hillsides and were hauled as logs to a sawmill propelled
by the same stream which the bridge crosses. So too with
lumber to build church spires which rise familiarly on Vermont
horizons, and wooden houses clustered around village greens,
and wooden fences, and spacious porches outside houses and
village stores, and town halls and schoolhouses. Brick is seen
frequently in local buildings, probably shaped in local kilns, and
wedges of granite serve as doorsteps, fenceposts, window
ledges, and the like. Entire houses are made of stone, especially
in Chester and along the Lake Champlain lowlands, and this

rock was extracted from local quarries. Vermonters made use of the immediate resources of their environment. The way they located their barns to serve hayfields and pastures, and connected sheds and outbuildings in a continuous sequence to their homes so they could do winter chores without tramping out-of-doors in snow or cold weather, suggests they learned long ago how to deal sensibly with their environment without destroying it. Simplicity and symmetry are evident in Vermonters' domestic architecture: Palladian windows fanning above broad doorways, framed in turn by corniced pilasters, suggest they had a sense of proportion about houses and the lives of their occupants.

The Vermont experience is heightened by the seasons. Summer days can be chilly at dawn and cool again at twilight with ample warmth in between—days for wearing a sweater and then shedding it but keeping it handy for later use. Summer days can also be hot and humid, with temperatures rising above 90 degrees Fahrenheit when southwinds blow up after a cold front has moved through from neighboring Canada. This is something to ponder in July or August, when it is 60 degrees or more above freezing, because in winter there are days that dawn 60 degrees and more *below* freezing, and all day for several days in a row the temperature may not rise above zero. Autumn foliage in Vermont is the most spectacular annual show of color on the North American continent. Spring, with lilacs and forsythia and apple blossoms, and new buds on greening trees, and fields turned yellow with dandelions, is the greatest hymn to renewal since the Christians first celebrated Easter.

Within the seasons the days offer dramas of their own. A thunderstorm on a torpid summer afternoon, with ominous dark clouds and bolts of lightning and gusting winds and a drenching downpour, can be majestic in its awfulness. But then it might conclude with a delicate rainbow of several soft colors that appears fleetingly over a valley becoming lucent again in filtered sunlight. On spring and autumn mornings the mist rises thickly in the valleys because the streams are much warmer or colder than the air of the changing seasons, and the way in which faint sunrays pierce the fog and then disperse it is as enticing to watch as the drama of fog and sunlight which San Francisco offers over its glorious Bay. In winter the blowing snow against the white light flickering from a street lamp, or cast through an unshaded window, is an engrossing sight. It is beautiful to see how the winds cause snow to drift, how the snow sticks heavily on the bent green boughs of pine trees, how it reflects shadows which are pink and purple on its crested banks, and how it glistens sharply and brilliantly on sunny days when the north winds from Canada have blown storm clouds away and framed the white earth against gaunt trees and a clear blue sky. Birch trees do droop as if the children in Robert Frost's poem have been climbing them and swinging back to earth. Icicles scintillate like diamonds when the morning sun pierces them and causes them to crack into pieces and roll like marbles down the slanting drifts.

Vermont is light and shadows—sunset hues against the clouds and hilltops, darkness in the valleys while the hilltops still glow in honeyed tints, and light momentarily diffused as summer clouds go skudding across the midday sky. In winter the shadows always lean northward, even at noon, as the sun rolls on an axis far to the south. Shadows cast by rooflines and chimneys and spires and trees seem always to be changing in their reach and intensity from sun-up to sun-down, from season to season.

The changes are barely perceptible day by day, yet they are continual despite a landscape which itself seems constant and unchanging. Vermonters can watch spring climb a hillside at the rate of one hundred feet each day and create varying shades of green as leaves bud first at lower elevations and become verdant while higher up they are paler, gentler, and more fragile until the promise of summer heat is no longer a dubious prospect but a certainty. Four months later they can watch autumn descend the same hillside, the top turning vermilion and carmine before the lowlands follow. When the leaves are off the trees Vermonters can see views that they had forgotten about when the spring and summer greenery had enclosed their world, and they can enjoy these widened perspectives to the horizons. They can watch the ponds and streams freeze over between Thanksgiving and Christmas in a mellow array of whites and dark blues, and then watch the ice go out, sometimes in a rampage, in March or April. They can feel the frost lifting out of the ground by Memorial Day, and can sense its imminent return anytime around Labor Day. Sounds accentuate the sense of change on the Vermont landscape and add awareness of the continuity of seasons. Spring is exuberant in its melody of birds returning northward, of frogs croaking and bees droning and light breezes blowing through tender leaves. Fall is crumpled leaves underfoot. Winter has its sounds, too—the crunch of footsteps on hard snow on sub-zero mornings, cars whining and wheels turning heavily on the hardpack, boughs snapping almost painfully as the falling temperature tightens them and makes walls and floors contract in the plunging cold, and ice on the ponds, spreading wider and deeper, with cracks like whip snaps, scaring skaters in the late afternoon.

And smells too—even the carrion odor of skunk cabbage at the advent of spring is refreshing. Then comes an earthy scent so thick that the whole state smacks of gardens and barnyards. In July and August there are sun-baked days so sweet-scented with new-mown hay that all of Vermont is dryly fragrant like one big hayfield. Autumn can be so succulent with the harvesting of pumpkins and apples and tomatoes that a heady aroma of apple wine is in the air. A person hasn't lived the Vermont experience until he has stood in the fall by a cider press and savored its redolence, or inhaled the sweet steam from the boiling of maple sap in a farmer's sugar shack in the spring.

Vermont was made for music, and each person with an affection for Vermont can associate his favorite composer or style with particular scenes on the landscape. For Ralph Nading Hill the view from a boat in the middle of Lake Champlain on a gorgeous day is "like a pipe organ with all its stops out." [7] For visitors to the Trapp Family Lodge in Stowe, it is the score from "The Sound of Music." For me the narrow road twisting

7. Ralph Nading Hill, *Lake Champlain: Key To Liberty* (Taftsville, Vt.: Countryman Press, in association with the *Burlington Free Press*, 1976), p. 277.

through Smugglers' Notch from Stowe to Jeffersonville, climbing around unmovable boulders and between sharp cliffs, is like the overture of a Wagnerian opera. Mrs. Walter R. Hard thought of Carl Ruggles's majestic tympany whenever she came northward on Route 7. "I never drive up the valley from Bennington to Arlington, watching the glorious chains of mountains marching ahead of me, that I do not think of Carl's *Marching Mountains* symphony," she has written. "He needs no recording of his symphony, in one sense, because centuries, millions of them, have already recorded it in the everlasting contours of Vermont's mountain beauty." [8] Driving past an empty bandstand on a deserted village green on a hectic day in 1980, trying to visualize the villagers and their children assembled there years ago for a twilight concert by the town band, and loving the melodies they heard in that innocent age before the radio and television inflicted raucous music and inane commentary on our banal lives, one listens for Charles Ives and his jumble of traditional hymn tunes and patriotic airs coming through the cacaphony, typical of our times, that he sensed and composed so imaginatively in his.

But primarily Vermont was made for Mozart or Haydn, and they could have composed for Vermont. Hearing the lilt and harmony of their melodies as played each summer at the Mozart Festival in Burlington, or at the Marlboro Music Festival, makes a listener realize that their tone and tempo are appropriate for the Vermont landscape. A summer resident of Thetford, William Hollis, caught this sense of music very aptly in a poem he wrote a decade ago entitled "Mozart in Thetford." Part of it reads:

> . . . on an evening like last night,
> When the sun settles slowly down the valley, and
> shadows
> Fall clean and sharp across a mown field, and
> Trees are like permanent

---

8. Margaret Hard, *A Memory of Vermont: Our Life in the Johnny Appleseed Bookshop, 1930–1965* (New York: Harcourt, Brace & World, 1967), p. 168.

Forms on the canvases of Tuscan artists, I
Want the quiet, assured sound of
Four instruments
Playing Mozart or something by Haydn.
I want the strings to replace, if only for a
Moment, the sound of wind, not in
Some quaint imitation,
But with their own sound that will fill
The valley with richness and cause the deer,
Who feed in the upper
Orchard, to pause and lift their heads high in wonder.
I would like to think, though I know
Better, that such
Music was written for a place like this.[9]

Hollis teaches literature at Drexel Institute near Philadelphia during the academic year; in the summer he not only hears music in Thetford but also senses the presence of the past. "As a historical note," he explains, "you might be interested in knowing that Mozart is played each summer in the particular hills where Mrs. Wallace did the plowing while her husband, Richard, went off swimming." He refers to Richard Wallace, Thetford's best-known Revolutionary War soldier, who set out after nightfall in July 1777 to swim two miles across Lake Champlain from Ticonderoga to the American troops on the Vermont shore, his clothes tied in a bundle around his neck, and treading water so quietly that the British ships anchored in the lake could not hear his strokes although he could clearly hear the "all's well" of their watchmen. His message for Gen. Benjamin Lincoln put the American troops in motion to the south in a chain of events which led subsequently to the military engagements at Hubbardton and Bennington. Mrs. Wallace continued to tend the farm in Thetford although most of her neighbors had abandoned their farms to seek safety from Indians and Tories who were marauding in the Connecticut River Valley. Hollis adds about the Wallaces that "though none of their build-

9. William Hollis, "Mozart in Thetford," *Massachusetts Review* 7 (1966): 85.
© The Massachusetts Review 1966. Quoted with permission.

ings are left, it pleases me to imagine that they built the walls
that still creep through the underbrush."[10]

Vermont residents today have ample reminders of such associations with the past. Indeed, the entire state is a reminder of
the American past, a remnant from the agrarian culture which
once we were. It is understandable why Americans come here
from other states in search of the mystic chords of memories,
and why some want to build a fence around Vermont in order to
preserve it as a specimen of Americana, a national park of the
Yankee spirit which infused our national psyche. "It was once
said that every cultivated man's second country was France,"
Allan Nevins wrote in 1949; "it can certainly be said that every
American's second State is Vermont."[11]

Here the first stars and stripes were carried as a flag into
battle—in Bennington in 1777—and here lies buried, in New
Haven, a man named Solomon Brown, said to be the first to
shoot down a British soldier at Lexington in 1775. Here was
killed in 1780, when the Indians raided Royalton, a soldier
named Giles Gibb credited with writing the lyrics of "Yankee
Doodle." Here lived Royall Tyler, the American dramatist who
created in *The Contrast* (1787) Brother Jonathan, the first homespun Yankee stage character to outwit a haughty, effete Brit-
isher in what was the first comedy to be professionally staged in
America. Here Horace Greeley came of age and learned the
printer's trade, in East Poultney, and later spoke the destiny of
the nation when he urged young men to go West and grow up
with the country. Here Eugene Field, the poet of American
childhood, played on the Newfane Green near his grandmother's rambling house, and in Barnard, Sinclair Lewis, the
mocker of small-town America, found what he termed one of
the few decent places in America to live. Here, appropriately,
stands the Shelburne Museum, forty-five buildings on thirty-five
acres assembled as "the Museum of the American Spirit." Here

    10. Quoted in *News and Notes* (the newsletter of the Vermont Historical Society) 18
(1967): 86.
    11. Allan Nevins, "Vermont—and the Other Forty-Seven," foreword to *The Ver-
mont Story: A History of the People of the Green Mountain State, 1749–1949*, by Earle
Newton (Montpelier: Vermont Historical Society, 1949), p. x.

Norman Rockwell found the faces he liked to paint for the front covers of the *Saturday Evening Post*. At one time no less than five artists working for the *Post* lived in Arlington, Vermont, and in his *Post* cover for Christmas 1948 Rockwell was able to include none other than Grandma Moses among his figures. How American! Entitled *Homecoming*, that painting hangs today in the Bennington Museum, as do many of Grandma Moses's primitive watercolors. There tourists can walk through the schoolhouse she attended as a youngster because it has been moved from its original site just across the border in Eagle Bridge, New York. In the Bennington Museum a visitor can see that first version of the Stars and Stripes. Vermont is strawberry festivals on the village green and small-town fireworks on the Fourth of July. It is where Calvin Coolidge was born in Plymouth Notch on the Fourth of July. "Vermont is perhaps the only place in America a stranger can feel homesick for," journalist Neal R. Peirce has written, "before he has even left it." [12] Vermont is benign neglect.

12. Neal R. Peirce, *The New England States: People, Politics, and Power in the Six New England States* (New York: W. W. Norton & Co., 1976), p. 233.

2

Behind the Beauty: Hard Living in a Hard Place

ERMONT is also a difficult experience to live and an expensive and inconvenient state to live in. A lot of Vermonters have left this state without feeling homesick for it. One doesn't have to be a cynic to cite Stephen A. Douglas's famous quip that "Vermont is the most glorious spot on the face of this globe for a man to be born in, *provided* he emigrates when he is very young." [1] Or Alphonso Taft's similar remark to his father in 1837—that Vermont is "a noble state to emigrate from"—when he decided to depart from Townshend and cast his future as the first of the Tafts to prosper in the bustling Ohio River town of Cincinnati. [2] For most of its history Vermont has been exporting its able and ambitious youngsters, and also many of its grown-ups, too, who became exasperated with too many rocks in its fields and too many storms in its sky. Vermonters today laugh ruefully about the "psychic income" they receive in the form of mountain vistas to augment the low wage scale in Vermont, which is seventeen percent below the national average. Many concede it is a good place to live but a poor place to make a decent living.

In winter many don't even concede that it is a good place to

1. Quoted by Robert A. Waller, "How Stephen A. Douglas Explained His Criticism of Vermont," *Vermont History* 42 (1974): 202.

2. Quoted by Ishbel Ross, *An American Family: The Tafts, 1678 to 1964* (Cleveland, Ohio: World Publishing Co., 1964), p. 6.

live. Let us consider a Vermonter who sets out for Montpelier on a frigid day, to testify and answer questions at a legislative hearing in the statehouse. He might first question himself about why he persists in living in this land of subzero temperatures and piercing winds. Direct democracy is a great virtue, and being able to testify on impending legislation means a citizen is in touch with government, but getting a car started on a cold Vermont morning makes it easy to understand why the Benito Mussolinis of this world are admired for getting the trains to run on time. A car is essential for rural Vermonters—a vital link to life in the 1980s, despite the high cost of fuel. Public transportation is scarce where people are not concentrated; in Vermont the railroad passenger service is limited to two Amtrak trains between Montreal and Washington, D.C., and each passes through Vermont in the dark hours of the night. A Vermonter must depend on his car, and except for the rare phenomenon of a snowless season like the "brown winter" of 1979–1980, the ordeal of getting through snow drifts to it may be the most pivotal task of the day. That means forsaking a warm bed before dawn has edged the winter skyline. Nowhere is it darker before dawn than in Vermont in January when the thermometer dips to thirty below.

If the car is garaged the doors may be frozen by ice formed by the drippings of yesterday's icicles, and chipping the ice away becomes the first chore. If the car has stood unsheltered all night in a driveway—and all-night parking on Vermont streets is prohibited from November to April so snowplows can push newfallen snow unobstructedly to the curbsides—the car may be covered with snow and refuse to start. That means cold feet and cold fingers in the cold dawn while a friend and a jump cord try to activate the frozen carcass by conveying sparks of life from one battery to another. Or one waits uselessly by the balky automobile until the man who runs the local gas station arrives like Yukon Jack in his four-wheel drive vehicle and gets things plowed and pumping again. To own a car with four-wheel drive in Vermont is a symbol of belonging—like wearing a ten-gallon hat in Texas. For Vermont men of middle age or older to shovel their own driveways may also bring a special distinction; the number of shovelers who collapse with coronary attacks is one of winter's grim statistics.

On slippery days a car may skid sideways on a modest hill and careen into a roadside ditch. That means getting a jack out of the trunk to raise the axle and pushing the car onto the road, or getting chains or ashes or an old scatter rug to put under the spinning wheels and hoping some helpful strangers will come along and risk muscle strains while shoving earnestly against the grudging hulk.

A Vermonter learns to drive slowly in winter, especially when approaching junctions where the snowbanks are gigantic pyramids which narrow the intersection, because an unseen car may be coming diagonally into the same intersection. A Vermonter will often tie a red or blue streamer to the top of the radio antenna so other drivers will see it flutter when snow drifts block vision of other cars. A Vermonter also learns how to drive a car like a cowboy astride a bronco—with neck craned over the steering wheel, and forehead bumping against the windshield so one can see left and right, even if warm breath has frosted the cold windshield and one really can't see much of anything.

Why go through this wintry torment? A Vermonter fantasizes that people in Florida and California are sliding behind their steering wheels, turning ignition keys and listening contentedly to purring motors and then heading down snowless streets which gleam in apricot sunlight. No wonder Alexander Solzhenitsyn remarked that his new home of Cavendish, Vermont, reminded him of the snows and winters of his native Russia. In Vermont a winter day may be consumed by waiting for tow trucks and auto mechanics, and after investing in snow tires and pouring quarts of antifreeze into the gizzard of a car it seems unfair. Nor does a Vermont winter end delicately. Frost heaves in March make roads look as if tanks have been driven over them. Then comes Mud Season (capitalized in Vermont), with mire so thick on unpaved roads that getting stuck in mud in late March and April is just as easy as getting stuck in snow in December and January—except it's more messy. Squally snow showers in April show that winter still has its grip on this climate. Almost every Vermonter has a tale to tell about a freakish May snowstorm which, as a final riposte in the duel with winter, causes drivers once again to fishtail into swirling whirlwinds of whiteness or spin to a halt on a hill suddenly too slick to climb. A Vermonter may conclude, without fear of paranoia, that getting from Thanksgiving to Memorial Day can be cruel and unusual punishment. Surely the framers of the Declaration of Independence did not have Vermonters in mind when they declared "all men are created equal," and the ordeal of winter in northern New England violates the national credo of equal justice for all.

New England is subjected to such broad variations of weather that it has been described as "a vast meteorological mixing bowl where diverse air currents converge and concoct atmospheric situations as varied as tossed salad." [3] Vermonters who try to fly in and out of this state on airplanes when the weather is unsettled know how it feels to be a piece of lettuce in a tossed salad. But those who keep their feet on the ground also know the peculiarities of Vermont's erratic weather, and undoubtedly it has shaped the character of people who live here. Dr. D. C. Jarvis of Barre was one of several persons to reflect on this aspect of the Vermont experience. "In our latitude the prevailing winds are westerly," he wrote.

Of the twenty-six storm tracks crossing the United States on their way to the Atlantic Ocean, twenty-three pass over Vermont. Consequently Vermont weather changes every few days the year round, and the Vermonter faces the major biological necessity of constantly adjusting his body to rapidly alternating heat and cold, high and low barometric pressure, and seasonal changes of humidity and air ionization. Every such adjustment to climate must be made by a change in the blood circulation. One day the skin is called upon to be a radiator, giving off heat. The next day it may have to be an insulator, retaining the body heat. This puts great strain on the heart and blood vessels.

He also commented that "Vermont might reasonably be described as the land of dizziness, for it is a common symp-

3. David Ludlum and the editors of *Blair & Ketchum's Country Journal, The Country Journal New England Weather Book* (Boston: Houghton Mifflin Co., 1976), p. 2.

tom.'' [4] The land of dizziness! Does a person have to be dizzy to live in Vermont? Maybe it helps.

A person driving to a legislative hearing in Montpelier on winter roads admires the workers who keep them clear. Vermonters know how to handle snow; this isn't like Washington, D.C., where a trace of snowfall can paralyze the capital city of the free world. Vermont roads are opened quickly so skiers can get in and milk can be trucked out. Even sidewalks will be plowed promptly. School sessions are rarely cancelled, and when they are called off it is more often for ice on the back roads where slickness can make it hazardous for school busses to travel their routes than because of snow.

Vermonters know too, as northcountry residents have long appreciated, that an early cold snowfall will insulate the earth and keep the frost from delving deeper. This means healthier grass for dairy cows in the spring and summer, and possibly an early start in the growing season. It also means that snow can insulate a house and reduce fuel costs if it's piled up around the foundation and left to stand high on rooftops. Homeowners who detect nails coming loose on shingled roofs will let the nails stand high rather than hammer them back down because those protruding nails may retain the snow better. But being wise in the ways of winter they will shovel it from the edges of rooftops; not to do so runs the risk of letting melted snow drip down between the walls, causing wood to rot and wallpaper to stain.

Vermonters may be savvy about the ways of winter, and road crews may be marvelously efficient in keeping the roads open, but the costs for such a small state are astounding. In an average winter the Vermont Department of Transportation dumps almost 100,000 tons of salt on nearly 6,000 lane-miles of highways, at a cost to the taxpayers of $3 million. The state's 246 communities spread another 125,000 tons of salt on 11,000 two-lane miles of pavement at a cost of more than $15 million. This means the state's 500,000 people are paying $18 million annually

4. DeForest C. Jarvis, *Folk Medicine: A Vermont Doctor's Guide to Good Health* (New York: Henry Holt & Co., 1958), pp. 6, 81.

just to salt winter roads—and making environmentalists unhappy because the salt seeps into water supplies and damages
the roots of roadside trees. The salt also pocks automobiles and
wears them out faster than normally; cars depreciate more rapidly in Vermont than cars driven on salt-free roads. Sand is also
used on Vermont roads, and in other ways the high cost of road
maintenance is visible as one drives a Vermont highway. Red-
dish snow fences in the fields, strategically implanted to dis-
sipate gusts of snow swirling across open spaces towards the
highway, must be erected each fall and dismantled each spring.
Snowplows work even on snowless days because in Vermont
there is always the brooding likelihood of more snow to follow,
day after day, and there has to be space to push the next ac-
cumulation. Snow removal continues long after nightfall, the
yellow lights of the trucks flashing like urgent heartbeats which
belie the calm of the icy starlight reflecting on the snow.

Vermont provides so many public services that one wonders
if this tiny state has overextended itself. Does Vermont really
need an interstate highway system which has 3.5 times more
highway mileage per resident than the national average, and a
per-mile traffic volume that is two-thirds the national norm?
Must this state spend so much for the pleasure of out-of-staters
who speed on their way to Pico Peak and Stowe and other ski
areas, and jam the highways southward when they head home to
the cities on Sunday nights? Does Vermont really need to support three state colleges, a technical two-year school, and a
community college in addition to a state university that includes
a college of medicine and other costly programs? It seems pre-
posterous that a state with the population of metropolitan areas
like Rochester, New York and Louisville, Kentucky should support its own correctional system, a public health program, a
state police force, and all the other services of state government.
Yet Vermont has one of the highest ratios of state-employed
workers to state population in the nation. Pima County, Arizona, has about the same geographic size and population as
Vermont; if America had been settled from West to East would
it make any sense for Pima County to be a separate state? Some

westerners have quipped that if the nation had expanded from West to East the Green Mountains of Vermont would only now be opening to settlement.

Nor is this a rich state, either. Vermont ranks forty-fourth nationally in per capita income, but nineteenth in per capita taxes. Vermont has the fourteenth highest state tax debt per capita in the nation. Yet Vermonters feel they are not getting what they should receive for their high taxes. Vermont youngsters who enroll at the University of Vermont pay the highest tuition in the nation for in-state students attending a state university. But of the six New England state universities the faculty with the lowest pay scale is at UVM. (UVM is shorthand for the University of Vermont, extracted from *Universitas Viridis Montis,* Latin for University of the Green Mountains, an appropriate cognomen and a refreshing classical touch in an age of sterile acronyms.) UVM is feeling the fiscal blues so severely that it and the University of Alaska are the only two state universities in the nation which don't field football teams each fall.

Besides their taxes Vermonters have to pay high prices for winter survival. Because gasoline and heating fuels are increasingly expensive, Vermonters are cutting their own firewood to burn in woodstoves. Winter in Vermont is an armor-clad season: heavy coats, scarves, sweaters, boots, gloves, all of which cost money. Storm windows must be put up each fall and taken down each spring, and other forms of insulation are needed to reduce heat loss through drafty doors and windows in houses which warp in the weather and shift their foundations in the spring mud.

Most Vermonters don't look like the sturdy homespun figures that Norman Rockwell painted. The men have leathered faces and look old before their time. Often their wives look haggard. Their kids have bad teeth. Their kids also have the lowest "aspiration rate" of high school youngsters in the entire nation, which means that proportionately fewer of them go beyond high school for further education than elsewhere. This isn't surprising because 100,000 adult Vermonters never finished high school.

Vermont can be a hard and brutal place. Tales occasionally

drift out of the backwoods about violent eruptions. In northern Vermont a man was hauled out of his jeep, on his own property, and beaten to oblivion by a group of twenty or more snowmobilers who wanted to cross his land despite his objections. A few miles away, fourteen snowmobilers intimidated an elderly couple who had bought twelve acres for retirement. "You build a house here and we'll burn it down," they were warned. In Morrisville a jogger was mistaken for a deer and shot through the leg; the hunter said he'd go for help but he didn't return. The injured man survived only by crawling through near-freezing rain for ten hours to a farmhouse at 3:40 in the morning.

Driving through Vermont one ponders how the landscape, as well as the people on it, don't fit the prevailing image of Vermont life. The state had 26,490 operating farms in 1945 but that number had declined to 9,247 in 1964 and further to 5,906 in 1974. By 1980 Vermont had only 3,209 farms selling milk and dairy products. The state has 6 million acres but in 1980 only 862,831 acres are actively tilled as croplands. To run a family farm is becoming almost impossible in Vermont; dairy herds have to be larger, equipment has to be mechanized, and substantial capital has to be raised since the average Vermont farm was appraised in 1978 at $219,290. All this is demanded at a time when land taxes are becoming more than a farmer can pay because his tax rate is determined by the value of his acreage on the open market. As sites for vacation homes, the property becomes expensive farmland. The landscape with its peaceful farms is symbolic of the Vermont way of life, but very few Vermonters make their livings from farming. Town halls in the villages are symbols of local autonomy, but town meetings are more ritualistic than effective as instruments of government. Haggling over school budgets and road costs will not deter the engulfing economic influences which affect the way Vermonters are employed.

Every major industry in Vermont is now owned by out-of-state firms, and most of these are big—such as International Business Machines and General Electric—or conglomerates such as one in Switzerland which bought the Vermont Marble Company of Proctor in 1976, or Colt Industries in Chicago, for whom the hallowed Fairbanks-Morse scales manufacturing plant in St. Johnsbury is now simply a division of the parent concern. The largest landowner in Vermont is the St. Regis Paper Company, with vast tracts of timberlands which it oversees from corporate offices in New York City.

Vermont is part of the modern world despite the rural landscape which belies the reality and the Currier and Ives imagery projected from the garish sides of maple syrup tins. Prof. Frank M. Bryan, the most sophisticated student of current Vermont politics, illustrates this truth from his own upbringing in Newbury: when a hay mower breaks down in a quiet meadow along the Connecticut River it means a call to St. Louis, Missouri, for parts, and that in turn activates a computer which alerts a factory in Japan about how many parts are needed to replace those being shipped from the warehouse in St. Louis. Bryan argues in *Yankee Politics in Rural Vermont* that "antenna politics," by which he means political image-making on commerical television, determines political choices among Vermonters as much as it does in large urban states. It is sad to realize that Vermont youngsters are addicted to the pap on television as incurably as kids who wake up on Saturdays and Sundays in the sprawling subdivisions of Los Angeles or any other American metropolis and turn on their sets for the cartoons in the morning and the game shows later. Vermont parents buy more at chain stores in shopping centers than at general stores or the little mom-and-pop stores which manage to survive. Vermont radio stations play the same rock and country western tunes as stations everywhere do, alternating the inane lyrics with the inane advertisements which have made us a nation of unsated consumers.

A Yankee storekeeper in Vermont is probably operating a modest venture and is cautious about stocking a plentiful supply of goods. "No, we don't have it," is a clerk's inevitable reply when a customer asks for an offbeat item, "but we can order it for you." For a person who wants to see the item before buying it, and maybe handle it, the alternative is hardly satisfactory. Local eateries can be as conventional as diners in middle America; in Vermont it isn't easy to get a good pastrami sandwich on fresh rye bread. Driving through many stretches of

Vermont with a craving for a hot cup of coffee can be frustrating because luncheonettes can be as sparse as gourmet restaurants outside of Stowe and the Mad River Valley and other ski areas. The restaurants often serve less than their menus proclaim because the luncheon specials may be gone before one o'clock, and the evening selections may be reduced by seven o'clock. Experienced diners learn to scan menus in Vermont restaurants for more than one choice of entree because waitresses invariably announce they just served the last platter of whatever appetizing fare most tempted the palate. Volume is light in Vermont restaurants, and the chefs don't want to prepare too much. On a Saturday they may say they are out of things or start to reduce portions because they want to put some aside for Sunday dinners—if indeed they are open on Sundays. Liquor stores are operated by the state and all but one are closed in the evening. All are closed on Sundays. In Montpelier there is only one movie theater in town, with only two showings each night, and chances of seeing a decent first-run film are almost nonexistent. If the theater in Montpelier gets more than a handful of paying customers for a week's showings the film will be held over week after week. Vermont is not for film buffs.

Despite the pastoral beauty of the Vermont landscape it is hard to get fresh fruits and vegetables in Vermont supermarkets. Except when the home-grown products are harvested in late summer and the early fall, the retailers generally truck in their produce from warehouses in New Jersey. Freshness has often faded, but the prices are high. It seems easier for the tourist traps to import knicknacks from Japan and Hong Kong than for Vermonters to buy quality food in their markets. The tourist traps pass themselves off as genuine country stores or old-fashioned Yankee emporiums, but most old-fashioned Vermonters scoff at these latter-day imitations.

The Vermont image suggests this is a land where oxen still pull plows in the planting season and horses still pull sleighs in winter in a preindustrialized arcadia. But the image is at war with the reality, and it is easy to be cynical about the way the imagery is cultivated to lure tourists and their dollars. Ethan Allen is romanticized as a dashing Robin Hood or Vermont equivalent of the Jolly Green Giant, and the Vermont Department of Development and Community Affairs has tried to interest Walt Disney Productions in making a film about him. But Ethan Allen and his brothers were also land developers—the Onion River Land Company they formed in 1773 was no piddling enterprise—and today's real estate agent or ski resort owner would admire how they shaped Vermont to fit their interests. The statue of Ethan Allen on the statehouse portico must warm every developer's heart.

Do the touring shutterbugs who snap pictures of scenic Vermont vistas ever wonder who lives in all the trailers and all the shacky houses they don't record on film? Do they notice the sad and ugly towns they drive through to get to the pristine villages which outsiders have restored? Bellows Falls, still sooty from its era as a railroad town, contrasts with charming Grafton, up the road; the shabby houses of Bridgewater, a forsaken milltown, sit next door to exquisite Woodstock; and decrepit Hardwick, a false-fronted town which looks transplanted from the mined-out silver lodes of the West, differs remarkably from Greensboro and Craftsbury Common, trim towns northward which gleam with bridal whiteness.

There is poverty in the squalid towns. There is poverty in the handsome towns, too; 23 percent of the residents of bucolic Weston have incomes below the minimum-income level. And there is poverty in the hollows and the backwoods and on the hillsides. Not all of Appalachia lies in West Virginia or eastern Kentucky. Vermont is Appalachia, too, as surely as the Appalachian Trail follows the crest of the Green Mountains until it crosses into New Hampshire. The poor mountain whites of the southern Appalachians are called "woodchucks" in Vermont—a derisive term used by newcomers and others who are middle-class or affluent. A "woodchuck" has the native's twang in his voice and a countryman's gait in his stride; he chops wood or does other manual labor or is unemployed. Everything about him is poor: his housing, his health, his nutrition, his schooling, his children and their schooling, the condition of his pick-up truck, and his behavior on Saturday nights after a ferocious round of drinking. He views the world with a sullen stare;

behind his back the comfortable world makes jokes about him—like the one that claims his idea of a banquet is boiled woodchuck and a six-pack of beer. The tourists don't see the poverty. When they see "woodchucks" they probably observe them as quaint archetypes of American Gothic. Visitors to Vermont who eat expensive dinners in a fancy restaurant that has been refurbished from a dairy barn don't know about the elderly farmer who toiled for years in that barn and now feebly survives on social security checks. People who love country auctions don't realize the pathos when all those worn and battered household items, often representing a widow's lifetime, are held up to public glare and sale. An auction can be a demeaning event at which the bargain hunters don't realize that the person who lived familiarly with those paltry goods may feel like a shriveled, caved-in body gradually reduced to nakedness as strangers bid piece by piece for the desiderata of a lifetime.

Many of the books praising Vermont as a beautiful place to live don't mention the poverty. In fact many of them seem to be written by people who move elsewhere after writing them. Many who have celebrated Vermont as a beautiful experience have afterwards turned to different subjects and lifestyles, as if coming to terms with Vermont were too harsh a challenge for a sustained commitment. For many Vermonters life is a predicament—a grueling ordeal of trying to scratch a living between a rock and a very hard place.

3

The Statehouse:
History in Granite

*W*HEN a Vermont citizen arrives at the Statehouse in Montpelier to discuss impending legislation with a state senator or representative, the legislator can't invite the visitor to the privacy of an office, duly barricaded by a secretary. Legislators have no offices. They have no secretaries. Instead a legislator and a visitor will sit on a Victorian sofa in the lobby outside the legislative chambers and talk over their kneecaps like neighbors on a porch bench back home. They will be readily overheard or interrupted because everybody in the statehouse is preoccupied with snatching stealthy glances at everybody else, and absorbing whatever fragments of conversation are audible in the hubbub. The mood resembles a fraternity house during rush week.

The legislator may be an older person living on a pension, or a middle-aged person with somebody back home tending the store or the insurance agency. The pay is low—$225 per week plus expenses each year from shortly after New Year's Day to around the opening of the trout season (the second Saturday in April)—and a legislator needs another income to survive. If a legislator is young he may be just out of college and not yet committed to a steady job and a definite career. Regardless of age or profession, the legislator may be a person of independent means, or married to a person with inherited wealth. Many of these privileged people have settled recently in Vermont, and they glitter like quartz which sparkles occasionally among the dull-colored stones and pebbles of the glacial rubble. Freed from measuring their days against the dollars they earn by their own labor they become active in public affairs, and probably use most of their Vermont incomes to pay their taxes. The independently wealthy enliven one of Vermont's favorite indoor games—gossip. The knowledgeable can reveal the secret of unfettered lifestyles on modest Vermont incomes by saying with authority, "Well, you know, she's a Parke of Parke-David," or "He's a Milbrook of Milbrook and McCloy," or "Her dad is what's-his-name who produces those shows on television." When the conduits of wealth aren't readily known the talk is more tentative: "Isn't she ketchup from Pittsburgh? Or is she catalogs from Chicago?" It's a game which thrives on inference: "If you think their house in Dorset is swank you ought to see the one they have on the main line near Philadelphia," or "I think her uncle is the angel who is bailing out the Sugar Glen Ski Area; that's why her boutique has space in the main lodge." Vermonters follow the private peregrinations of these monied neighbors with interest: "Now that she's divorcing him I guess he'll have to stop living off his father-in-law." But a lot of the coupon-clippers show up in Montpelier to serve on various boards and commissions, for which the state ordinarily pays the magnificent sum of thirty dollars per day as an honorarium, plus mileage. At that rate the people of independent means are invited to run the state.

It makes a person wonder: is this the best way to conduct state business? And why is Vermont a state, anyhow? Its statehouse looks down on two "No U Turn" signs right on State Street, near the walkway leading to its portico. Inadvertently those signs suggest that Vermont, like many of the small towns within its borders, is only a wide place in the road, and travellers need to be told which way is straight ahead and not get turned around. They emphasize the effrontery of Vermont's venture in statehood. And if Vermont truly aspired to be an equal member of the sisterhood of states, why did it locate its public heartbeat between the narrow valley walls of a dinky, overgrown village called Montpelier?

Actually, Montpelier can shimmer like a golden nugget ensconced in boughs of green. That is literally true when one drives to the valley floor from the hillsides surrounding Montpelier: "to the city" reads one sign in a rare example of Vermont hyperbole. The gold leaf of the statehouse dome reflects the sunshine while the green of the pitched hillside behind it marks the setting. Ceres, the goddess of agriculture, stands in white splendor atop the dome with sheaves of wheat tucked under her arm. She was carved from wood by Dwight Dwinell, a former sergeant-at-arms for the legislature below, when the original by Larkin G. Mead, the famous sculptor from Brattleboro, had become so weatherbeaten on that exposed perch that it needed to be replaced. Dwinell was eighty-seven years old when he carved that statue. Whittling has long been a talent and a pastime for Vermonters like Dwinell; the first statehouse, a wooden structure built in 1808, only three years after Montpelier had been designated as capital of the young state, had literally been carved to ruins, so the story goes, by farmer-legislators who needed to occupy their idle hands while their colleagues droned away the hours on lawmaking.

The statue of Ceres has been interpreted in various ways by different people at different times; women libbers of the current age say it's typical of the Vermont power structure to put a woman on a pedestal away from the place where she can participate in state business on her own merits. (A rejoinder is to note that the Vermont Legislature, early and easily, approved the proposed Equal Rights Amendment.) Back in the 1930s Ceres was said to be Dorothy Thompson, the newspaper columnist who lived with her (then) husband, Sinclair Lewis, in Barnard, on her way to deliver a copy of the *New York Herald-Tribune* to the Republican loyalists down below. Ceres is also the goddess of brewing, and some think that is appropriate for Vermont because in its early days, and recent days also, Vermonters have kept themselves warm and have jollified occasions by drinking prodigious amounts of intoxicants. Montpelier during legislative sessions has seen its share of inordinate drinking. Local folklore recounts how newsmen walking along State Street in front of the statehouse one evening came upon a legislator draped over the iron fence that enclosed the statehouse green. (Alas, the fence was dismantled and contributed to a scrap metal drive during World War Two.) The legislator was unable to hold the vast quantity of liquor he had imbibed. "What's the trouble?" asked the newsmen. "Can we help you? What are you doing here?" The sufferer raised his head and between spasms groaned woefully: "I'm tryin' to represent the town of Mount Holly in the Legislature—but I dunno but it'll kill me before I'm done with it!" [1]

When he was writing *Inside USA* John Gunther characterized the Vermont Statehouse as perhaps the "most charming" of all the capitol buildings in all the states. [2] The present statehouse stands on a ledge which was blasted by dynamite from the hillside east of the Winooski River; today that hillside is part of Hubbard Park, 134 acres owned by the city of Montpelier and thick with greenery whenever leaves are on the trees. Framed in green—or brown trees or gray ledges or white snow in other seasons—it is not unusual for legislators to look through their chamber windows to see deer nibbling for food in the clefts among those rock outcroppings. In winter, looking from the statehouse across the narrow valley to the opposite hillside, legislators can occasionally see youngsters from the Montpelier High School Ski Team practicing their skills on a ski jump.

On the front the statehouse is rimmed by terraced lawns which rise gradually from State Street to the building itself. It is granite, appropriately, with steps formed by granite blocks in a series which Montpelier youngsters traditionally try to navigate backwards with their eyes closed as George Dewey did in the 1850s when he was a boy living in a white clapboard house directly across State Street from the statehouse. It is a challenging dare to accept from a boyhood companion because it requires a steady route, backwards and sightless, while trying to remember how many steps to take on each of the plateaus, which vary in uneven lengths between the steps themselves. And being hewed from granite the steps themselves are craggy and unevenly

---

1. Note in the papers of Dorothy C. Walter, gift of Mrs. Walter Nelson, Vermont Historical Society Library, Montpelier.
2. John Gunther, *Inside U.S.A.* (New York: Harper & Brothers, 1947), p. 910.

placed. A tumble is likely, and not gentle either on those hard and sharp-edged surfaces.

The present statehouse was built after a January fire in 1857 destroyed its predecessor, which in turn had been built between 1833 and 1837. Some of the exterior of the 1833–1837 structure was left standing and incorporated into the 1857 structure. The two buildings are similar—a central square with a dome on the top and a Doric portico with six fluted pillars on the front, each pillar being about six feet in diameter at the base. The portico is modelled after the Greek temple of Theseus in Athens, an excellent choice for Vermonters to copy because Theseus was the mythical patron of Athenian democracy and the person who supposedly transformed Attica from congeries of villages into a single city-state. Vermont's emergence as a state—and a very democratic one in character—has parallels to that classical antecedent. Behind the portico the central building is almost 73 feet in width and almost 96 feet in depth. Wings on each side are 52 feet long. Classical and austere, the structure is shaped like a Greek cross.

The previous building stood as a monument to the Vermont commitment to work. The structure required 22,000 feet of granite, and Capt. William Bradford was paid eight cents per cubic foot for drawing the stone to Montpelier from quarries on Millstone Hill and Cobble Hill in Barre. Teams composed of four horses and a yoke of oxen left Barre each day at 4:00 A.M. for the quarries and loaded the granite with skids and rolls (they had no derricks in those days). Then they drove to Montpelier to unload the granite. Then they returned to Barre, arriving home at about 10:00 P.M. Altogether that required a round-trip of twenty-five miles and a day's work that took eighteen hours.

Inside the statehouse the tessellated marble floors, in which white blocks alternate with black blocks in a checkerboard design, contain traces of prehistoric gastropods. The marble was quarried at Isle La Motte, the island just below the Canadian border in Lake Champlain where Vermont's first permanent settlement was established by Frenchmen in 1664 and where Vermont's first religious service, a Roman Catholic mass, was conducted. The white wall paneling is hand-carved and often ornate in a gentle, subdued way. The high-molded ceilings are coffered and also white, and the doors are thick and dark and swing heavily. Doorknobs are a shiny golden and silver. The staircases are iron and intricately designed, and their curved steps are carpeted and adjoined by shiny dark banisters. Even the iron radiator covers are intricately cast; antique collectors eye them enviously.

A huge bust of Abraham Lincoln dominates the downstairs hall which intersects the main hall that runs end-to-end across the front. The Lincoln sculpture was done by Larkin Mead and is identical with the one at Lincoln's tomb in Springfield, Illinois. It seems appropriate to find Lincoln here, casting his somber presence over those whose footsteps echo off the statehouse walls, his gaunt mien personifying the mystic chords of memory which he invoked in his effort to preserve the Union. Vermonters were supporting the newly born Republican party in the 1850s before Lincoln had become a Republican himself, and in 1860 they cast 75 percent of their votes for him as the Republican candidate for the presidency. That was a higher percentage than he received in any other state in that campaign, and Vermonters mustered that tremendous support despite the alternative of voting for Stephen A. Douglas, the Democratic candidate and a native Vermonter. Vermont has been the most loyal Republican state in the Union since Lincoln became the first Republican president. Lincoln freed the slaves, in popular memory, and that also seems appropriate for Vermont because it was the most abolitionist state in sentiment in pre–Civil War days. Curiously, Lincoln never once set foot on Vermont soil nor had any Vermont antecedents in his family background; for a Kentucky-born stranger who was raised in Indiana and practiced law in Illinois to occupy such an august position in the Vermont Statehouse unintentionally negates the importance that native Vermonters attach to being born in Vermont.

Inscribed on the white walls along the corridor approaching the Lincoln bust are pithy statements, lettered in black scroll, which epitomize Vermont. In their stark and simple way they convey a clear sense of the forthrightness and independence of this mountain fastness:

> Out of storm and manifold perils rose an enduring state, the home of freedom and unity.

(This is from the gravestone epitaph of Vermont's first governor, Thomas Chittenden; the "freedom and unity" serves as Vermont's official state motto.)

> If the spirit of liberty should vanish in other parts of the Union and support of our institutions should languish, it could all be replenished from the generous store held by the people of this brave little state of Vermont.

(This was the concluding line in an extemporaneous speech given by Calvin Coolidge in Bennington, Vermont, on September 21, 1928.)

> I am as determined to preserve the Independence of Vermont as Congress is that of the Union and rather than fail I will retire with my hardy green mountain boys into the caverns of the mountains and make war on all mankind.

(This is Ethan Allen—pure Ethan Allen!—in a letter he wrote to the Continental Congress on March 9, 1781.)

> They hewed this state out of the wilderness, they held it against a foreign foe, they laid deep and stable the foundation of our state life, because they sought not the life of ease, but the life of effort for a worthy end.

(This is President Theodore Roosevelt, during a 1902 visit to Vermont.)

> That frequent recurrence of fundamental principles, and a firm adherence to justice, moderation, temperance, industry, and frugality, are absolutely necessary to preserve the blessings of liberty and keep Government free.

(This is a passage from the Vermont Constitution.)

The record of Vermont as a resolute champion of individual freedom, as a true interpreter of our fundamental law, as a defender of religious faith, as an unselfish but independent and uncompromising commonwealth of liberty-loving patriots, is not only unsurpassed, but unmatched by any other state in the Union.

(This was stated by George Harvey, a native of Peacham, Vermont, who became publisher of *Harper's* Magazine, a behind-the-scenes manipulator in presidential nominating politics, and U.S. Ambassador to Great Britain during World War One.)

One can have fun in the Vermont Statehouse by imagining other pithy statements which might replace some of the classics already inscribed there. A Vermont chauvinist might submit Bernard DeVoto's little gem, "There is no more Yankee than Polynesian in me, but whenever I go to Vermont I feel that I am travelling toward my own place." Another with a puckish sense of humor and an anti-promotion mentality might borrow a motto which has turned up on bumper stickers on cars driven by outlanders who have come to Vermont and love it but don't want others to follow and ruin it. It is simply, "Keep Vermont a Secret." Disdainful natives have their bumper stickers, too— "Flatlanders, Go Home"—and that might counterbalance what a Wall Street banker has said: "Vermont is the only place within a day's drive from New York that's fit to live in." Those who want either to resist or resign themselves to the influx of New Yorkers could choose John L. Garrison's 1946 statement: "Vermont is a land filled with milk and maple syrup, and overrun with New Yorkers." To characterize Vermont's sparse population there is the comment of a schoolgirl who wrote, "I like Vermont because the trees are close together and the people are far apart." Those who admire how Vermont is contrary country might cite the dictum from folklore which says: "If a Vermonter fell into a river he would float *up*stream."

The entire statehouse bespeaks a sense of history. Away from the inscriptions the walls are full of portraits and plaques. Flags carried by Vermonters in the Civil War are clustered in a tattered and confused dignity behind glass cases. Some of their staves were scarred by Confederate bullets, and the flags themselves were stained by the blood of young Vermonters who fought beneath them. The flag of the "Old Brigade," for example, was carried into Civil War battles that today ring vividly in memory for bloodshed and carnage—the Wilderness, Spotsylvania, Cold Harbor, Winchester, New Market, Cedar Creek, and others. In a span of slightly more than five months a total of 3,116 Vermonters were killed or wounded while following those flags. During the entire war Vermont lost 5,237 of its men; 350 of them died in Andersonville Prison, the Confederate Dachau in Georgia. Comparative estimates are difficult to derive, but along with Michigan and Kansas, Vermont gave as high proportion of its manhood for the Union cause during the Civil War as any state in the nation. Some historians claim Vermont had the highest ratio of all.

Vermonters looking at those flags in glass cases in the statehouse can understand what Gov. Erastus Fairbanks meant in 1861 when, responding to President Lincoln's request to the Union governors for troops, he replied with cool assurance: "Vermont will do its duty." Or why Gen. John Sedgwick at the battle of Gettysburg had confidence in the Green Mountain troops and issued his famous order, "Put the Vermonters ahead and keep the column well closed up." No Vermont flags were captured in battle by Confederates during the Civil War, and when Richmond fell in 1865 the first Union troops to enter the Confederate capital were Vermonters. These flags are emblematic of such proud words and deeds.

In the governor's reception room on the second floor of the statehouse is Julian Scott's large (20 feet by 10 feet) painting of the Old Vermont Brigade at the battle of Cedar Creek on October 19, 1864. A native of Johnson, Vermont, who enlisted as a drummer boy and later was wounded, Scott wanted to paint a scene of the bloody cornfield at Antietam where the Old Brigade fought valiantly, but Vermont veterans persuaded him to choose Cedar Creek in the Shenandoah Valley because more Vermont regiments were under fire in that encounter than in any other Civil War engagement. In detail Scott showed Vermonters in the last victorious charge at the end of a desperate and bloody day of fighting. Framed in dark oak, the painting itself is dark and difficult to comprehend in its entirety because the reception room is narrow. The painting deserves to be up high and well-lighted, and viewed in a room as large as its dimensions require, but the statehouse doesn't have ample space. (Generally Vermonters don't build large rooms with high ceilings; smaller spaces are easier to heat in winter.) But Gen. Philip Sheridan liked it when he visited Montpelier shortly after the Civil War to give a speech in the house chamber. He studied Scott's painting intently and then praised it for its realism because, he said, it "made the boys as they were, going in."

The Statehouse walls are so crowded with portraits and plaques that all available space seems occupied. Things are exhibited in a chock-a-block fashion; the array is splendidly disordered like the upstairs living quarters of the mansion of some landed family whose deep roots entwine the history of the state. In a sense the statehouse furnishings give an impression of the homestead of Vermont's most prominent family. Pompous former governors and senators look sternly through Victorian chinwhiskers from their portraits. Memorabilia abounds. Absorbed as a whole, they make a visitor realize that Vermont is a place on the calendar as well as a place on the map, and the calendar has a nineteenth-century date on it. But the elegant portraiture doesn't conflict with the clean and simple lines of white paneling and dark polished wood. Instead the atmosphere denotes stability through time, a stiff-necked adherence to those traditional virtues of industry and frugality epitomized by Theodore Roosevelt as the "life of effort" in the inscription on the downstairs wall by the Lincoln bust. Vermont has become an island in space and time.

In the senate chamber with its thirty seats, and in the much larger representatives hall with 150 seats, the dark desks are arranged in a semicircle around the well of each house. They also speak, like the building itself, with a quiet solemnity and sturdiness of purpose. Some think the senate chamber is the most beautiful room in the entire state. In each chamber the presiding officer stands at a rostrum decorated with a carved rendition of the Vermont coat of arms, and this is appropriate for Vermont, too. The coat of arms shows a green landscape with the outline of Camel's Hump (Vermont's third-highest mountain) and Mount Mansfield (Vermont's highest peak, at 4,083 feet) rising in blue majesty against a yellow sky. In 1861 Charles Heyde, a Burlington artist, was commissioned by the Vermont Historical Society to depict the coat of arms for formal and official state uses, and he sketched these two mountains as they were probably seen from Lake Champlain by Samuel de Champlain in 1609. A pine tree rises from the base of the shield and reaches nearly to the top; on one side is a cow, and on the other are three sheaves of wheat. On the crest is the head of a buck deer, and below is the state's motto, "Vermont, Freedom and Unity," which neatly expresses the fact that Vermont was independent before joining the Union, and persisted in freely choosing its own stance on issues despite the constraints of being one of the United States. Luxuriant branches of pine support the shield, and these evergreens represent the sprigs of pine worn by Vermonters who went to fight at Plattsburgh, New York, during the War of 1812, and later went southward to fight in the Civil War. The Vermont state seal is a simplified version of the coat of arms.

Outside, on the portico of the statehouse, the statue of Ethan Allen stands bigger than life next to the main entrance. For Ethan to stand on the portico of the Temple of Theseus is appropriate because both were state-builders and capable of prodigious feats of strength. The reputations of both also, are largely legendary. The original statue of Ethan was carved by Larkin Mead and dedicated in 1861; the current statue is a duplicate by Aristide Piccini and replaced the original when it weathered. Ethan has his arm upraised and a scowl on his face; he is depicted in the audacious act of demanding the surrender of Fort Ticonderoga from the British on May 10, 1775. Standing on a circular granite base he represents the verve and zeal of Vermont's defiance in the days of its emergence and uncertain status as a separate republic and later as a contrary-minded member of the United States. Suitably, a brass cannon captured from Hessian mercenaries at the Battle of Bennington in 1777 stands across the portico from Ethan Allen. By a quirk of history the cannon had been part of the ordnance of Gen. William Hull in the War of 1812 and was recaptured by the British when Hull surrendered Detroit to the British. But the following spring, when American troops defeated General Vincent's Britishers at Fort George, near the mouth of the Niagara River, the cannon was recaptured. It was sent to Washington where Henry Stevens, the famous bibliophile from Barnet, Vermont, discovered it outside an arsenal in dismantled condition where it had been discarded as obsolete. Being a lover of Vermont (he often signed himself as G. M. B.—for Green Mountain Boy—when he took up residence in London, England, and became a renowned book dealer), he found a way to get the cannon to Vermont for display.

Down from the portico, on a terrace of the statehouse lawn, stand two large cannons from the Spanish cruiser *Castilla,* which was sunk by George Dewey's squadron in Manila Bay, the Philippines, on May 1, 1898. Thus Dewey's famous command, "You may fire when ready, Gridley," reverberates from that long-ago war across this spot where Dewey played as a youngster.

The Dewey home was moved in 1947 from its original location across from the capitol to a site down State Street to the west, where it served as an antique shop and gradually became so dilapidated that it was demolished and replaced by a parking lot. An office building occupies the original site. A similar fate might have befallen the Pavilion Hotel, to the east of the capitol, just beyond the granite Supreme Court Building (which also houses the Vermont Department of Libraries). Instead a compromise was reached, after three years of controversy, by those who would preserve the structure and those who would demolish it. As with all compromises it satisfied everybody except the uncompromising purists at both extremes. The preservationists wanted the old hotel renovated, and the resolute modernists insisted that a new glass-and-steel office building or parking structure would be the only way to serve efficiency. The solution was to build a new office building with the same exterior style as the 1876 "Steamboat Gothic" structure. As a consequence, the statehouse green is still bordered by "the grand old lady of State Street," as the five-story Victorian landmark was called, its two-story white porch set against red brick walls suggesting grace and stability. Flower boxes overflow the railings in the summertime, and benches invite the modern world to slow its pace and sit awhile.

The lobby of the 1876 hotel has been restored as a remnant of the decades when this structure was called "Vermont's third house" because many legislators lodged there and state business was conducted informally in its rooms. Behind the lobby the museum of the Vermont Historical Society allows a visitor to roam among a mishmash of Vermont artifacts, ranging from Ethan Allen's rifle to the stuffed carcass of the last panther shot in Vermont—killed in Barnard, in 1881. Inside the Pavilion and outside, up and down State Street, other red brick buildings and Victorian houses now used for state offices add to Montpelier's aura of permanence and tranquillity. Even the tippling spots within an easy walk of the statehouse bear names reflecting Vermont symbols—the Thrush Tavern is named for the Hermit Thrush, Vermont's state bird, and the Justin Morgan Lounge in the Montpelier Tavern Motor Inn honors the Morgan horse, Vermont's official state animal. This horse came to Vermont from Massachusetts in 1791 with its owner, a singing-master named Justin Morgan, and sired a line of sturdy descendants. The Morgan, it has been said with pride by Vermonters, could outrun, outpull, and outlast any other breed, just as you would expect a Vermont horse to do.

4

Vermonters and Their Government:
Small is Beautiful

*O*N a warm day it is worthwhile to sit on the statehouse steps and ruminate on the fact that Vermont exists as a state and Montpelier as its capital, and the statehouse serves as the official locus of state business. That defiant statue of Ethan Allen and the cannon, and that hard rock cut from granite quarries, suggest that Vermont, perhaps more than any other state in the Union, lives its present with a pervasive sense of its past.

Montpelier is quiet: a visitor from noisy parts of the nation might notice this whereas a native might assume it is a natural characteristic and not mention it. State Street can become crowded with cars when state offices empty at 4:30 P.M. on workday afternoons, but even with a long line of cars waiting to escape the bottleneck in downtown Montpelier and get home to the hills and surrounding towns, the absence of a single honking car horn is remarkable for anyone who has heard what a traffic jam sounds like on one of Manhattan's major arteries.

True, when there is nothing else to do at twilight or later on a summer evening the kids go roaring back and forth on State Street on their motorcycles and in their cars with all the undirected energy of aimless young Americans. When not riding they stand around their parked vehicles, talking about their speed and wild escapades, or sit on the porch of the Pavilion Building, drinking beer and wine and generally being loudly obnoxious. Oldsters no longer sit there on summer evenings, wait-

ing for the movies to start or for a bus to arrive at the little depot
across the street. But still there are times, after working and
commuting hours, when the quiet is marred only by occasional
street noises. Otherwise the breeze can be heard wafting gently
around corners and through the trees.

For a long time Montpelier must have persisted as one of the
last places in the United States where adults could walk after
dark without any fear of getting mugged and homeowners didn't
lock their doors at bedtime. That is changing now: youngsters
who formerly left their bicycles carelessly on lawns all night
and still found them undisturbed in the morning are now being
told of unlocked bikes which have been stolen, even from
porches. Ever since Olene Doyle had her purse snatched in the
supermarket parking lot, the fear of crime has become real. For
years a window in the statehouse was deliberately kept unlocked
because George Aiken, when governor, liked to return to his office at night but often forgot his keys. Thus the "Aiken Window" became a secret entry to the statehouse and until the late
1960s was used by members of the press corps who were then
quartered up under the dome and wanted to get inside after-
hours. All that is different now; the statehouse has an electronic
monitoring system which includes televised surveillance of visitors moving through its far corners.

Yet Montpelier is still a town where coins left in the pocket
of a suit sent to the cleaners will be returned safely when the
suit is ready to be picked up. It is where the public tennis courts
are likely to be free without a long wait, even at five o'clock on a
Friday afternoon in summer. It is where it is safe to assume that
a person approached on the sidewalk is an acquaintance from
some introduction made in the misty past and not a stranger,
and it would be wiser to say "hello" rather than pass by without some nod of recognition.

Montpelier is where a driver can expect to find a parking
space in front of the statehouse at midday, except during the
legislative session and at the height of tourist traffic during the
summer and foliage seasons. This is even more remarkable
because the Vermont Division of Motor Vehicles has its

quarters on the first floor of the office building directly across from the statehouse, and its location generates continuous on-street parking needs as Vermont newcomers and others come regularly to Montpelier to register their cars and otherwise tangle with bureaucrats in various state departments. Montpelier is small, just as Vermont is small. Its 8,700 residents make it the smallest state capital in the nation. Even Juneau, Alaska, has 5,000 more residents, and places like Cheyenne, Wyoming, Pierre, South Dakota, and Carson City, Nevada, are at least twice as large. As in small towns everywhere, there is little anonymity in Montpelier. Thus the husband of one of my secretaries at the Vermont Historical Society was a clerk in Montpelier's state liquor store (there is only one in town), and could gauge both my drinking tastes and my consumption rate. The husband of another secretary was the person who gave me my driver's examination when I applied for a Vermont license.

Anecdotes are told about Vermont as a whole to emphasize its smallness. William Allen White once told Dorothy Canfield Fisher that he finally figured out why Vermont politicians were such honest souls. The explanation, said he, lay in the fact that there were not many nickels circulating in Vermont, and because everybody knew where they were at any given time it was nearly impossible for any state official to steal one.

Because Vermonters are few in number it is wise to assume that in Vermont the person you are conversing with is related to, or acquainted with, the person you are talking about. Even in Burlington, Vermont's largest city (a metropolitan area of 125,000), this premise can be painfully true. Marguerite Hurrey Wolf came to Burlington when her husband accepted a position on the faculty of the medical college at the University of Vermont. "We were fresh from the impersonal towers of Manhattan," she has recounted, "and it never occurred to me that half the population in Burlington knew what houses were on the market, their approximate values and who lived in them. I was gaily telling one colleague's wife about the monstrosity that I had visited that day, describing its ugly woodwork, antiquated kitchen and exorbitant price. I thought she cooled perceptibly and I asked her if she knew the house. 'Every newel post,' she replied, 'that's my family homestead.' " [1]

Vermont contains an estimated population of 500,000, which is an increase of about 60,000 from the 1970 federal census. Nevada passed Vermont in size of population in the 1970 census; that means that only Wyoming and Alaska contain fewer people. For the present, only one American of every 458 is a Vermont resident. Put another way, only .00218 percent of the American population lives in Vermont. Subtract the 125,000 Vermonters who live in greater Burlington, and another 50,000 who live in Rutland, Barre, Brattleboro, and Bennington, and the number of Vermonters who live in rural or village Vermont goes down to 325,000. Half of Vermont's population lives in twenty-four of its 246 towns. The U.S. Postal Service zip code directory lists all of Vermont's zip codes on a single page, with space to spare.

Forty-fourth in geographic size among the fifty states, Vermont covers more land than Connecticut, Delaware, Hawaii, Massachusetts, Rhode Island, and New Hampshire. The state's eastern boundary runs 157 miles from the Canadian border to the Massachusetts border along the mean watermark on the Vermont bank of the Connecticut River, which means the stream officially is in New Hampshire. On the west the border separating Vermont from New York runs 120 miles down Lake Champlain. Mountain ranges ordinarily serve as barriers, and this was true in Vermont until fairly recently. In *The Green Mountains of Vermont*, W. Storrs Lee called the mountains an "eternal barrier" because they divided eastern Vermont and western Vermont into separate sections. Historically the east was more conservative; nineteen of the first twenty-one Congregational churches in Vermont were in the Connecticut Valley, whereas Ethan Allen and his irreligious freethinkers located on the western side. Even today Vermonters on the east side speak with more of a Boston accent in their voices, whereas westerners

---

1. Marguerite Hurrey Wolf, *How To Be A Doctor's Wife Without Really Dying* (Coral Gables, Fla.: Wake-Brook House, 1967), p. 101.

sound more like upstate New Yorkers. Eastern Vermonters say "bahn" for "barn"; western Vermonters say "barrn." Until recently the "mountain rule" in Vermont politics was an understanding that the governorship would alternate between the east side of the mountains and the west side, and that Vermont's two senators would represent opposite sides of the barrier.

In 1980, sitting on the statehouse steps, one is impressed with how accessible Montpelier is to a large number of Vermonters. Its accessibility is generally due to Interstate Highway 89, the Vermont portion of which was completed in 1969, and which enters Vermont from New Hampshire at White River Junction, one hour of driving time south and east of Montpelier. An hour's drive north and west from Montpelier, and a motorist is into Burlington or beyond, heading towards the international border station at Highgate and only ninety minutes or so from the St. Lawrence River and Montreal's Dominion Square. One aspect of driving in Vermont which brings a self-satisfied smile to the face of a Vermont driver is the contrast between driving on an uncrowded road while the car radio, tuned to a New York or Montreal station, gives the latest report of the congestion on the West Side Highway in Manhattan or the Jacques Cartier Bridge in Montreal. In such moments Vermonters realize how close they are to major metropolitan areas but also how distant they are from the everyday exasperations of big-city commuters. It is easy to be smug in such moments, but it makes a person wonder how much longer Vermont can enjoy the best of these two worlds.

In Vermont commuters to Montpelier drive from as far away as St. Johnsbury near the New Hampshire border, and from Rutland to the southwest near the New York border. If Vermont citizens have something to say in Montpelier at a legislative hearing they can drive up from Brattleboro or Bennington in the southern corners, or down from St. Albans or the Northeast Kingdom, and still be home for supper.

In Vermont citizens don't look upon their two senators and congressmen in Washington as strangers. Citizens probably know their state representative—or the representative knows where constituents work, or live, or who their children married.

A familiar greeting is often overhead: "You must be the fellow who bought the Marsette House." (Vermonters attach names to homes when a family moves *out;* the past is not far from the present in their thinking. It is also an oblique way to remind newcomers of their status as new arrivals, and regardless of how congenially they fit into the community, and aspire to social acceptance, they will long be categorized as recent arrivals or temporary residents.) In many instances Vermont legislators probably decided to stand for election because the legislative club didn't seem difficult to aspire to, provided a person had the time and income and, until recently, the Republican pedigree. Individual members can achieve amazing accomplishments. Theodore Riehle of South Burlington was one: he proposed to ban off-premise billboards along Vermont roadsides, and through promotion and persuasion and tireless effort he overcame a stiff lobbying campaign against the bill which billboard proponents organized.

Vermont at times appears to be David, slaying the Goliath of the Big Interests. In 1970 the Vermont legislature approved the most far-reaching environmental legislation passed to date by any state when it added Act 250 to the Vermont statutes. The act requires all land developments of more than ten acres (or as small as one acre in towns which lack zoning and subdivision controls) to abide by the State Land Use and Development Plan. The real estate agents howled and predicted disaster but they couldn't defeat the measure. It requires developers in Vermont to guarantee before they build that water sources and sewage disposal are adequate, that pollution and erosion won't occur, that natural resources, scenic areas, and historic sites won't be harmed, and that roads can bear the traffic and schools can absorb the children when the population grows. An environmental board and seven district commissions implement the plan. This severe crackdown on uncontrolled development has given Vermont an antibusiness reputation, in some circles, but Vermonters continue to believe the plan is not too stringent despite the efforts of developers to weaken it.

Achievements like Act 250 cause Vermonters to smirk at the big states. With mock pity they note it is easier to pass forward-looking legislation in Montpelier than it is for Manhattan residents to make their voices heard in Albany, or for a good-government type in some other big city to carry a torch of righteousness to the state capital. In Vermont the immediacy of government suggests that the state is a textbook on how civic affairs can operate responsively.

This direct democracy can be discouraging, too. A game biologist with the Vermont Department of Fish and Game may persuade a legislator to introduce a bill reducing the size of the Vermont deer herd to a number where the animals are able to survive the hard winters of less available leaves, berries, and forage. A public hearing will be held in the evening in the house chamber, and deerhunters for miles around Montpelier will fill the galleries and spare seats, after filling themselves with beer, and noisily deride those advocating a reduction in the number of deer. The chairman of the committee considering the bill may get exasperated or testy and threaten to adjourn the hearing unless decorum is maintained. But legislators get the message and act on it regardless of personal views about the size of the deer herd. All those hunters, so visibly exercised by what they term an infringement on their autumnal rights to plod through the leaf-strewn woods and shoot their bucks, convey a clear warning to legislators who might dally with voting for the deer instead of the hunters.

The same scenes occur when snowmobile owners descend on the statehouse for hearings about controlling those noisy intruders in the winter stillness. There are 36,000 registered snowmobiles in Vermont, plus others which are unregistered or brought in by out-of-staters. "If you want to meet a seventh-generation Vermonter," a seventh-generation Vermonter remarked bitterly, "you'll see him astride his snowmobile, steering through somebody's field, full of beer and as thoughtless as a teenager with a new driver's license and unrestricted use of the family car for an evening. He'll come through your land at night if he has a mind to, circling your house and making that infernal noise even if your house is dark and normal people might assume at that late hour that you're trying to sleep." He adds his disdain for the way snowmobilers let their dogs chase the deer on the hard-packed snowmobile trails, the deer already near exhaustion because their nourishment during the winter is limited. "To hell with them," he says curtly about the snowmobilers. But in those statehouse hearings their numbers and their vociferous attitude must cause Ceres, up atop the dome, to smile. It *is* democracy, and they do drink a lot of beer!

Lobbyists, to be sure, are evident in Montpelier, and stories are told about olden days when one would sit in the legislative gallery, leaning on the white railing with a folded piece of paper in his hands, which he used to signal instructions to lieutenants on the floor. The stories have more drama in them than truth. Vermont has never been dominated by the "interests" to the extent that railroads once dominated New Hampshire or the copper barons ruled Montana. More typical is George Aiken's custom of holding down his expenses for re-election to the Senate to less than $20 in each campaign. In 1968 he spent $17.06. Aiken said he spent only that much to make a few phone calls, mail a few letters, and buy some gas to get to some Grange Hall or other meeting place to say a few words (not necessarily about politics or his candidacy) and shake hands all around. When expenses would rise a few dollars above what he spent six years before, Aiken would explain by noting a gallon of gas cost more, or the postal service had raised its postage rates.

Press coverage by Vermont daily newspapers and the wire services is detailed and often probing. This watchfulness keeps bureaucrats and politicians alert and responsive. Donors who contribute as little as $5 to a candidate are likely to find their gifts listed as news in the *Rutland Herald,* thus causing their friends to wonder why they didn't contribute more, and causing them to regret they didn't give more instead of appearing tight-fisted. When the Vermont Department of Highways opens bids from contractors for road construction or repair projects the specific amounts from all the bidders is broadcast during the noon hour by Vermont's most influential radio station, WDEV in Waterbury. Robert Stafford learned how words become newsworthy, a lesson which his experience as a Vermont governor and five-term congressman had not taught him. One year he won the Democratic nomination for Congress in addition to the

Republican nomination (another example of how a small number of Vermont voters can exert inordinate influence), and in a speech to the Rutland Lions Club he extracted all the humor he could from the fact that he was opposing himself in the run-off campaign. "I've traveled throughout the state in the past three weeks, but the fellow on the other side of the ballot has gone everywhere I've gone," he lamented with mock seriousness. "He's shaken every hand I've shaken." And then he added: "Besides that, my wife is sleeping with him." This reference to his conjugal situation was duly recorded in the next morning's edition of the *Rutland Herald*.

It is hard to keep a secret in Vermont, even if some are trying to keep Vermont a secret from the rest of the world. This is as true of personal characteristics as it is of public behavior. Shortly after Ernest William Gibson had resigned in 1949 as governor of Vermont in order to accept a federal judgeship, he was awakened at home in Brattleboro one night by a call from a police chief in a southern town. The chief said one of his officers had picked up four men in a cemetery, and the four had clearly been imbibing for a good share of the evening. They claimed to be innocent of any mischief; they said they were attending a major meeting of the Grange and in the course of the evening they decided to visit the grave of a founder of the Grange and pay homage at his tombstone. While wandering through the cemetery they were seen by a policeman driving by, and the officer of the law decided to bring all four to the stationhouse as suspicious characters. One of the four protested his innocence by emphasizing he was Harold A. Arthur, governor of Vermont, and didn't deserve to be treated that way. The chief agreed to telephone the previous governor of Vermont to ascertain if the gentleman in his custody was indeed Vermont's highest-ranking constitutional officer.

Judge Gibson recalled sleepily that Governor Arthur was an excellent whistler. "Can he whistle?" the judge asked the chief. The chief asked back, a tone of disbelief in his voice, "Can he whistle?" The question seemed silly. But the judge was insistent. "Yes, can he whistle? Ask him to whistle." The judge heard the chief lower the telephone and say in a muffled voice,

"Hey, bud, can you whistle?" The retort was a mellifluous and sprightly whistling up and down several octaves. "He sure can whistle!" the chief said emphatically. "Well," said the judge with equal emphasis, "he sure is our governor!"

5

Vermont and New Hampshire: Two Roads Diverged

$\mathcal{O}$UTSIDERS tend to pair Vermont with New Hampshire, and the two states are sometimes called the Twin States—at least in the Connecticut River Valley where many people live, shop, and work on different sides of the river and don't give a thought to interstate commerce as part of their daily lives. Radio stations beam into both states, and newspapers have subscribers who read the same regional news, although they look to Concord or Montpelier for state news. The first school district in the United States to unite towns on opposite sides of a state boundary is the Dresden School District, which joins Norwich, Vermont, with Hanover, New Hampshire, and which takes its name from the original name for Hanover. The combination really isn't extraordinary, because Norwich has long served as a bedroom community for faculty members at Dartmouth College, just as nonprofessional employees at Dartmouth, such as janitors and maintenance men, often live in White River Junction, Vermont, because they can't afford the high cost of real estate in affluent Hanover. Similarly, youngsters north of Hanover in Lyme, New Hampshire, have been crossing the Connecticut River for generations to be educated at Thetford Academy. Historically, more Vermont students attended Dartmouth College than the University of Vermont until the 1870s when the proportion shifted to UVM.

Robert Frost once described Vermont and New Hampshire as "yoke fellows" and said New Hampshire was one of the two best states in the nation to live in, Vermont being the other. New Hampshire claims Frost because he lived a long time in that state; Vermonters retaliate by noting that the Vermont Legislature in 1961 designated Frost as its official poet laureate, that Frost left New Hampshire to live in three different Vermont towns—Concord, Shaftsbury, and Ripton—and that he chose to be buried in the historic churchyard at Old Bennington. Arguments about Frost's regard for New Hampshire versus his affection for Vermont seem pointless to outsiders. It is natural to wonder why northern New Englanders should make an issue about a Californian born south of Market Street in San Francisco, named after Gen. Robert E. Lee, and forced to go to England (not *New* England, mind you) to publish his first widely known volume of verse.

Outsiders confuse Vermont with New Hampshire and don't seem perturbed when they do. Evan Hill, a writer who lives in New Hampshire, tells how he has dealt for twenty years or more with an editor at *Reader's Digest* who couldn't distinguish New Hampshire from Vermont. "And how are things in Vermont?" the editor would ask Hill in greeting. "New Hampshire," Hill would reply. Later, while discussing a manuscript, the editor would say, "Now when you get back to Vermont, why don't you add a paragraph or. . . ." Hill would interrupt to say "New Hampshire." And upon leaving the editor would say, "Have a good trip back to Vermont." Hill would try again: " 'New Hampshire,' I say, but it does no good. And perhaps that's just as well. It's not truly sinful to be confused with a Vermonter." [1]

But for Vermonters it is important not to be confused with New Hampshiremen. Vermonters contend that the two states are remarkably different—and that the differences are noticeable upon crossing from New Hampshire into Vermont. They love to hear statements like one by Elizabeth Forbes, coauthor of *New*

1. Evan Hill, *The Primary State: An Historical Guide to New Hampshire* (Taftsville, Vt.: Countryman Press, 1976), p. xiii.

Hampshire: A Bicentennial History: "I'm always surprised when I cross the Connecticut River into Vermont, to see the differences in look between the two states. New Hampshire looks beat and tired and bedraggled in places, while Vermont is neat and well-tended." [2] Vermonters attribute the difference to the ice sheet: it scraped more severely at the New Hampshire peaks, leaving them stony and exposed. Also, geologic action thrust up more granite in New Hampshire than Vermont, and granite has an acidic quality which reduces the fertility of the soil. Vermont is underlaid more with limestone, gneisses, and schists—indeed, green schist is the official state rock—and these sweeten the soil. Thus, Vermont is greener than New Hampshire, and that is why it looks more pastoral and tidy. For Vermonters the logic of this analysis leads inescapably to the conclusion that the Green Mountains are more beautiful than the White Mountains, and that Vermont as a state is much more beautiful than New Hampshire.

Vermonters contend also that their state is more sensible than New Hampshire. They argue that a right-wing governor like New Hampshire's Meldrim Thomson, Jr., elected to three consecutive terms in the 1970s, could never win a single state-wide election in Vermont, and that a right-wing newspaper like William Loeb's *Manchester Union Leader* would never exert influence in Vermont like it does in New Hampshire. In New Hampshire the *Union Leader* plays a major role in defining issues and in persuading some prospective state-wide candidates to put themselves forward and dissuading others from doing the same. Decent people are reluctant to expose themselves and their families to being pilloried by Loeb's relentless and often personal criticism in his newspaper. In Vermont there is no evidence that any newspaper exerts influence on the process of candidate selection by either major party.

Vermont has been spared almost all the anguish of McCarthyism in the years since World War Two, but New Hampshire has nurtured several petty McCarthyites, each encouraged by Loeb's incessant clangor about subversion from within. In

2. Quoted by Jeanne Paul, *Humanities* 6 (1976): 4-5.

Vermont in 1953 a bill was introduced in the general assembly to authorize an investigation of textbooks in use in Vermont schools on the suspicion that subversive ideas were imbedded in some of them and should be rooted out or the books should be discarded. Former Congressman Charles Plumley had persuaded a Northfield neighbor of his to introduce the bill, and Plumley and the few supporters of the bill who spoke in favor of it hinted darkly that "Vermont was a testing ground for the Communists" and that the conspiracy was symbolized by the fact that Alger Hiss had been known to summer in Peacham. The bill was referred to the House Education Committee, which reported it, "without recommendation." It went to the House Appropriations Committee because it called for state funds to establish a board of censors to examine and decide what schoolbooks were acceptable. The House Appropriations Committee voted against the bill by a tally of 14 to 1. On the house floor, in that year when McCarthyism was inflaming the nation, the bill to protect Vermont youngsters from schoolbook subversion was defeated overwhelmingly. Two hundred and two house members voted against it; only eleven voted for it. "Anybody who tries to bore from within in Vermont is going to strike granite," is how one editor summarized the matter.[3] Prudence, caution, reasonableness, and a refusal to be scared into repressive legislation carried the day in Vermont. The episode allows Vermonters to lament, to the discomfort of those in New Hampshire who are sensitive to barbs about their state's behavior, that the Granite State could be more granite-like in opposing gibberish in public dialogue.

Whenever Vermonters become dismayed at the pettiness or obtuseness of their general assembly they sigh with relief that not Vermont but New Hampshire is burdened with a legislature so large, cumbersome, and underpaid that it is as slow as cold maple syrup in its deliberations. In fact the New Hampshire Legislature is the largest in the western hemisphere and the fourth largest in the world, with four hundred members sitting in its lower house.

3. Quoted by Dorothy Canfield Fisher, *Vermont Tradition: The Biography of an Outlook on Life* (Boston: Little, Brown & Co., 1953), p. 397.

A favorite way for Vermont chauvinists to illustrate the differences between New Hampshire politics and Green Mountain politics is to emphasize the contrast between New Hampshire Sen. H. Styles Bridges and Vermont Sen. Ralph Flanders. While Bridges was blustering about all sorts of subversive influences undermining his vision of a properly conservative America, his colleague from Vermont, Ralph Flanders, had the courage to stand up in the Senate and call for an end to Joe McCarthy's unfounded and unprincipled red-baiting. Flanders was a conservative, too, but in the bedrock sense of a man personally committed to the traditional values of a nation which meant what it proclaimed in the Bill of Rights.

New Hampshire has neither a sales tax nor an income tax, and as a result it has minimal state services. Vermont ranks twenty-third among all the states in state expenditures per citizen, while New Hampshire ranks forty-second. To New Hampshire Vermont is spendthrift; to Vermont, New Hampshire is tightwad.

New Hampshire has about 300,000 more residents than Vermont, and its growth rate—because of its low tax rate—is among the highest of all states in the Union. But Vermonters have a rejoinder to economic data like that; they point out that the average weekly earnings of production workers in manufacturing in New Hampshire are far below those in Vermont. And to twist the knife they like to mention that concern about the public good in New Hampshire isn't as spirited as it is in Vermont; in 1968, for example, Vermont outscored New Hampshire in voter participation by six to one. Ask a Vermonter why people choose to live on the New Hampshire side of the Connecticut River and he or she might quote Maxfield Parrish, the artist who lived in Cornish, New Hampshire, across from Windsor, Vermont: "I live in New Hampshire so I can get a better view of Vermont."[4] Nor was that just a rodomontade by Parrish; the outline of Mount Ascutney, south of Windsor, looms in the background of many of his paintings.

For Vermonters to tease their neighbors across the river gives

4. Quoted by George E. Holman, "Maxfield Parrish Looks at Vermont," *Vermont Life* 6 (1952): 12.

all the pleasure which comes to a little brother when he taunts a big brother. Vermonters relish these occasions. When the Vermont General Assembly was debating a bill authorizing a state appropriation of $10,000 to assist repair and preservation of the Bedell Covered Bridge, which spans the Connecticut River between Haverhill, New Hampshire, and Newbury, Vermont, some opponents emphasized that the bridge actually was New Hampshire's because New Hampshire's jurisdiction extends to the mean low-water mark on the Vermont side of the river. Why should Vermont spend its money to help repair New Hampshire's bridge, opponents asked, when New Hampshire refused to appropriate even one dollar in state revenues to support its own bridge? Why be generous in times of austerity when New Hampshire was being tight-fisted? Others sided with Rep. Allen R. Foley of Norwich, a retired Dartmouth College history professor who preferred to live in Vermont and look through the back windows of his house towards New Hampshire than live there. "I was born in Massachusetts," Foley explains, "educated in New Hampshire, and found peace and contentment in Vermont." But on the floor of the house, when the Bedell Covered Bridge bill was up for discussion, Foley rose to resolve the issue. "Let's raise it from $10,000.00 to $15,000.00," he suggested, "and shame the bastards."

A Vermonter is likely to admit, with a sigh of relief and a skyward look to thank the lucky stars, that fate has been kind to Vermont by not burdening it with a paper as extremist as the *Union Leader*. There is irony in that because Loeb, the *Union Leader* owner, got his start as a newspaper publisher by buying a couple of Vermont dailies, and he is still owner of the drab *St. Albans Messenger*. Vermont's largest newspaper is the *Burlington Free Press*, with a circulation of about 46,000 across northern Vermont, and although it is conservative in a shrill and fustian way, its influence is counterbalanced by the smaller but energetic *Rutland Herald*. The *Herald* company also owns the *Barre-Montpelier Times-Argus*, and the two provide a searching treatment of Vermont politics. The *Herald* is admired among newspaper professionals as one of the best small dailies in the nation. Vermont has only three television stations, and one of these, fortunately, is the noncommercial outlet for quality programming by the Public Broadcasting System. One of the commercial channels, WCAX-TV, can reach 75 percent of all the households in Vermont which possess TV sets. It is staid like the *Free Press* but too stodgy to lure a following. Vermont is susceptible to saturation by the right-wing media—perhaps even more so than New Hampshire. Vermonters aren't exposed to Boston-based television news and newspaper reporting, whereas southern New Hampshire is now within the outer fringes of suburban Boston and attuned to Boston's liberal mix of journalism. A press baron who wanted to dominate a state by buying a major newspaper might think that Vermont would be a better prospect than New Hampshire and that Loeb's success could be emulated in the state next door. But to date it hasn't happened and it probably won't.

A look at history suggests the differences between New Hampshire and Vermont can't be attributed primarily to the impact of the media serving each state. The states have been different in major ways at critical periods in the nation's history. Before the Civil War Vermont was a hotbed of abolitionist sentiment but New Hampshire was as unmoved about the plight of Negro slaves as any state in the North. Vermont and Massachusetts were the two strongest Whig states before the Civil War while New Hampshire was the strongest Democratic state. Antimasonry became a major political force in Vermont in the 1830s—indeed, Vermont was the only state in the nation in 1832 to instruct its presidential electors to cast their ballots for William Wirt, the Antimasonic candidate for president, while antimasonry made no impact on New Hampshire politics. In 1912 Vermont was one of only two states (the other was Utah) to stick with William Howard Taft when Theodore Roosevelt's third-party candidacy disrupted many traditionally Republican states and permitted Woodrow Wilson to win. Vermont did not support Franklin D. Roosevelt during his four successful campaigns for the presidency; New Hampshire retained its traditional Republican allegiance in 1932 but then voted for FDR in 1936, 1940, and 1944. Perhaps the differences go back to the beginning; New Hampshire was settled initially in its coastal lowlands, and maritime wealth nurtured an aristocracy in Portsmouth that made it similar to Salem, Boston, and Newport. Vermonters were upcountry people from the outset and plainly democratic in ways unlike the seaport residents. Ethan Allen said it to New Yorkers but the remark applies as well to Vermont-New Hampshire relationships: "The gods of the hills are not the gods of the valley."

Understandably Vermonters do not acquiesce gently when people from afar assume that all of northern New England must be pretty much the same country. For outsiders the similarities are confusing. New Hampshire is nicknamed the "Granite State" but the world's largest granite quarries are at Barre, Vermont. A rock formation in New Hampshire's Franconia Notch called "The Great Stone Face" or "The Old Man of the Mountains" has mistakenly been credited as a Vermont configuration, possibly because stone faces and craggy profiles are what people expect to see when they see Vermonters.

So too with New Hampshire Sen. Charles Tobey; this tart, Bible-quoting old Yankee was so sharp-tongued and indignant during the well-televised Kefauver hearings on illegal gambling and big-time criminal activities during the early 1950s that viewers across the nation assumed anybody who talked like that must come from Vermont. Old-fashioned moral standards are thought to survive longer in Vermont than in citified places. Sherman Adams, also, has been labeled a Vermonter by outsiders because this former New Hampshire governor who became President Dwight Eisenhower's key White House aide was a tight-lipped, no-nonsense type of administrator who wasn't hesitant to say no, bluntly and unequivocally. In Adams's case, however, there was good reason to make the Vermont attribution; he was born in Dover, Vermont, in 1899.

An American doesn't know the diversity of his country until he has experienced that remote upper pocket of it called Vermont. Likewise, a Vermonter doesn't know Vermont if he hasn't experienced some other regions of the country. All good Vermonters should leave home. They need to walk in warm January sunshine in the sunbelt in order to appreciate what a cold and snowy winter does to people in the snowbelt. They need to see how fertile soil and a long growing season make farming a less grueling venture when the climate is gentle. They need to see life in the city streets and sense the anomie which plagues millions of urban dwellers. They need also to know how cities can nurture the arts and give spice to life—from theater to exotic foods—and contrast this heterogeneity with their small-town fare. They need to drive the New Jersey Turnpike and the Santa Monica Freeway, and risk riding the New York subways at rush hours in order to appreciate the fact that Vermont is civil and sparsely settled.

Vermonters and Americans everywhere need to understand that Vermont is unlike the rest of the nation. That fundamental truth can be stated simply and directly: Vermont is different. Those three words—terse, taut, and unadorned—could also be inscribed on one of the statehouse walls.

Part II

History

6

Hillside Perspectives and Mythic Figures

ERMONT is different because its history is different. People who equate the significance and relevance of a state's history with its role in national affairs can be amused at the prospect of someone writing a history of Vermont. Viewed from a national perspective the story seems as sparsely populated by major events and trend-setting developments as Vermont itself has been sparsely inhabited since it was settled. Some see Vermont's formation and early development as the only events in its past worth attention, as if Vermont's history itself has been rolling downhill since early in the nineteenth century and isn't worth retrieving. "A history of Vermont?" A California author laughed with disbelief when he learned I was writing this book. He writes big handsome volumes about the desert and mountainous West and has bold adventures of exploration and ambition to describe against a backdrop of dramatic landscapes. "What can one say about Vermont after 1820 or 1825?" he asked. Samuel Proctor of the Florida Historical Society put it pretty much the same way. "Just write about the Green Mountain Boys," he advised, "and then finish it off with a couple of chapters." Others have asked seriously, looking at Vermont's history in the context of American history, "does Vermont have any history?"

Vermonters retaliate at sallies like these by citing some famous American who was born here or some invention or other "first" which occurred here. Like citizens of every state Vermonters tend to identify important elements in state history with the main currents of American history. By looking for similarities they miss the differences. While teaching an introductory survey course in American history at the University of Vermont a few years ago I pointed out to the assembled freshmen and sophomores that their textbook, a compact one-volume chronology by Charles G. Sellers, Jr., and Henry F. May of the University of California at Berkeley, mentioned Vermont only twice while narrating American history from the arrival of Christopher Columbus to the departure of Richard Nixon. The first was a reference, in parentheses, to Vermont's admission to the Union in 1791. The second illustrated the surge of industrialism between the Civil War and 1900 by noting: "Yet nobody, from the most isolated farm in Vermont to the sleepiest village in Mississippi, was wholly unaffected by the power of industry." [1] To couple backwoods Vermont with backwater Mississippi as examples of rural stagnation, while much of America was pulsing with wealth-making energy, caused some grimacing and a stir of shifting feet in the lecture hall. But the point is valid even if Vermonters are discomforted by it. Just as Sinclair Lewis once wrote a novel with a Vermont setting which he entitled *It Can't Happen Here*, about the threat of fascism in America in the 1930s, so too could one write a book about Vermont's role in American history and borrow from Lewis for a title to fit the hard truth: *It Didn't Happen Here*.

No puritan divines thundered ominously from their pulpits about sin and salvation in Vermont from 1620 to 1763, the era Carl Bridenbaugh has labeled "The Neglected Period in American History." No major encounter between white invaders and native Americans was ever fought on Vermont soil. Only one battle of the American Revolution occurred in Vermont—a minor rear-guard action at Hubbardton on July 7, 1777, when Seth Warner's Americans were retreating from Fort Ticon-

---

1. Charles G. Sellers, Jr., and Henry F. May, *A Synopsis of American History*, 2nd ed. (Chicago: Rand McNally & Co., 1969), p. 210.

deroga and were surprised over breakfast by an advancing British regiment. The skirmish, from first to last, was fought in less than an hour. The Battle of Bennington, which occurred the next month, was actually fought west of Bennington, across the New York border in East Hoosick, New York. The Bennington Battle Monument stands today in Vermont because it marks the site of the munitions and other supplies that Gen. John Burgoyne was intent on capturing.

No body of constitution-makers from several states met in Vermont to deliberate and formulate an instrument of government for the self-declared young nation. Ratification of the constitution proposed at Philadelphia in 1787 was of little concern to Vermonters nor a matter of urgency to those who wanted to solidify the new nation because Vermont claimed to be an independent republic and never had been one of the original thirteen colonies. George Washington never slept in Vermont. Vermonters who became presidents of the United States did so after they left Vermont for New York and Massachusetts—states which often do produce presidents.

Marching armies did not devastate the Vermont countryside during the Civil War. The only Civil War engagement fought on Vermont soil occurred on October 18, 1864, when a band of Confederate soldiers came down from Canada to rob banks in St. Albans and hurry back across the international border with their loot. Only one Vermonter was killed in this escapade, and the action hardly qualifies as a Civil War "battle." It resembles the type of bank holdup or train robbery Jesse James and his brothers attempted in obscure Missouri or Kansas towns.

The populism of William Jennings Bryan never inspired Vermonters with messianic visions of better times if silver could be coined at a sixteen-to-one ratio with gold. Progressivism did not spread nationally from any bold or imaginative action taken by Vermont legislators or governors between 1900 and 1914. When the nation loosened some of its moral and social inhibitions in the 1920s it was a native Vermonter, Calvin Coolidge, who presided over the scene as a nostalgic embodiment of the traditional virtues persisting from a more strait-laced past. As the character of the American people changed from being "inner-directed" to "outer-directed" (in David Riesman and Nathan Glazer's terms) it was the Vermonters "who stood still themselves while the society did the transitioning." [2]

When the Great Depression of the 1930s caused hardship throughout the nation some Vermonters were heard to admit they didn't realize times were so harsh since they never knew that times were supposedly good before the Crash of 1929. Vermont and Rhode Island were the only two states which did not experience bank closures between January 1, 1931, and February 1, 1932. When the Bonus Army marched on Washington, D.C., in 1932, only one Vermonter joined that horde of unemployed and discontented citizens, and when he informed Vermont Sen. Ernest Willard Gibson that he was in town, the senator promptly invited him to Capitol Hill for lunch. Franklin D. Roosevelt teased James A. Farley, chairman of the Democratic National Committee in the 1930s, that it wasn't safe for Farley to walk around after dark in Vermont, when he came back from visiting his son, Jimmy, in summer camp in New Hampshire, because Vermont and Maine were the only two states which didn't vote for FDR in 1936. When Harry S. Truman went whistle-stopping in the 1948 campaign he didn't give hell to anybody in Vermont. He simply ignored it. Vermont was the only state of the forty-eight then in the Union which President Truman didn't visit at least once between April 1945 and January 1953.

Vermont is not where Chicago or Pittsburgh or Detroit or other large cities grew. It is not where stockyards and slaughterhouses spread along the railroad tracks, or steel mills darkened the skies with smoke, or automobiles rolled off the assembly lines to be sold to a nation in love with cars. It is not where gold-seekers or silver-seekers clamored for the riches to be extracted from beneath the crusts of the earth, or where men dug for coal or sank oil wells to extract the energy to fuel this urban-

---

2. David Riesman, in collaboration with Nathan Glazer, *Faces in the Crowd: Individual Studies in Character and Politics* (New Haven: Yale University Press, 1952), p. 273.

industrial nation. It is not where throngs of Irish immigrants and others who fled peasantry in monarchial nations across the oceans crowded so intensively into the industrial rookeries of this nation that they threatened the dominance of Yankee culture by erecting their own churches (with crosses on the top, not weathervanes or clocks) and electing their own kind to public office. It is not where black slaves were imported to pick cotton in the fields or where their descendants were shunted into ghettoes when they fled the rural South and tried to fashion new lives in the urban north and west. (Only 761 blacks were living in Vermont in 1970.) It is not where police and pickets met repeatedly in bloody warfare outside manufacturing plants which labor unions were trying to organize. It is not where the Okies went after they were plowed off their land by the corporate farmers, or where Iowa farmers went when they retired, or where the moviemakers went when they wanted ample sunshine for outdoor filming. It is not where corporate men of decision met to decide how goods should be made and sold, where the Madison Avenue hucksters contrived ways to induce us to buy them. It is not where men of war and their business associates decided what weapons should be made and manned and launched. No astronaut ever said goodbye to Vermont soil as he climbed into the nose of a space capsule and prepared to rocket to the moon. Nobody who worked for "Mission Control" ever cleared his desk at the end of a day's work and headed for home on a Vermont road towards an old farmhouse with an old wood stove in the kitchen, horses and sheep and goats in the barnyard, and fields stretching out to woods beyond.

No presidential aspirant ever hinged his future on an effort to win the voters of Vermont in a primary campaign. The media has never made an event of what Vermonters might do in an impending election, or how victory for a candidate here should be interpreted nationally. How Vermont delegations at national political conventions decided to cast their votes has never held the interest that the Ohio delegation commanded, or the Texans, or Mayor Daley's flunkies from Illinois. On election day every fourth November the pundits who perform for the major television networks have never spoken in a tone of foreboding about the meaning of a cold rain or early snowfall moving across the Green Mountains and how that storm might affect voter turnout among the Republicans and Democrats of that mountain stronghold. The lights in American homes never burned late into the evening, to midnight and beyond, on those quadrennial election days when the nation sat by its television sets and radios for news from states where the outcome was uncertain, and the focus narrowed to the old Green Mountain Republic, and the overriding question steadily emerged: "Which way, Vermont?" The tone in Walter Cronkite's voice never became ominous when he mentioned that the returns from Vermont were too close for even the CBS computer to call. The question simply has not been important enough to ask because Vermont isn't big enough to figure in the larger scheme of things.

Vermont has been apart from the American mainstream for the past two centuries and more. As in geography so in history: Vermont lies upstream, on high ground, away from the major currents which have shaped the American destiny. It has its own history, its own relationship to the American story.

To know this history, moreover, is difficult because many of the people who lived the Vermont experience did not document why they came to Vermont and what they did here, and what it meant to live in this state. Some who were mindful of the history in their lives and did record portions of it have been victimized by an uncaring posterity; Ira Allen wrote a memoir, for example, but the early chapters of it, "with an account of my brothers and sisters," was mislaid in the early nineteenth century and has never been located. These historical accounts would be enlightening today if found buried at the bottom of old trunks or discovered back on the dusty shelves in the closets of old farmsteads.

But historians need to know Ira well enough, and know others who were important in shaping Vermont, to be skeptical when reading the documents which do survive. They created some of these sources to deceive posterity as well as contemporaries about their true intentions. Historians of Vermont have often portrayed these early Vermonters as heroes, as mythic figures larger in size and ability than ordinary humans, accepting their own words to explain their motives and goals and opponents, and trying to defend their reputations as resolutely as the Allen brothers and others did on their own behalf in their own time. Most Vermont historians have opposed the Yorkers as diligently as Ethan Allen did, and have gloried in the capture of Fort Ticonderoga as much as he did. They have tried to explain away his dalliance with the British in the 1780s, a ploy which might have put Vermont back in the British Empire, as earnestly as he did. The story can never be extracted from the myths which encompass it and reconstructed satisfactorily from the literary remains which depict it.

The problem is as old as Vermont's recorded history. It started with Samuel de Champlain when he sailed into the lake bearing his name in July 1609, the first European to see this marvellous expanse of blue water and the looming mountains rising to the east and west of it. When his party routed the Iroquois on the beach and meadows below the future site of Fort Ticonderoga, on what became the New York side of the lake, he made a drawing of this encounter. The brief battle was an important event because it intensified a century of conflict between Algonquins and Iroquois, and it hardened the alliance of the French with the Algonquins and the English with the Iroquois for more than a century to follow.

Champlain was not much of an artist but the scene as he depicted it is a valuable document for all who try to visualize what happened. However, he sketched all the Indians as fighting in the nude, even though the Algonquins and the Iroquois were clothed in their usual garb on that fateful day. Why a nude encounter? Because it was customary in the earliest illustrated books about the New World to picture aborigines in North America as naked. This is what European readers expected to see when they saw renditions of these Indians, and Champlain simply abided by this fashion in his drawing. In addition he planted some palm trees in the scene he sketched, although neither then nor since have palm trees graced the shores of Lake Champlain with tropical lushness. He was exercising artistic license because on an earlier exploration he had seen palm trees in the West Indies, and he wasn't hesitant about transplanting them to the Champlain Valley in his drawing since, after all, the New World was pretty much the same, north and south, in the minds of the folks back home in Europe.

For a long time historians weren't sure that Champlain was the first European to see Vermont. In a sand pit on a bank of the Missisquoi River near where it empties into Lake Champlain in Swanton, Vermont, two workmen uncovered a lead tube in 1853. Inside, on coarse brownish paper protected by a gummy substance inserted into each end of the tube, was this message:

Nov. 29 AD 1564

> This is the solme daye
> I must now die this is
> the 90th day sine we
> lef the Ship all have
> Perished and on the
> Banks of this river
> I die to (or, so) farewelle
> may future Posteritye
> knowe our end

Johne Graye [3]

Who was Johne Graye, and how did he get to Vermont in 1564? The question stirred the nineteenth-century imagination in Vermont and beyond, but twentieth-century analyses of the paper, ink, script, and spelling by Samuel Eliot Morison at Harvard University and by the Huntington Library in San Marino, California, discredit the document—Vermont's equivalent to New York's Cardiff Giant and Minnesota's Kensington Stone. Furthermore, efforts to link Johne Graye with a sixteenth-century voyage to the New World were fruitless; Martin Frobisher's first recorded voyage was in 1576, twelve years after the date on Graye's message to posterity. To complicate the issue further, both the document and the pipe have since been lost, not a

3. Quoted by Ralph Nading Hill, "Where Did the Sailor Die?" in *Mischief in the Mountains*, ed. Walter R. Hard, Jr., and Janet C. Greene (Montpelier: *Vermont Life*, 1970), p. 33.

surprising outcome, because both had been treated casually and examined by several people, and even had been displayed on an office wall and may have been borrowed from the Highgate Library, where they remained for a while, as if they were no different from a book lent to a library patron. Most likely a Vermonter, perhaps as far back as the eighteenth century, perpetrated the hoax. Possibly this person was the first to initiate a custom which persisted through the nineteenth century and continues today.

For Vermonters the put-on has become a folk art, particularly when victims of it are outlanders. (As an aside it is worth noting here that the most famous Vermont hoax, first launched from Calais in 1887 to beguile the public, is a tale about human hibernation. It tells how Vermonters would freeze their oldsters for the winter and thaw them out in the spring in time to help with the planting of crops. The tale still circulates in the guise of truth, and outlanders ask incredulously if it is true. The answer given is yes, of course it is true.)

A current puzzle in Vermont centers around forty cave-like stone huts found in twenty-one different towns. Some think they were built by early Vermonters to serve as root cellars or for some similar agricultural purpose. Others argue that they were built by early Celtic settlers who came to the New World from Ireland in about 800 B.C. One investigator, Barry Fell, has deduced that these are "traces of a vanished civilization that had once flourished there," and that the "old Celtic highroad" ran through South Woodstock. "Truly the mountain pastures of Vermont are hallowed soil," he exclaims.[4] His critics think his assertions are nonsense. The controversy provides Vermonters with a new issue to discuss on cold winter nights.

How Vermont got its name is also befogged by time and conflicting claims of authorship which can't be verified. The honor is claimed by the Reverend Samuel Peters, an Anglican clergyman who in 1807 said he was travelling through Vermont in 1763, baptizing men, women, and children, when he decided

---

4. Barry Fell, *America B.C.: Ancient Settlers in the New World* (New York: Quadrangle/The New York Times Book Co., 1976), pp. 139, 154.

to baptize the state itself. Peters, who also had a sharp eye for land speculations and a talent for telling prodigious lies, wrote that he and his party in the late fall ascended "a high mountain, then named Mount Pisgah, because it provided to the company a clear sight of Lake Champlain at the west, and the Connecticut River to the east, and overlooked all the trees and hills in the vast wilderness at the north and south." While pouring a bottle of spirits on a rock he dedicated the wilderness with "a new name worthy of the Athenians and ancient Spartans—which new name is Verd Mont, in token that her mountains and hills shall be ever green and shall never die." Afterwards, according to Peters, "the company descended Mount Pisgah, and took refreshment in a log house . . . where they spent the night with great pleasure." Vermont deserved a christening like that, but unfortunately the baptism may never have occurred. At least Peters's detractors doubt his word on this and practically every other adventure in his life. Peters insisted that his claim was valid, and he insisted that he named the state Verd Mont, for Green Mountain, not Vermont, which translates from the French as "Mountain of Maggots." Piqued at his critics he curtly observed: "If the former spelling is to give way to the latter, it will prove that the state had rather be considered a *mountain of worms* than an ever green mountain!"[5]

The naming of Vermont is usually credited to Dr. Thomas Young of Philadelphia, a radical of extreme views who wanted the Revolution to be a social revolution, with a realignment of property, not solely a rebellion from England. A strident propagandist like his two friends, Thomas Paine and Samuel Adams, Young has been called "America's first professional revolutionist" by historian David Freeman Hawke, a role Young played by sending a copy of the radical Pennsylvania Constitution to the inhabitants of what he called "Vermont" and urging them to declare their independence. The Windsor Convention of 1777, which adapted Vermont's first constitution, also accepted Young's suggestion for a name of the state.

5. Samuel Peters, *History of Hugh Peters, A.M.* (New York: printed for the author, 1807), pp. 94–95.

But what inspired Young to propose "Vermont" as a suitable name for the Green Mountains has never been adduced. Zadock Thompson, in his 1842 history of Vermont, stated the name "Verdmont" was in use before Samuel Peters allegedly conducted his baptismal ceremony in 1763, but neither Thompson nor any other historian has cited definite instances of such usage.

To complicate the matter further, a 1774 map found in the Sherburne town clerk's office by the late John Clement of Rutland, a president of the Vermont Historical Society, shows Killington Peak in that town to be labeled as Mount Pisgah. On a clear day in the autumn, when the leaves are down from the trees, a person on the top of that peak, the second highest in Vermont, can clearly see Lake Champlain to the west and possibly see a brief stretch of the Connecticut River glimmering to the east. Samuel Peters may have been a liar all his life, but he may have told the truth about that ceremony atop the mountain in Sherburne.

Trying to establish how Vermont became a state is more difficult than ascertaining how it was named. For that we can thank Ethan and Ira Allen; the two men who did more than any others to shape Vermont into a separate entity were equally adept at determining what history would know of them. Ira was twelve years younger than Ethan, shorter in stature (his nickname was "Stub"), and a devious character. According to Ethan's biographer, Charles A. Jellison, Ira "proved himself to be without peer in his mastery of deceit." When Ira and Ethan negotiated with the British in the 1780s about delivering Vermont back into the British empire, they shrouded this hazardous intrigue by drafting several versions of the same documents. "As for the Vermont records, official and otherwise," Jellison wrote of this clandestine venture, "the less said the better. They are for the most part so beclouded with confusion and subterfuge as to be decidedly undependable." [6] Ira was elated when his cunning enabled him to elude or confound his enemies, a frequent occur-

6. Charles A. Jellison, *Ethan Allen: Frontier Rebel*, 2nd ed. (Taftsville, Vt.: Countryman Press, 1974), p. 252.

rence in a long career full of machinations. In 1781 Vermont legislators became increasingly suspicious of his coy dealings with the British and called on him to explain himself before the legislature assembled in the Bennington meeting house. Lesser men might have quailed, because Ira knew that spies from Canada were in the gallery, together with emissaries from other states concerned about Vermont's negotiations with the British in Canada. Every word he spoke would be weighed by the Vermonters in front of him and reported soon afterwards to the British in Quebec City and the Continental Congress in Philadelphia. But Ira chose his words adroitly, and sixteen years later, when writing his *Natural and Political History of the State of Vermont*, he recalled smugly how he outwitted everybody. Referring to himself in the third person he wrote:

> All seemed satisfied that nothing had been done inconsistent to the interest of the States and those who were in the interest of the United States paid their compliments to Colonel Allen for his open and candid conduct. In the evening he had a conference with the Canadian spectators on the business of the day and they appeared to be as well satisfied as those from the neighboring states and Vermont. Is it not curious to see opposing parties perfectly satisfied with one statement, and each believing what they wished to believe and thereby deceiving themselves!" [7]

Ira's *History* was the second published history to chronicle the formation of Vermont, and historians have relied on it so excessively from that time to this that they demonstrate the hallowed truism that history doesn't repeat itself but historians certainly repeat each other. Moreover, Ira may have censored the first history of Vermont, Samuel Williams's *Natural and Civil History of Vermont*, published in 1794, thus exerting an even more constricting influence over what posterity would know of his deeds.

The same is true of Ethan, who was often the only witness to

7. Ira Allen, *The Natural and Political History of the State of Vermont, One of the United States of America, to Which Is Added an Appendix Containing Answers to Sundry Queries Addressed to the Author* (London: J. W. Myers, 1798), as published in *Collections of the Vermont Historical Society* 1 (1870): 428.

important events in his life, or the only one to record an account of these events. Ethan was a prisoner of the British for thirty-two months, from his capture at Montreal in September 1775 until his release in May 1778, and what we know of that segment of his life is derived almost totally from his own version, *A Narrative of Colonel Ethan Allen's Captivity*, published in 1779. Did he demand the surrender of Fort Ticonderoga in May 1775, "in the name of the Great Jehovah and the Continental Congress," as generations of school children have been taught ever since? Probably not. It is more likely he cursed and shouted something like "Come out you damned rascals and surrender," which is less glorious but more credible.

Ethan was in love with his own imagery, and posterity has loved it, too. He was a swaggering and blustery giant who spoke with awe and terror and whose strength made him invincible. Ethan probably invented some of the tales told about him—how he lifted two adversaries off the ground, one on each arm, and beat them together until they begged for mercy, how he could shoot the horns off a buck deer at a distance of one hundred yards, how he strangled a catamount that leaped from a tree onto his shoulders, and how he chewed nails into bits. Vermont folklore is full of tales like these, and Vermonters love to recount them. Some emphasize Ethan's cleverness as well as his hardiness. Once he captured two New Yorkers, so the story goes, and locked them in separate rooms on the same side of a house. During the night he made an effigy and tied it to the limb of a tree outside their windows, and in the morning he told each one, individually, to look through the window and see what happened to his companion. Each was allowed to escape believing the other was hanging from that tree, and afterwards each was startled to see the other walking down a street in Albany.

Another story relates how he and Ira managed to postpone a well-attended sheriff's auction of a farm in Charlotte because they wanted to obtain the property without bidding much for it. In league with the sheriff they announced the sale was rescheduled for "one o'clock tomorrow." The crowd dispersed, planning to return at one o'clock the next afternoon. But at one o'clock in the morning the sheriff met at the farm with Ethan and Ira and asked for bids. In the dark Ethan bid a dollar for the house, barn, and one hundred acres. Ira bid two dollars. "Sold," said the sheriff, "to the short man in the coonskin cap."

The upshot of these tales is to confuse the real Ethan Allen with the mythic figure of legend, and complicate the task of explaining how Vermont was born and reared. Ethan's words, for example, were more vigorous than his actions; while his language could scorch like brimstone he was careful, throughout his encounters with Yorkers and Britishers, to prevent anybody from being killed or severely injured. The only serious bloodshed during those Yankee-Yorker altercations occurred when Ethan's cousin, Remember Baker, had his thumb cut off by a Yorker sword. Fort Ticonderoga was captured from the British without a single casualty on either side. Similarly, by keeping the spotlight on himself Ethan has deterred historians from explaining how the Green Mountain Boys, all living on the west side of the mountains, were able to induce the eastsiders, who were twice as numerous and who were more stable settlers, to support the Allens in launching Vermont as a separate state. The story has enough perplexity without Vermont chauvinists adding more. H. Nicholas Muller III, an excellent historian of early Vermont, has aptly summarized the challenge of exploring it:

> Conceived in a bewildering mix of geographic ignorance, conflicting and even larcenous land claims, and the reckless ambitions of colonial land speculators, Vermont was finally born in the swirling confusion of complex local, national and international events. Her genesis and first years as a struggling but independent republic have presented problems which only a few historians have really tackled and which even fewer have succeeded in solving.[8]

8. H. Nicholas Muller III, "Appraisal and Appreciation: An Introductory Essay," in *The Reluctant Republic: Vermont 1724–1791*, by Frederic F. Van de Water, 2nd ed. (Taftsville, Vt.: Countryman Press, 1974), p. iv.

7

The Gods of the Hills: Ethan Allen and the Vermont Republic

*T*o probe Vermont's history is to venture into a heart of darkness. Vermont itself was a heart of darkness before it was much of an experience for anybody to live. Unnamed and largely unsettled, these woody hills and valleys were a land in-between. The natives clustered in the adjacent lowlands—in the Saint Lawrence Valley to the north with access to Vermont through the Richelieu River and Lake Champlain; in the Hudson-Mohawk river valleys to the west; and in the Connecticut Valley to the east. Some Indians did settle in Vermont, and village sites and burial remains are continually unearthed along the lakesides and river banks. But these settlements were probably small and transitory; primarily the Indians knew Vermont as a place to hunt and fish. Their war parties also knew it as a place to cross—partly on water until streams like Otter Creek and the Winooski River became too shallow for their canoes, then on foot along the valleys and over the ridges through the thick forests.

So too with the Europeans as they moved into this land in-between. The French built a fort on Isle La Motte in 1666, and two years later Bishop Laval came by canoe from Quebec to say mass, but within eight years this post was abandoned. Some Dutch settlers were squatters in Pownal in the 1720s. In 1690 a Dutchman, Jacobus Ten Warm, led a British expedition against the French and erected a fort and trading center at Chimney

Point on Lake Champlain, but that outpost didn't survive for long. The French laid out sections of land called *seigneuries* in the Champlain Valley, but attempts to settle farmers on these parcels never succeeded. Reflecting on the long-range consequences of this failure, Ralph Nading Hill has noted, "If the French had shown as much vigor in settling the land as the British did elsewhere in New England, the fortunes of this great valley might have been different." [1]

The British from Massachusetts established the first permanent settlement in Vermont by erecting Fort Dummer in the southeast corner in 1724. Sixteen years later another fort, unimaginatively called Number Four, was constructed thirty miles upstream on the Connecticut River at Charlestown, New Hampshire. For the British to erect forts as they penetrated this heart of darkness was necessary because until 1760 the area was part of a larger scene of conflict. Canada had been British in 1629, but five years later the French won it back in the Treaty of Saint-Germain. When the French tried to annihilate the Mohawks and Iroquois the British retaliated by leading the Iroquois against the French and Algonquin settlements south of Montreal. In 1704 the French led a band of Indians across Vermont via the Winooski Valley and the Connecticut River and destroyed Deerfield, Massachusetts, in a raid that left 47 dead and another 120 taken as hostages. In 1709 and 1711 the British tried to invade the Champlain Valley but failed. In 1731 the French built a stockade called Saint Frederic (which the British, when they captured the site in 1759, renamed Crown Point) and strengthened it in 1734 and 1742.

In 1755 the French also built a fort called Carillon where Lake George and Lake Champlain were separated by a narrow piece of land the Indians called Ticonderoga. In 1758 the British launched a massive attack against this fort but failed to dislodge the French. As a reprisal for several depradations by Indians, Col. Robert Rogers and his men in 1759 killed two hundred In-

---

1. Ralph Nading Hill, *Yankee Kingdom: Vermont and New Hampshire*, a Regions of America book, ed. Carl Carmer (New York: Harper and Brothers, 1960), p. 23.

dians and burned the village of Saint Francis on the Saint Lawrence. At that time also the British under Gen. Jeffrey Amherst advanced northward from Lake George to move the French out of the Champlain Valley. The French destroyed their fort at Ticonderoga as they retreated northward, but Amherst rebuilt it and others abandoned by the French. That fall Gen. James Wolfe defeated the Marquis de Montcalm on the Plains of Abraham above Quebec City, and the British finally controlled Canada. By the Treaty of Paris in 1763 the heart of darkness became part of the British Empire.

But which of the king's colonies in North America would have jurisdiction over this land in-between? Nobody had cared enough to address this question while the land was wild and unsettled and endangered by French and Indian maurauders. In 1664 it had presumably been part of the large grant made by King Charles II to his brother, James, the duke of York (who later became King James II). At least New York later presumed that all land west of the Connecticut River belonged to it because of this grant. But the duke's charter was based on a hazy awareness of the geography of the region and didn't conform with other royal charters to other colonies, nor with descriptions of boundaries separating different grants.

Moreover, practical adjustments of boundaries often modified early grants. For example, in 1700 the British crown had determined that New York's border with Connecticut would parallel the Hudson River along a north-south line twenty miles east of the river. This decision prompted uncertainty about New York's border with Massachusetts. Did it lie along the west bank of the Connecticut River (as New York claimed, citing the 1664 charter to the duke of York), or did it, like New York's border with Connecticut, extend only twenty miles east of the Hudson? Despite the 1664 charter some New York officials in the early eighteenth century seemed willing to concede that Massachusetts, like Connecticut, extended to a line twenty miles east of the Hudson. This boundary also seemed sensible because settlers from eastern Massachusetts had already moved westward across the Connecticut River into the Berkshire Hills. Fort

Dummer was built on the west side of the Connecticut River, above the northern border of Massachusetts, and an order-of-council of September 6, 1744, instructed New Hampshire to maintain the fort. This order implied that the crown was not opposed to an extension of New Hampshire's jurisdictional rights west of the Connecticut River. The situation was further complicated by New Hampshire's failure to garrison the fort adequately (even in the 1720s New Hampshire scrimped on expenditures for the public good), so Massachusetts continued to maintain it while pleading with New Hampshire to pay for its upkeep.

All that uncertainty about the land lying west of the Connecticut River and north of Massachusetts stirred the fertile imagination of Benning Wentworth, New Hampshire's royal governor. He was a man of modest income but expensive tastes, and his ambition to enrich himself was enormous. During a lull in the colonial wars in November 1749, he asked the royal governor of New York, George Clinton, how far east of the Hudson and north of Albany the New York borders lay. Wentworth said he was being pressured to grant land in New Hampshire "in the Neighborhood of your Government." Probably he was trying to prompt a concession from New York that its eastern boundary was a northern extension of the Connecticut-Massachusetts line twenty miles east of the Hudson. Possibly this interpretation is undeservedly constrained as an estimate of his purpose: he may also have been probing to ascertain if New York's jurisdiction did not extend north of a line running west through Albany from the Connecticut-Massachusetts line. If it did, he could then claim—and grant—lands west and north of Albany in today's Adirondack Mountain region. This prospect may have intrigued him for years; in 1762 a group of New Hampshire surveyors were discovered on the western side of Lake Champlain.

But one step at a time: on January 3, 1750, Wentworth granted a township six miles square to relations, friends, and political henchmen—none of whom planned to settle there. The place was called Bennington, a humble toponym for the governor to choose, and he reserved 360 acres in it for himself. Bennington was located forty miles west of the Connecticut River, in the uninhabited far side of the Green Mountains, less than twenty miles from the Hudson River. No settlers would locate in Bennington until 1761, but the governor's imperiousness in granting this township was a bold stroke of audacity. If he hadn't named Bennington for himself the place afterwards should have been called Wentworth to commemorate his effrontery.

Not until April did the Yorkers reply to Wentworth's letter of the past November, and then they conveyed their understanding that New York's eastern border extended to the west bank of the Connecticut River—just as Charles II had told the duke of York in 1664. Wentworth argued for a northern extension of the Connecticut-Massachusetts line twenty miles east of the Hudson. But New York was oddly laggard about asserting its claim, and Wentworth was blithely unconcerned by doubts about his jurisdiction west of the Connecticut River. He continued to grant townships in the region—sixteen by 1754. Then the renewal of warfare made the issue of jurisdiction a dormant question. But in 1760, with the region at peace again, Wentworth renewed his grant-making—sixty-three towns were designated in 1761. By 1764 Wentworth had granted 138 towns, containing about three million acres, of which he assigned about sixty-five thousand to himself. Often he would designate his parcel in a town to be contiguous with parcels in adjoining towns, thus giving him generous units conjoined across town boundaries. He sold to cronies and to speculators; his father-in-law, Theodore Atkinson, had parcels of 350 acres or more in fifty-seven towns, and he ignored the king's orders that grants in the colonies be made solely to groups of fifty families or more who intended to settle the land themselves. Most of Wentworth's customers bought at an average of less than a half-cent per acre and afterwards resold to settlers, who in the early 1760s started to pour into the area. There were so many of them that the land in-between was being called the "Hampshire Grants," or simply "the Grants."

In 1764, in an effort to resolve the confusion, the king-in-council declared the border between New Hampshire and New York "to be" the west bank of the Connecticut River. For holders of the Wentworth grants this meant trouble. In many instances their grants overlapped grants made by New York officials to New York settlers, and the Hampshire holders might have to move from the fields they had cleared and planted and the homes they had built. Those who could stay would have to pay New York quit rents and answer to New York authorities, who were appointed rather than elected as was the custom in New England. In the summer of 1765 New York survey teams were stretching their chains across farms in Bennington and Shaftsbury, farms tilled by Hampshire grantees. The settlers argued that the king's decree pertained to jurisdiction and not to the validity of land titles. The crown had said the boundary was "to be" the Connecticut River, wording that could be interpreted to mean New Hampshire's authority was valid for grants made before 1764. In one of those quiet moments in history that could have turned the future in a different direction, the New Yorkers or the crown could have resolved the issue simply by confirming the Wentworth grants.

Instead the Yorkers demanded that the New Hampshire settlers pay fees in order to legitimize their claims to the land they were occupying. Although these fees were low they were often twice the purchase prices paid by the Hampshire claimants, and the Yorkers required payment in cash from people tilling the soil who rarely had any cash. The Hampshire grantees petitioned the king for relief in 1767, and he ordered New York authorities not to issue any more grants in the area and not to molest the Hampshire settlers already there.

This royal order buoyed the hopes of the Hampshire settlers. More arrived. New York watched passively until 1769 and then, unable to restrain its frustration any longer, decided to defy the king's decree. Rather than see the land fill with Hampshiremen the New Yorkers issued titles to 600,000 acres in the disputed territory. Harassment started again. In mid-October a Yorker survey team appeared on James Breakenridge's farm in Bennington. He and sixty of his neighbors, some armed, told the surveyors to get off his land. Ire was escalating, and violence seemed possible.

In June 1770 a series of nine ejection suits, filed by Yorker grantees against Wentworth settlers in the Bennington area, were scheduled to be heard by the New York Supreme Court at Albany. The Hampshiremen organized a defense of the settlers, called the Bennington Nine. To co-ordinate their efforts they elected Ethan Allen, a zealous, quick-witted, and fast-talking man of thirty-two who had been footloose since selling his share of an ironworks in Salisbury, Connecticut, and who had hunted frequently in the Green Mountains since 1767. Allen went to Portsmouth to obtain land certificates and other documents supporting New Hampshire's grants in the disputed territory, and then went to New Haven, Connecticut, to hire Jared Ingersoll as the attorney to represent the Wentworth settlers. But in Albany, Chief Justice Robert Livingston (who held New York titles to parcels in the Grants, but wasn't bothered by that conflict of interest) wouldn't accept the Wentworth titles as admissible evidence because New Hampshire, he reasoned, had no authority to grant land within New York's jurisdiction. This ruling, coming in the first case, prompted Ingersoll to rise and, with Ethan trailing behind, leave the courtroom. All the cases were obviously hopeless, Ingersoll told Ethan, if the Hampshiremen couldn't present their evidence.

Ethan tarried at his Albany tavern before going home to the Grants. There he was joined by James Duane and John Taylor Kempe, one the New York lawyer who had prosecuted the ejection suits, and the other the attorney general of the province. The Yorkers apparently suggested that they would make it worthwhile for Ethan if he would persuade Hampshire settlers in the Grants to accept the court's ruling and not oppose New York's authority. Ethan, as he recounted the conversation later, replied with his famous assertion, "The gods of the hills are not the gods of the valley." Asked to explain this cryptic comment Ethan simply said "If you will accompany me to the hills of Bennington, the sense will be made clear." Wrote historian Richard Carlson: "If every society needs to possess a mythical moment of creation, this was Vermont's." [2]

---

2. Richard G. Carlson, "Vermont's Heritage of Independence," in *The 1976–77 Official Vermont Bicentennial Guide*, ed. Peter S. Jennison (Taftsville, Vt.: Countryman Press, for the Vermont Bicentennial Commission, 1976), p. 7.

Ethan then rode by himself to Bennington. Shortly thereafter, at landlord Stephen Fay's tavern on the hill, called the Catamount Tavern, he organized about two hundred men into a band to protect their land titles by force since justice, as they viewed it, was not forthcoming from the New York Supreme Court. When the governor of New York heard of this band of insurrectionists he scoffed at their brazenness and said he would drive them out of the Green Mountains. At Fay's tavern on the hill in Bennington Ethan Allen and his cohorts were disdainful of the governor's boast and began calling themselves, proudly, the Green Mountain Boys. The Yorkers called them the "Bennington Mob."

The Green Mountain Boys organized themselves into a regiment with several local companies. Committees of safety were also formed in the various towns, and these were co-ordinated by a central committee of safety in Bennington. Meeting often in the taproom of Stephen Fay's tavern, these men resolved that no surveyors from New York would be allowed onto any land in the Grants, nor could Yorker sheriffs remove anybody from the Grants without first receiving permission from the committee of safety in Bennington, nor could any Wentworth grantee accept confirmation of title from New York. Outside Stephen Fay's tavern a stuffed catamount, facing westward on a platform atop a twenty-foot pole, glared defiantly at the Yorkers.

The symbol was ideal for the Green Mountain Boys because catamounts roamed the forests when the Grants were being settled, and tales were often told of how these powerful but stealthy panthers would lurk unseen and unheard and then pounce suddenly on unsuspecting humans and strike with death-blows before the victims could scream in terror. Panthers were best left undisturbed and must never be provoked: this was the sage advice which accompanied the telling of these tales. That was the message conveyed to the New Yorkers by the stuffed catamount—don't trifle with the Green Mountain Boys. They would be as fierce and nimble as panthers protecting their territorial rights if roiled by New Yorkers trying to evict them from the Grants. Vermonters still admire these slinky felines and like to attribute to themselves the sinewy prowess which panthers embody. When UVM meets Middlebury College in athletic competition it is the UVM Catamounts versus the Middlebury Panthers. And catamounts are still stalking the woods, Vermonters will tell you today; the 1881 carcass in the Vermont Historical Society Museum may be the last to be shot in Vermont but surely it is not the last to wander where trees are thick and humans rarely venture. Tales now are told about coming around a bend in the road or over a hilltop and seeing a panther slink furtively into the leafy underbrush or behind some rocks. These sightings are momentary glimpses, always too quick to be captured by the lens of a camera, but in the 1770s the Yorkers learned that the west-looking catamount on the hill at Bennington was a serious symbol, not just a figment of the fanciful.

In May 1771 a New York surveyor named William Cockburn came over to the Grants and ran his chains in Pittsford. Ethan and some Green Mountain Boys rode up and told Cockburn and his crew to get off the Grants unless they wanted to be murdered. Cockburn fled to New York and recounted to his governor that he was unable to execute his survey. A few days later Ethan sent one of his lieutenants, Robert Cochran, and about a dozen Green Mountain Boys to Poultney, where they drove some New York settlers off land which was theirs under a New York title. In early July, Sheriff Henry Ten Eyck of Albany, with a force of about 150 men, tried once again to remove James Breakenridge from the land he was tilling in Bennington. On his way to the Breakenridge farm the sheriff learned that about 300 Green Mountain Boys, all carrying rifles, were scattered through the woods in well-placed groups. Ten Eyck turned back to Albany. In October, when some Scots with New York titles started to clear land in Rupert, Ethan and his men descended upon them, burned their cabins, and drove them back to New York with orders never to return to the Grants. "Go your way now," Ethan thundered, "and complain to that damned scoundrel your Governor. God damn your Governor, Laws, King, Council, and Assembly."

When this outburst was conveyed by the chastened Scots to the authorities in Albany, the Yorkers issued warrants for the arrest of the "abominable wretches, rioters and traitors" who had committed the outrage. In November Ethan and his cohorts were declared outlaws by the governor and council of New York and rewards were offered for their capture. Early in 1772 Ethan and his lieutenants countered by offering a reward of their own for the capture of key New York officials. In March the Yorkers came after dark one night to Remember Baker's house in Arlington and smashed down the door. Blood flowed when Baker's thumb was severed in a scuffle, Baker was tied in a sleigh, and the group hastened towards Albany. Mrs. Baker got word to the Green Mountain Boys, and after a furious chase they overtook the Yorkers halfway to Albany and drove them off while releasing Baker.

That spring the Yorkers tried to deflate the rising crisis by suggesting the Green Mountain Boys send representatives to New York City to discuss their grievances with provincial authorities. Stephen Fay and his son, Jonas, were sent. But the prospects for conciliation collapsed when the Green Mountain Boys drove several families of Jerseyites off land in Panton they were settling with a New York title. Then the surveyor Cockburn was found again, this time in Bolton, and captured and carried to Bennington. When the governor heard about the Panton and Bolton episodes he accused the Green Mountain Boys of breaching the good faith that prompted the negotiations with the Fays in New York City. Ethan said the breach was Tryon's fault; Cockburn should not have been surveying in the Grants while the negotiations were underway. Tryon said Ethan was insolent.

Tryon began making grants to land claimed by Hampshire proprietors and simultaneously urged Wentworth settlers to confirm their holdings at half the established fee. Ethan drove Yorker settlers from Clarendon, held a mock trial of the chief Yorker in that town, Benjamin Spencer, and as punishment for upholding New York law on New York jurisdiction it was determined his house should be burned. Benjamin Hough, who succeeded Spencer as the Yorker justice of the peace in Clarendon, was arrested by the Green Mountain Boys, tried, and sentenced to receive two hundred lashes on his back for his "crimes" of upholding New York authority and then banished from the

Grants. Tryon increased the rewards for capture of Ethan Allen and his outlaw companions, and the New York Assembly passed an "Outlawry Act" to prevent "tumultuous and riotous assemblies" by the Green Mountain Boys and authorized the governor to demand they surrender within seventy days or be shot on sight. Ethan, always a skillful propagandist, labeled this "the Bloody Act," and so it became known in the Grants. A convention at Manchester in April 1774 forbade all inhabitants of the Grants from holding office under New York authority and those already empowered were ordered to suspend their functions "on pain of being reviewed" by the Green Mountain Boys. Early in 1775 the fears of oppression by the Grants settlers began to wane because Governor Tryon had not chosen to act as authorized by the Bloody Act, and he had left for England.

But on March 11, 1775, tensions were inflamed again, this time on the east side of the mountains, at Westminster. Here local farmers tried to prevent a New York Court from sitting in the Westminster Courthouse because times were bad and legal foreclosures on farms seemed unavoidable. The crowd was unruly; the Yorker sheriff and his deputies fired their guns. One man was killed on the spot; another was mortally wounded. The affair was dubbed the "Westminster Massacre," and the victims became martyrs. Not only did the affair inflame the Hampshire settlers against New York authority, but it also united east-siders and west-siders in common discontent. Ethan was delighted; the next month he was present when a convention in Westminster voted to renounce New York authority and ask King George III to allow them to be "either annexed to some other government or erected and incorporated into a new one."

A week later, about one hundred miles south and east of Westminster, British soldiers sent to Lexington and Concord were repulsed by colonials called Minutemen. Less than a month after the Westminster convention the Green Mountain Boys had captured Fort Ticonderoga from the British and repulsed the British from the Champlain Valley.

Why did the Green Mountain Boys attack the British Empire by seizing Fort Ticonderoga? New York was their enemy, not

England; by attacking the British they allied themselves with the Yorkers in the rebellion. The crown had restrained the Yorkers from making grants in the disputed territory and thereby kept alive the hopes of the Hampshire grantees. In 1772 and 1774 the home government had refused Yorker requests for troops to end disorders in the Grants, telling the Yorkers to use their own troops to calm the turmoil in what London perceived as a local problem. At the time the Revolution started, the crown was rumored to be kindly disposed towards the Hampshire grantees and would issue an order confirming settlers on the Wentworth lands. "By all that was right and reasonable," Charles A. Jellison has written about the Green Mountain Boys in the spring of 1775, "they should have remained loyal to the King." [3]

On the other hand, the Onion River Land Company owned 60,000 acres in the Champlain Valley. Formed in January 1773 by four of the Allen brothers (Ethan, Ira, Heman, and Zimri) while wintering in their old haunts in Salisbury, Connecticut, the company also involved an Allen cousin, Remember Baker, as a fifth partner. This loosely organized venture in land-dealing numbered Thomas Chittenden of Salisbury among its first purchasers. He would become Vermont's first and only president while Vermont was a republic (except for one term out of office), and after statehood in 1791 he would be Vermont's first governor.

As speculators these men had risked their fortunes that the Wentworth Grants would be recognized as valid. They viewed their plight in a reasoned series of premises: whoever controlled the valley would control the company; whoever controlled Lake Champlain controlled the valley; and whoever controlled Ticonderoga, Crown Point, and St. Johns controlled the lake. If the British controlled the lake militarily the consequences for the Onion River Land Company might be as doleful as acquiescing to New York's command of the lake. If the rebelling colonies to the south won control of the lake, and did not believe the Green Mountain Boys were committed to American independence and

---

3. Charles A. Jellison, *Ethan Allen: Frontier Rebel*, 2nd ed. (Taftsville, Vt.: Countryman Press, 1974), p. 102.

would exert themselves for it, the consequences for the Wentworth holders in the Grants would be dismal. It was not unusual in the 1770s and 1780s for the Allens to seize property or capture prisoners and return them as exchanges in negotiations. If London was about to confirm the titles of settlers on the Wentworth Grants, but not of speculators who held titles to land they had not settled (and this the Allens feared), to offer to return forts in the Champlain Valley would strengthen their bargaining. The same would be true if the colonies achieved the incredible by defeating the British and winning independence as a new nation.

Among leaders in the Hampshire Grants in late April and early May 1775, it was evident that somebody, sooner or later, would seize Fort Ticonderoga, and better that it be sooner, while the fort was undermanned and poorly prepared to withstand attack, and better that it be done by the Green Mountain Boys. Heman Allen brought news from Connecticut that a Capt. Benedict Arnold was marching with militia to seize Ticonderoga in order to transport the cannon from the fort to Boston where the rebels needed artillery for their seige of the British. Leaders of the Connecticut expedition wanted the Green Mountain Boys to assist Arnold's troops in the attack. Undoubtedly the Allens realized that the value of the prize would be greater if the glory of taking it were not shared with others. Ethan allowed Arnold to accompany him on the raid and enter the fort with him, but aside from this courtesy Ethan did not concede to Arnold's insistance that his authority be recognized. Ethan later excluded Arnold from the account of the victory he wrote in *A Narrative of Colonel Ethan Allen's Captivity*; the glory of that luminous day at Fort Ticonderoga was too splendid to allow upstaging by Arnold or anyone else.

Ethan explained the decision to capture Fort Ticonderoga as springing from "a sincere passion for liberty," and while it is easy to dismiss this motivation, it may be true that he acted because he valued independence for its own sake. But it seems more likely that he valued independence as fitting the larger view of things he foresaw for the Hampshire Grants. He and Philip Skene, a retired major in the British army who held

30,000 acres at the south end of Lake Champlain, had discussed for two years the prospect of creating a separate province that would extend from the Connecticut River to Lake Ontario, with the Mohawk River dividing its northwest section from New York and the 45th parallel marking its border with Canada. Ten days before Fort Ticonderoga was captured, Allen had also written to Oliver Wolcott in Connecticut suggesting independence for the Grants. The seizing of Fort Ticonderoga seemed impulsive, and historians have often remarked that Ethan Allen seemed to act impulsively. Yet as early as February 1775, Allen had let it be known secretly to the Boston Committee of Correspondence that the Green Mountain Boys would attack Fort Ticonderoga as soon as possible after rebellion started.

But if Ethan Allen envisioned independence for the Grants, free from New York and the British Empire, he did not foresee that he would be captured by the British and deprived of his freedom while Vermont was struggling to maintain freedom for itself. In fact he probably wondered if he would survive his captivity, just as his associates in the Grants wondered what outcome the convulsion in North America would engender. Late in 1775 his cohorts notified inhabitants of the Grants to send representatives to a meeting in Dorset on January 16, 1776, "to see whether the Convention will consent to associate with New Yorkers, or by themselves, in the Cause of America." A committee of five, headed by Heman Allen, was appointed to go to Philadelphia and petition the Continental Congress to allow the controversy about the Hampshire Grants to be deferred until the war with Britain had ended. They said they were "not willing to put ourselves under the honorable, the provincial Congress of New York in such a manner as might in the future be detrimental to our private property." The Congress referred their petition to a five-member committee, which recommended that the petitioners "for the present" submit to New York authority until "the present troubles" had ended, adding "such submission ought not to prejudice the rights of them or others to the land in controversy." This was not what the Hampshire holders wanted. Allen withdrew the petition, ostensibly he said, because he had "left at home some papers and vouchers necessary to support allegations therein contained," but most likely because he feared the Congress would approve the resolution suggesting the Grants submit temporarily to New York.

Another convention was called at Dorset, and after deciding not to align with the government of New Hampshire it was moved, with only one dissenting vote, "that application be made to the inhabitants of said Grants to form the same into a separate district." The association was formed and the inhabitants of the Grants were invited to subscribe to it. Those who spurned the invitation were, by unanimous vote, "deemed enemies to the common cause of the New Hampshire Grants." The convention pledged support to the new American nation.

This convention adjourned until September and took steps to form "a separate district" and to raise troops, control loyalists, send delegates to the Continental Congress, and organize in other ways. Meeting again at Westminster in January 1777, the convention voted on the 16th "That the district of land commonly called and known by the name of the New Hampshire Grants be a new and separate State; and for the future conduct themselves as such." In this Declaration of Independence the new state was named "New Connecticut," but since some Connecticut settlers on the Susquehanna River in Pennsylvania had already applied that name to their locality it was decided, at the next meeting in Windsor in July, to replace it by accepting Thomas Young's suggestion that the new state be called Vermont. The name stuck.

The Windsor convention called for elections to be held in Vermont in December, but these were postponed until March 1778. Ira Allen explained the delay by saying it was difficult getting Vermont's new constitution printed—although he found a way to print a lengthy pamphlet defending the constitution during that time. When the constitution was printed it was distributed only a few days before the March elections. Although some Vermont towns did ratify the constitution, some did not, and since 1778 it has been uncertain if Vermont's frame of government was duly approved by the people who then were calling themselves Vermonters and living in a self-proclaimed republic. Procedural niceties did not disrupt the process; in March the first Vermont Legislature was elected and assembled, and Thomas Chittenden was elected president. The Allen Junto was firmly in control of the fledgling government.

8

Statehood and the Hand of Destiny

*B*UT security did not come with independence. Indeed, those who see the hand of destiny controlling events in Vermont from 1777 to 1791, guiding the republic inevitably towards statehood, misconstrue how precarious the situation was in those years. The hand of destiny was turning a kaleidoscope, and the shifting pieces of time, place, and interest rarely persisted in any enduring pattern of symmetry. It is not only Vermont's climate which induces the dizziness Dr. Jarvis referred to; Vermont's history from 1777 to 1791 is a dizzy chronicle to disentangle.

New York opposed the impudence of this upstart republic and prevented the Continental Congress from recognizing Vermont and admitting it to the Union. Besides, the Congress had a Revolutionary War to tend to. The British with their Indian allies attacked a blockhouse at Shelburne in March 1778, and that autumn they devastated the few settlements near Lake Champlain which had not already been abandoned. Families withdrew southward below forts at Castleton, Rutland, and Pittsford which, in a line continuing on to Newbury, defined Vermont's northern frontier during the Revolution. Fear of sudden depredations were common in what today is called Central Vermont, and the burning of Royalton by British-led Indians in 1780 proved that the danger was real.

While northern Vermont emptied of settlers, eastern Vermont gained new residents. Sixteen towns on the New Hampshire side of the Connecticut River petitioned in 1778 to join the Vermont Republic; they felt they were underrepresented in their government at Exeter, and they shared common interests with their Vermont neighbors across the river. The Allen Junto really didn't want the New Hampshire towns to unify with Vermont because they would strengthen the east side in Vermont's government and jeopardize the junto's control. But to refuse union with them might provoke their Vermont neighbors to withdraw from Vermont and form a separate state in the Connecticut Valley or join New Hampshire and give the valley towns more power at Exeter. Vermont did accept the New Hampshire towns and, predictably, angered New Hampshire officials who previously had not been adverse to an independent Vermont.

Massachusetts decided to revive a long-dormant land claim to southern Vermont, which meant the Continental Congress had three members—New York, New Hampshire, and Massachusetts—opposing the Vermont Republic. The Congress decided to let these states resolve Vermont's future but excluded Vermont from playing a role in determining the outcome. The Congress also ordered Vermont not to grant land within its borders or confiscate the property of those who expressed allegiance to New York or New Hampshire. From Vermont came a firm assertion that Congress had no authority to interfere in the internal affairs of an independent republic.

Talk was heard that New York and New Hampshire would divide Vermont along the ridge of the Green Mountains, with each state taking all on each side of this imposed boundary. In the New York Assembly this plan failed because Yorkers living east of the mountains didn't want to become New Hampshiremen any more than they wanted to become Vermonters; they persuaded their legislators in Albany not to abandon their claims. In 1779 these Yorkers in southeastern Vermont refused to be drafted or to pay a sum in lieu of providing men for military service (as Vermont law allowed), and Governor Chittenden dispatched Ethan Allen to quell the troubles and arrest the insurrectionists. Again in 1782 Ethan Allen crossed the mountains into southeastern Vermont to subjugate rebellious New Yorkers. In that year also the talk recurred about dismembering the republic along a mountaintop boundary, with New Hampshire taking the eastern half and New York the western side. Discontent always seemed virulent: critics of the junto complained they were unfairly accused of being loyalists and having their property confiscated; legislators grumbled that the junto was exceeding its executive authority.

Vermont expelled the New Hampshire towns early in 1779, in fear that the Congress would "annihilate" (Ethan Allen's word) the young republic if it did not. (Allen tried to soothe the Congress by saying union with the New Hampshire towns had been "inadvertent.") Cries of betrayal from the representatives of the sixteen New Hampshire towns, and their Vermont allies, were mingled with threats about creating a separate valley state, and the lieutenant governor of Vermont, Joseph Marsh of Norwich, was among the New Hampshire representatives when that spurned contingent walked out of the Vermont Legislature. In 1780 relations between Vermont and New York were improving; there was sentiment in both states for arbitrating their differences. With only one dissenting vote the New York Senate agreed it was inexpedient to pursue New York's rights in Vermont, and the house was warm towards giving its approval to this resolution when Governor Clinton threatened to prorogue the house (and he had authority to discharge this body if he chose to do so) if it voted for conciliation. The governor's personal enmity towards Vermont (where he, too, held New York claims to land) was unyielding, and it deterred conciliation for another nine years.

In 1781 Vermont took those sixteen New Hampshire towns back in together with eighteen more. It also claimed the territory lying in the twenty-mile stretch between Vermont's western border and the Hudson River. This muscular show of imperialism ignited more fury from New Hampshire and New York. Militiamen from Vermont and troops from New York lined up against each other across the Walloomsac River in the disputed twenty-mile corridor, but the Vermonters outnumbered the New Yorkers and the latter withdrew. The Continental Congress was fearful that New York might not pay its taxes or reassign its troops if the Congress didn't act against Vermont. The Congress assured Vermont it would be admitted as a new state if it relinquished its territorial ambitions. Vermont once again expelled the New Hampshire towns and withdrew its claims to the twenty-mile strip, but Congress did not act as it promised. The defeat of Cornwallis at Yorktown put the Vermont question in a new context. Southern states, then and later, were opposed to the admission of a new northern state. States with claims to western lands were cool towards letting Vermont establish a precedent by becoming a new state. Nor was Vermont any longer essential in the defense of the rebelling colonies against the British in Canada.

Although the defeat of Cornwallis was the undoing of the British in their effort to subjugate the rebelling colonies, the surrender at Yorktown also undid a complicated set of negotiations between the Allen Junto and the British in Canada which centered around Vermont's reunion with the British Empire. The British had been trying to wean Americans away from the cause of independence since the disastrous defeats the mother country suffered in 1777 and the failure to negotiate a peace in 1778. Benedict Arnold's defection was the most significant and dramatic achievement in this effort to subvert the Americans. The British wondered if Arnold's companion at the capture of Fort Ticonderoga in 1775 might be equally warm towards defection, especially if the Allens could be assured that their land titles would be secure and Vermont would have status as a separate province in the empire. Lord George Germain told Sir Henry Clinton, commander in chief of the British armies in North America, in March 1779, that by "discrete management" the Vermonters might be detached from the revolutionary cause. John Beverly Robinson, a Virginia loyalist who tried to persuade Connecticut's Rufus Putnam to defect, twice wrote Ethan Allen that Vermont might win several advantages if it rejoined the empire. Robinson's first letter arrived in Arlington in July 1780, at the same time that Governor Chittenden informed the Continental Congress that Vermont, being fully independent, was "at liberty to offer or accept terms of cessation of hostilities with Great Britain without the approbation of any other man or body of men."

That October the British agent assigned to negotiate with Ethan Allen arrived at Allen's headquarters in Castleton. He was Justus Sherwood, then a captain in the Queen's Loyal Rangers but formerly a Green Mountain Boy who had not been reluctant to defy Yorker authority; he had been one of Remember Baker's rescuers on that March night in 1772 when the Yorkers kidnapped Baker and tried to hustle him to Albany. But Sherwood became a loyalist when the Revolution started, and he and Ethan walked together in the Castleton woods that day, beyond earshot of the others, in order to recall old times and talk about the future.

Sherwood suggested that Vermont join the British because the Continental Congress would never recognize Vermont or admit it to the Union but instead, sooner or later, would force it to submit to New York's authority. By aligning with the British the Vermonters could have status as a separate province, recognition of the Wentworth titles, free trade with Quebec, and their own troops commanded by their own officers. Allen said he would not agree to any "dam'd Arnold plan to sell his country and his honor by betraying the trust reposed to him." If the people of Vermont knew that he was talking seriously about reunion with Britain, Ethan said, they would "cut off his head" for supporting it. Allen insisted that Vermont could do no more to help the British than be neutral even if Lt. Gen. Frederick Haldimand, governor of Canada, promised to dispatch troops to help Vermont repel any force sent by the Congress. Allen and Sherwood agreed to keep their negotiations secret and to terminate them if the Continental Congress recognized Vermont's independence. Sherwood promised that the British would suspend offensive operations in Vermont and northern New York. Allen and Sherwood would negotiate, they agreed, under the guise of trying to arrange an exchange of prisoners.

Late that fall Governor Chittenden wrote to Governors Clinton and Trumbull of New York and Connecticut, respectively, suggesting that the three states unite against a British invasion if

New York and Connecticut would concede their claims to Vermont. If they refused, Chittenden hinted, and if the British did invade Vermont, the only recourse for Vermont would be to accept British terms. It was clear that the Vermonters were encouraging both the Continental Congress and the British to seek their support, and that Vermonters would align themselves with whoever offered the most security—and whoever also assured the Allen Junto its land titles and authority would be safe. Rumors that the Allens were discussing terms with the British were conveyed to General Washington. Suspicions were further aroused when Vermont repealed its statutes banishing Tories.

But the Allens, while professing to the British a firm desire to rejoin the empire, were also finding ways to delay and complicate the process. The ice on Lake Champlain impeded travel, Ira told Sherwood, and he couldn't get to Isle aux Noix, the narrow island in the Richelieu River only a few miles above Lake Champlain where they agreed to meet. When he did get there in May 1781, he said the time wasn't ripe for reunion. Vermonters were warm towards admission to the Union of American states, he claimed, and they would have to be "educated" about rejoining England. Nothing could be done until after the legislature had met in June. Ira argued that the people of Vermont deserved the right to elect their own governor and not be forced to accept a royal appointee. Why hadn't the Parliament passed legislation favoring Vermont, he asked, probably knowing full well that Parliament had other concerns which demanded more attention than an irksome backwoods republic somewhere in the dark interior of North America. Ira wanted a copy of Haldimand's instructions to Sherwood but the captain demurred, suspecting Ira was sly enough to give the instructions to Congress to document how serious the British were in trying to entice the Vermonters into the empire. Ira exasperated Sherwood by saying he wanted to talk personally with Haldimand, who was in Quebec City. When Sherwood suggested Ira put in writing his reasons for not pursuing reunion, Ira did so, but then balked at signing the statement he had drafted. Sherwood, in a dispatch to Haldimand's secretary on May 11, 1781, showed an acute judgment as well as growing exasperation when he referred to the negotiations as "this perplexing and shuffling business."

They agreed to talk some more in July, and in July they agreed to talk some more in September. The British were impatient; they hinted they might use force if the Vermonters didn't act on their own to reunite. The Vermonters were fidgety, too. Rumors were flying about disloyalty in high places. Ira and Jonas Fay went to Philadelphia to urge Congress to recognize all of Vermont's claims, but the British were told what some Vermonters suspected—that Ira neither expected nor wanted the Congress to accede to their requests. Instead they wanted rejection in order to move opinion in Vermont towards reunion with England. Congress refused to discuss Vermont's claims until the east and west unions were dissolved. Back in Vermont after this encounter Ira went over to Skenesboro and proposed to Sherwood that when the next legislative session convened in October, Haldimand should issue a proclamation of the terms the British were offering Vermont for rejoining the empire. It was agreed that a British force would be at Fort Ticonderoga when the proclamation was released, in case British troops were needed to protect Vermont or quiet dissent within the republic. The British were optimistic about the way the negotiations were culminating, but in case the Vermonters rejected the offer the British spoke direly of "melancholy consequences" which would smite the fickle Yankees.

In October, only a week after the legislature had convened in Charlestown, Gen. Barry St. Leger, with two thousand British troops, arrived at Fort Ticonderoga. He was carrying Haldimand's proclamation, and he was waiting to hear from Ira about its release date. When Ira sent no word, St. Leger decided to send a message to him by capturing a Vermonter and sending the prisoner to Charlestown as a courier. But capturing a Vermonter proved more difficult than anticipated; a party sent over to Mount Independence exchanged shots with some Vermonters and accidentally killed Sgt. Archelaus Tupper. The general was horrified when told of this. Despite the fact that war existed between the British and the Vermonters, just as it did between the British and the colonials elsewhere in North America, St. Leger had been warned by Haldimand that "every appearance of hostility must be carefully avoided." St. Leger wrote a letter of apology to Governor Chittenden and invited the Vermonters to come over for the grand funeral he promised to give Sergeant Tupper. The sergeant's clothes were bundled and sent to his widow. When the news reached Charlestown there was consternation about why a British general should apologize for the death of an enemy soldier. Once again the Allens were tested by angry questions implying duplicity with the British. Once again the Allens were able to alibi. "Good men are sorry when good men are killed," Ira said. The next day they sent a message to St. Leger asking that he not issue the proclamation until tempers had cooled. On the same day St. Leger received this message he learned also that Cornwallis had been defeated at Yorktown. The next day, realizing that events were shaping a different future for the British in North America, he sailed for Canada.

The episode was a gentle graze with destiny. If St. Leger had not been tardy by a week in reaching Fort Ticonderoga, the scenario might have occurred quite differently, and Vermont's fate might have been turned in another direction. As it was, although the British abandoned realistic negotiations for obtaining Vermont as part of the empire after Yorktown, the Allens kept hopes alive by continuing to talk about reunion. Probably they feared that the colonies would now unite against them and abolish their authority and titles. In the summer of 1782 Ethan Allen wrote to Haldimand, "I shall do everything in my power to render this state a British Province." Once again Vermonters expressed their suspicions of what the junto was up to; Samuel Herrick, a former Green Mountain Boy, led an angry mob to Governor Chittenden's doorway to ask again if secret negotiations with the British were underway, and the governor was able to assure them that their suspicions were unjustified.

With the fall of Lord North's government in London, and the beginning of peacemaking by the Shelburne government, the prospects for reunion faded rapidly. In the Peace of Paris of 1783 the British included Vermont within the territorial boundaries of the United States and did not offer any trade advantages which were not offered equally to the Continental Congress.

Still the Allens had visions of securing some sort of favored status with the British so their land titles would be guaranteed and their trade with Quebec would flow freely. At the time the United States Congress was negotiating to admit Vermont to the Union, Levi Allen, himself a loyalist during the Revolution, was in London advocating that Vermont be brought into the empire. He arrived back in Vermont two days too late to mount a campaign against the movement for statehood. In 1796 Ira was transporting 20,000 muskets and twenty-four pieces of artillery from France to Vermont, ostensibly to equip the Vermont militia but actually to arm Vermonters and French Canadians in an uprising which would result in a new state called *United Columbia*. Ira hoped this plot would result in commercial and diplomatic benefits for his dream of empire, but the plot collapsed when the British alertly intercepted the ship carrying these arms (ironically named the *Olive Branch*) and impounded them. The great days of adventuring by the Allen Junto were over.

The formation of the new federal Union in 1787 and 1788 again put the future of Vermont into a different context. Alexander Hamilton and others in New York were ready to recognize reality and acknowledge that Vermont would not be reunited with New York. Yorkers in southeastern Vermont had been given land in the Chenango Valley of New York to compensate for the futility of defending New York claims in what in 1781 became Windham County, Vermont. New leaders were emerging in Vermont to replace the Allen Junto. Ira Allen was under a cloud of suspicion because some Vermonters thought he had enriched himself as state treasurer. Even Thomas Chittenden was defeated as governor and was out of office while Moses Robinson served for one year. Federalists in Vermont like Isaac Tichenor and Nathaniel Chipman were espousing viewpoints which Federalists in New York were pleased to hear. New York wanted to be the locus of the new government; the capital was already in New York City and more support from nothern states to keep it there would be helpful. Kentucky wanted to join the Union; by admitting Vermont and Kentucky the North and South would counterbalance each other's power.

The New York Legislature passed a bill proposing a commission to settle the issue. The Vermont Legislature passed a similar bill, and by coincidence sent it to the governor and council for concurrence on October 19, 1789—twenty years to the day after the Yorker surveyors on James Breakenridge's farm had been told to lift their chains and get off that land. The commission suggested that Vermont pay New York $30,000 to compensate New York for surrendering its claims to Vermont. Both states accepted this proposal. On March 4, 1791, the Congress accepted Vermont as the fourteenth state, the first of thirty-seven to join the original thirteen, and only one of two (Texas is the other) which were independent republics before joining the Union. Achieving statehood for Vermont was a long and arduous task, but when it finally happened it seemed to happen easily.

It is fitting to contemplate the gods of the hills while sitting high in the hills themselves. By getting onto a hilltop or mountain summit and seeing this beautiful state spreading below to the blurry horizons a person can appreciate why Vermont in the early days was called "the old roof-top state." [1] One can also understand how travelers like William Dean Howells could rhapsodize that a sunset over Lake Champlain was more resplendent than a sunset over the Bay of Naples. Many Vermonters have their favorite hill or mountain vista tucked away in their memories and renew their fondness for them each year by putting aside other business on a glorious day and ascending to where the views open up, or by walking along a favorite stretch of the Long Trail, a well-maintained footpath along the mountain ridges which extends 261 miles from the Canadian border to Massachusetts. Some are scornful of valley-dwellers anyhow: "If you're going to live in Vermont you ought to get up high where you can see a hunk of it," a lady on Montpelier's Towne Hill told me, nodding towards Camel's Hump down the Winooski Valley. For others, getting up to the views can be as

1. Benjamin H. Hall, *History of Eastern Vermont, From Its Earliest Settlement to the Close of the Eighteenth Century* (New York: D. Appleton & Co., 1858), p. vii.

easy as driving to the top of Mount Equinox in Manchester, or lolling up the chairlift at Mount Mansfield; or as strenuous as climbing up Camel's Hump; or as simple as walking up any convenient slope in this serrated state.

My favorite viewing spot is in the town of Brookfield, just north of the geographic center of Vermont, where a man named Wallace S. Allis gave some land on Bear Hill to the state in 1932. At Allis State Park towards twilight on a warm summer day, when the promise of a beautiful sunset is in the sky, the view from Bear Hill is superb. There is a rickety fire lookout tower, about fifty feet high, which rises above some cleared but rocky land among the pine trees in the center of the park, and as the Federal Writers Guide to Vermont aptly noted in 1937, it "affords a truly magnificent view, a sweeping panorama over forest and mountain grandeur." The tower also gives me a queasy feeling, the heebie-jeebies as I tell my children when they scamper up it. "Hey, Dad, look up here!" they shout from the observation platform triumphantly. I can hardly bear to do so. Youngsters often climb the tower, and get down safely, and the whole adventure, in a vagary of metaphor, is reminiscent of those early Vermonters with their lofty ambitions and hazardous climbings and descents. With Vermont as with youngsters in general: in the process of coming-of-age it is a wonder that survival outlasts adolescence.

The view from Bear Hill is mostly southward, and one can see the interstate highway billowing as a ribbon lying on the folds of land, heading towards New Hampshire but providing the option, at the serpentine road intersection blasted from the rocks at White River Junction, of heading down towards Windsor and Westminster and the other history-soaked towns along the west side of the Connecticut River. In the opposite direction the land gives way to the Winooski Valley watershed, and rainwater falling there drains northward into the system which empties down the Saint Lawrence into the Atlantic Ocean. Rain falling on the park heads southward, and flows down the Connecticut River into Long Island Sound. There are no major associations in Brookfield to events or heroic personalities of Vermont's formative years, but the vista from that hilltop gives a sense of Vermont as an entity. A viewer looking directly at Killington Peak thinks of Samuel Peters's stirring dedication "in token that her mountains and hills shall be ever green, and shall never die." Even if Peters was a charlatan he had a gift for apt phrases.

Pondering Vermont's history from a hilltop causes a person to contemplate how it might have happened differently. History doesn't reveal its alternatives, but the evolution of Vermont as the fourteenth state suggests the possibilities. These also come to mind while driving along the Vermont side of the Connecticut River, looking across New Hampshire's river at New Hampshire's land. Could those towns on the other side be ours if the two unions with the New Hampshire towns had not been undone by the Allens? Could our towns be theirs? Likewise, while quietly crossing Lake Champlain on one of the ferryboats which still ply the lake, and trying to estimate precisely where in those lapping waters the boundary-makers separated Yankees from Yorkers, one wonders if this lake could have become entirely a Vermont lake. Or could it have been a Canadian lake? Would people crossing now into Vermont from Massachusetts be stopping there at Canadian immigration stations if the Haldimand negotiations had produced an agreement? Would we all now live in *United Columbia?*

Other places physically embody the history that made Vermont. Fort Ticonderoga still looms massively on the headland separating Lake Champlain and Lake George because John H. P. Pell and his forebears have devoted themselves to preserving and restoring that imposing fortress. The Constitution House at Windsor has been moved from its original site and used for various purposes for two centuries, and now has a porch on the front which it didn't have in 1777, but it stands on the Main Street and welcomes visitors. Standing by Thomas Chittenden's grave in Williston, or by Ethan Allen's monument in Burlington's Green Mount Cemetery, a historian wonders what undisclosed secrets they carried into the earth forever.

So many of those early Vermont leaders lived vigorous lives, but they died painfully or prematurely. Remember Baker was killed and beheaded by Indians in 1775, at age thirty-eight, and the Indians paraded with his head atop a pole until Britishers persuaded them to return it for burial by his body on the eastern shore of the Richelieu River, not far from Isle aux Noix. Seth Warner, at age forty-two, was racked by tuberculosis and strapped to his bed as his failing mind refought the battles of the Green Mountain Boys. Ethan Allen was barely fifty-one when he was stricken by a sudden illness while crossing on Lake Champlain's frozen surface on a cold February morning. His hayrack was just entering the iced-over mouth of the Winooski River when he said, "It seems as if the trees are very thick here." These were his last words; they sound as if Ernest Hemingway could have written them for one of the hard-living, hard-drinking characters in his fiction.

Isle aux Noix has been expertly restored by the Canadian Park Service and a visitor pauses to imagine Ira Allen meeting there with Justus Sherwood in 1781. Standing on Isle La Motte one can try to picture Champlain and all the other Frenchmen who sailed into the lake and dreamed of a Gallic empire ringing that valley. Today one has to visualize where much of the history occurred. The dam at Vernon on the Connecticut River raised the waters to a level flooding the site of Fort Dummer; the courthouse at Westminster where Vermont declared independence no longer stands. Nor does the house in Salisbury, Connecticut, where some historians believe a meeting to form the Onion River Land Company planted the seed that became the state of Vermont. Nor the tavern near Albany where Ethan Allen told the Yorkers about the gods of the hills, nor Stephen Fay's tavern at Bennington where Ethan organized the Green Mountain Boys.

If they had divided Vermont along the crest of the Green Mountains in 1779 or 1782, with New Hampshire taking the eastern portion and New York the western, Bear Hill would probably be just within the New Hampshire border. If that had happened a visitor would not muse about Samuel Peters and the Allens and all the other figures of early Vermont but would contemplate William Loeb instead. At such times it is more pleasant to ruminate about Vermont's problems.

Actually at Allis State Park we don't get cerebral but instead bring a softball and a frisbee to toss while waiting for the firewood to glow with enough heat for grilling hot dogs and hamburgers. Afterwards, when the twilight is long in June and July, we head down the dirt road which crosses the interstate highway (where a cloverleaf, fortunately, was not built to spill traffic along country roads of white farmhouses). There is time to catch the last of the sunset rays on the houses on the east side of Colts Pond (also called Sunset Lake and Mirror Lake, appropriately). The medley of colors, some splashing off the water onto the white clapboard of those houses, is irridescent.

A floating bridge that crosses the pond is 320 feet long and buoyed by barrels which serve as pontoons. People fish from the bridge and swim from the far shore where a tumbling outlet once provided power for a little pitchfork factory that is now a cozy restaurant. Crossing the bridge is slow and limited to one car at a time. The bridge can't bear the weight of trucks or tour buses, and in the winter it is unusable because vehicles would cause the frozen pontoons to crack. But the bridge is a charming remnant from the past even if it isn't efficient by current standards of the automobile age. There has been a floating bridge at Colts Pond since 1812, and townsfolk insisted on keeping it when the Vermont Department of Highways, with the itchy compulsion of roadbuilders in every state, suggested that a new one built overhead would be better. In fact the highway department proposed to blacktop some of Brookfield's dirt roads in the early 1970s but opponents rose in wrath against what they dubbed "the Brookfield Massacre," and the department relented and agreed that the village itself could retain its unpaved roads. Vermonters still are not to be trifled with.

From the bridge the road curves around a white church with a tapering steeple which, on nights with a refulgent moon, points like a finger directing the moonrise into the dark sky. Up the road we stop in Williamstown for ice cream cones. This is the town where Robert L. Duffus was born and raised, and left for Stanford University in California and newspapering and a long career as an editorial writer for the *New York Times*. When he retired he wrote *Williamstown Branch*, a delightful memoir of boyhood in his turn-of-the century Vermont, and listening to the frogs and crickets of Williamstown, one thinks how far New

York City is from all the hamlets in Vermont like this one, and how far from our time was the era of Duffus's adolescence.

But those thoughts don't survive for long as we head for home on the Barre-Montpelier Road. This is a dreary stretch of shopping centers, car showrooms, outdoor theaters, and a bowling alley, with Harry's discount house, Colonel Sanders' fried chicken, and McDonald's hamburgers, and all the other gratifications which fast food and prepackaged America can offer its citizens. The road already carries more traffic than it can safely serve; its special turning lanes and directional signals try to sort out the cars and prevent havoc. Years ago, when few people owned cars, a trolley line connected Barre and Montpelier and ran through open fields where now the stores and parking lots are spread. On excursions people got off the trolley by those fields and walked up to the shady swimming hole where Benjamin Falls cascaded down the hillside; today that spot is mostly obliterated by the access road to the interstate highway which rises up the hill from Howard Johnson's restaurant. The Barre-Montpelier Road is in the town of Berlin, but Berlin has lost its identity as a community to the road which bears the names of its big-shoulder neighbors, impounding it from both ends. This is modern Vermont, just as it is modern America. It is the Vermont spewing out the Shelburne Road and the Williston Road from Burlington, and extending along Route 7 approaching Rutland and Bennington, and captivating even tiny Morrisville, where a shopping center on the outskirts of town makes the village center look forlorn. Surely this heart of darkness deserves a destiny different from neon-lighted drive-ins along slurpy strips of highways which lead to huge shopping centers and acres of asphalt for parking lots. Vermont is different? The question is asked sardonically. The trouble with Vermont is that Vermont isn't different enough.

9

High Hopes and Earnest Toil

*M*UCH of Vermont's history has been a quest to cultivate home-grown prosperity, and the result has often been disappointing. Vermont history is a chronicle of high hopes and earnest toil, but many of the hopes never propagated among the rocks, and many of the toilers or their offspring decided that fecund lands elsewhere offered more fertile opportunities than stony Vermont. An aura of tragedy seems to hover over the Vermont landscape; you sense it on seeing a crumbling millrace once built to channel the tumbling water where an enterprising Vermonter tried to manufacture wooden bowls or iron kettles; in the beeches and balsam grown up in what was once somebody's pasture; in the long list of casualties on the plinth of a Civil War statue in a small town; in space left in the family burial plot for the youngster who went West and never came home, not even to be laid to rest.

But in the springtime of its youth Vermont was a yeasty place. It had a population of 85,425 when it joined the Union in 1791, a remarkable growth from the estimated 20,000 to 30,000 inhabitants of the Grants when the republic was formed in 1777. Growth continued after statehood: in 1800 Vermont contained 154,465 residents (an increase of 80.8 percent over 1790), and in 1810 it expanded to 217,895 (up 41.1 percent over 1800). It was the fastest-growing state in the nation in the years before the War of 1812 and continued to increase its numbers after the war ended in 1815. But the rate slowed in the middle years of the nineteenth century, and between 1840 and 1850 it was the slowest-growing state in the nation. The 314,120 counted in 1850 grew by only 978 (0.3 percent) in the next decade as the nation grew by 35.6 percent. Its population when the Civil War started was 315,098, and this increased by less than 50,000 by the time World War Two started. In one of those decades the state grew not at all; in two others (1910–1920; 1930–1940) it actually lost population. At the end of World War Two Vermont contained about 360,000 people, but postwar prosperity caused it to grow modestly to 389,881 by 1960. Only in the past twenty years has the rate of population growth matched the increases of the early nineteenth century, and still the state has only a half-million people. The numbers are stark, as is the story they tell.

But for the people who came to Vermont in the early nineteenth century, or stayed here, the vitality and promise of growth must have been exciting. It was a young person's country: two-thirds of all Vermonters in 1800 were less than twenty-six years old. It demanded the energy of youth: they felled trees to make clearings and farmhouses; erected sawmills, gristmills, carding mills, and tanneries along streams; and connected towns with roads. And every town of size seemed to have at least one distillery or brewery. Iron was forged at Vergennes, Tinmouth, Brandon, and elsewhere. Logs were driven down the Connecticut River to papermills and woodturning plants; as early as 1805 Brattleboro was becoming a printing center. On Lake Champlain timber was floated northward to port cities along the St. Lawrence. A newspaper was started at Westminster in 1780 and another at Bennington in 1783. Higher education was served by the founding of the University of Vermont in 1791 and of Middlebury College in 1800. The first patent issued by the United States Government was assigned to a Vermont potash maker, Samuel Hopkins of Pittsford, who devised a process of leaching wood ashes to produce a lye used in making soap and glass.

The first charter for the building of a canal in the United States was issued in 1791 so boats could bypass the rapids on the Connecticut River at Bellows Falls. Men who talked about

Vermont's prospects for prosperity talked about the need to build canals, even one connecting the Connecticut River with Lake Champlain which would carry boats across the Green Mountain barrier. By 1823 the Champlain-Hudson Canal linked Lake Champlain at its southern end with the Hudson River, thus reversing the natural flow of trade northward, with the waters emptying through the Richelieu into the St. Lawrence and obviating the obsession of the Allens to contrive a government unifying those interconnecting waterways. Not only did Vermont have an outlet to the Hudson River towns all the way to New York City and the Atlantic Ocean, but in 1825 the Erie Canal extended this network westward to the Great Lakes.

Steamboats were speeding the movement of people and goods. Samuel Morey in 1793 had operated a small steamboat on the Connecticut River between Orford, New Hampshire, and Fairlee, Vermont, and in 1808 a steamboat named *Vermont* was launched on Lake Champlain. The next year regular service between Whitehall, New York, and St. Johns, Canada, was initiated. Canals on the Connecticut River were dug to open this stream to shipping from Long Island Sound to Barnet, Vermont.

But the aspirations embodied in opening Vermont to commerce were repeatedly frustrated by practical setbacks. The first steamboat to navigate the Connecticut River, optimistically christened the *Barnet*, was welcomed to Brattleboro in 1826 by a big celebration, but it ran aground on the rapids. Dragged over the shallows, it couldn't get through the locks at Bellows Falls because it was too wide. Another steamboat tried in 1829 and got above White River Junction but grounded there. A third, in 1831, navigated to Wells River but got stuck on a sandbar north of the village, and no steamboat ascending the Connecticut River from the south ever passed this point. Ironically, across Vermont the Champlain Canal adversely affected Vermont farmers because the wheat and other grains they produced in great quantities were forced to compete with wheat grown in the Genesee Valley and elsewhere in the west and shipped eastward on the canals. Also, the opening of the canals made it easier for those migrating from Vermont to leave the state.

The years immediately preceding and following the War of 1812 provided all sorts of troubles for Vermont. In 1800 the east side of the state was stricken by drought, and west of the mountains the same happened in 1805. Heavy rainstorms in 1811, 1825, and 1830 caused streams to swell and carry away barns and bridges and mills and crops. A plague of grasshoppers followed the storms of 1811, and this in turn was followed by the spread of wheat rust. Epidemics of human diseases began in 1813 when "spotted fever" (cerebrospinal meningitis) carried by soldiers in Burlington infected citizens and struck down entire families. The terror of uncontrollable illnesses is vivid to anyone who strolls through old cemeteries in Vermont and reads the inscriptions and death dates on gravestones in family lots. For many who did not stay, the series of cold summers that began in 1812 and lasted until 1818 may have been the impetus for leaving. The worst came in 1816 and thereafter was remembered as "Eighteen Hundred and Froze to Death," or "the Poverty Year," or "the Year Without a Summer." On June 6 a cold wave moved eastward across Lake Champlain and dumped a foot of snow on some Vermont towns. Frost followed, and recurred on July 8 and again in mid-August. Vermonters bundled in winter clothes and looked in dismay at their stunted crops. The town of Worcester was abandoned by all but one family, and no town meetings were held until the town reorganized itself with the arrival of new settlers in 1821.

The War of 1812 also disrupted Vermont's economic life. When President Thomas Jefferson extended his 1807 embargo on trade with England to cover inland trade with Canada, he was attempting to foreclose the major economic outlet of the Champlain Valley. Understandably the war was extremely unpopular in Vermont, and many Vermonters simply ignored the embargo and smuggled goods across the Canadian border in defiance of federal prohibitions against trading with the enemy. In some instances soldiers stationed along the border helped citizens to get their goods across surreptitiously. Sir George Prevost, governor of Canada, estimated in 1814 that "two-thirds of the army in Canada are at this moment eating beef provided by

American contractors, drawn chiefly from the States of Vermont and New York.'' Vermonters even floated naval supplies to Isle aux Noix and St. John for the British to use at their shipyards.

The British sent ships into Lake Champlain and lofted some shells onto the battery that had been built to protect Burlington. Some towns along the northern border were pretty much abandoned during the war in fear of British depredations. As in the Revolution the British planned to attack the United States through the Champlain Valley, and they anticipated ample support from Vermonters who were unsympathetic with the war. Among Vermont federalists there was talk about Vermont aligning itself with Canada. But the defeat of the British fleet on Lake Champlain by Lt. Thomas Macdonough's hastily constructed ships in the Battle of Plattsburgh, 1814, ended the threat from the north. The British withdrew into Canada and stayed there.

Smugglers had prospered during the war, and so had the owners of mills who provided cloth. But with peace in 1815 the British flooded the United States with cotton goods they could manufacture cheaply. This and a general deflation following the war caused hardship in Vermont; the state's manufacturing wealth in 1810 had exceeded $5 million, but by 1820 it had declined to less than $1 million. Not until 1840 would it rise again to the 1810 level.

After the war, moreover, it was becoming clear that Vermont was depleting its resources. The timber of the Champlain Valley was pretty much exhausted by 1830. Even the fish in Vermont streams and the animals in its woods were approaching extinction. By 1820 there were no otters in Otter Creek. In many places the thin topsoil, subject to annual planting, was declining in fertility, and the cutting of trees allowed soil to wash away when freshets occurred. Historians tend to date the turning point in Vermont's economic development as 1808, or 1810, or with the War of 1812. Springtime in Vermont has always been a short season.

Still, Vermonters dreamed that commercial wealth could be nurtured in their mountain fastness. They built railroads with the same fervor they lavished earlier on the building of canals because they could see how railroads were vital in southern New England for the manufacturing and marketing of products. The first railroad train in Vermont was run in June 1848 on twenty-six miles of track just laid from White River Junction to Bethel, and its arrival was greeted by a joyous celebration. The following year both the Rutland and Burlington Railroad and the Vermont Central completed tracks to Burlington, providing two routes between that city and Boston. Soon the network was extended by connecting Vermont lines with Albany and Troy, and northeastern Vermont was served by the Grand Trunk Railroad, which linked Montreal with an all-weather open port at Portland, Maine. But once again the enthusiasm for industrial development did not bring all that Vermonters hoped for. The railroads brought cheaper products made elsewhere that could be sold for less than the small country manufacturers in Vermont needed to stay solvent. And the railroads allowed discontented Vermonters to leave even more easily and speedily.

Vermont farmers began raising sheep during the War of 1812, and they believed that demands for wool would guarantee prosperity. The boom began in 1811 when William Jarvis, formerly the American consul at Lisbon, Portugal, brought four hundred Spanish Merino sheep to his model farm at Weathersfield Bow on the Connecticut River and demonstrated to neighboring farmers that the Merinos, with their thick long folds of wool, were well-suited to the Vermont climate and landscape. Prices soared during the war when wool was needed urgently, but afterwards they collapsed. In 1825 the boom began again. Protected by the high tariffs of 1824 and 1828, and eagerly purchased by the New England mills producing broadcloth, the price of wool climbed steadily, suffering a temporary decrease in the Panic of 1837 but recovering to reach a new high in 1840. The sheep craze was becoming a mania; Vermonters believed the fleeces were golden, and they transformed their state into a vast sheep run. "Not even the lower South in the heyday of 'King Cotton,' " wrote the late Lewis Stilwell of Dartmouth College, "was more thoroughly committed to a single crop than was the Vermont of the '30's.'' [1] By 1840 there were six sheep per person in Vermont, and Addison County was raising more sheep and producing more wool in proportion to both its population and territory than any other county in the United States. But prices tumbled when Democrats in Congress removed the high tariff protecting fine wool, and by 1848 and 1849 Vermonters were slaughtering their flocks in order to sell their hides and mutton for whatever prices they could get. The Civil War caused a brief revival of sheep raising, but by 1870 the production of wool as a staple in Vermont was economically hopeless.

Those years of economic uncertainty and upheaval may explain why Vermonters tended to view questions of human destiny with intense seriousness and fervid debate. Calvinists of various persuasions pitted themselves against deists who proclaimed a natural rights liberalism, and the result was a "constant warring," as historian David Ludlum put it. It started with revivals in 1800 when the Connecticut Missionary Society of the Congregational Church launched a big campaign to convert the sinful Vermonters from their misguided ways. "Vermont belongeth to the world," announced the Connecticut missionaries, "and Christ can never rule the world until Vermont is subject to His truth."

That might appear to give the Vermont infidels more attention than they deserved, but soon the Green Mountains were traversed by preachers in search of souls to save. The Congregationalists found themselves competing with Free Will Baptists, Methodist circuit riders, and confident Universalists, and even oddball sects like the Dorrilites, who believed that living in filth was virtuous. Since Vermonters were independent and contentious in matters of religion, the Green Mountains became a natural place for spawning Joseph Smith and Brigham Young and other leaders of Mormonism, and also for nurturing critics of Mormon polygamy who were as harsh and indignant as any in the nation. Understandably Vermont cultivated utopian visions like that espoused by John Humphrey Noyes of Putney in 1838,

1. Lewis D. Stilwell, *Migration From Vermont* (Montpelier: Vermont Historical Society, 1948), p. 172.

who believed men could devise an ideal community if they mutually shared property in a form of pure communism—a theory which led to the mutual sharing of wives, too. Not surprisingly, that was viewed as unabashed promiscuity by Noyes's neighbors, and in 1847 they drove him and his so-called Perfectionists to Oneida, New York, where they made excellent silverware in addition to communal love. A belief that the Second Coming would occur in 1843 or 1844 prompted William Miller, a revivalist born and raised on the Vermont–New York border, to exhort his followers to assemble on hilltops and in church belfries to greet the Judgment Day. But when Gabriel and his angels did not sound trumpets and descend with news of the Great Day, the Millerites went home to the ridicule of their taunting neighbors.

In sectarian squabbles, as well as religious controversies, the Vermonters demonstrated that their society was more productive than their soil. They bought barrels of New England rum and distilled so much of their own potato whiskey and hard apple cider that every occasion was enlivened by the hoisting of jugs. Ministers lubricated their tongues before preaching from the pulpit. In Cabot in 1806 the town meeting voted to lock all the liquor in a closet for thirty minutes so issues of town government could be addressed before the imbibing freemen were totally confused about which way they were voting. Abuses were so prevalent that temperance advocates grew in number and persistence, and in 1852 Vermont became the first state to follow Maine in prohibiting liquor. Vermonters were more suspicious of the secrecy and political power of Masonic Lodges than Americans in any other state when the anti-Masonic movement spread in the late 1820s, and in 1831 Vermonters elected William Palmer, an anti-Masonic candidate, to the governorship and re-elected him three times. When abolitionists in Vermont first advocated freedom for Negroes they were hooted and even disrupted by unruly crowds, but by the late 1830s Vermont was more abolitionist in sentiment than any other state. The Georgia Legislature passed a resolution suggesting a squad of Irish laborers be hired to dig a canal around Vermont and float "the thing" out to sea. Vermonters roiled against the annexation of

Texas and the War with Mexico, and they sent money to aid Yankee settlers in "Bleeding Kansas" to win that territory from the South. When the Civil War began they became soldiers in a holy crusade.

The war exhausted their fervor, and afterwards they did not beset themselves with turbulent and volatile arguments about proper forms of social organization and behavior, and routes to spiritual salvation. Vermont became as placid as a cow meandering across a rolling pasture and nibbling at wisps of grass, an apt analogy because dairy herds supplanted sheep as the primary activity of Vermont farmers. The first state-wide dairy association in the nation was founded in Vermont when about a hundred farmers gathered at the statehouse in 1869, and in that year the first silos to be built in America were constructed in Vermont barnyards. As Boston and New York increased their demands for milk and dairy products Vermont became their major provider. By the end of World War One only Wisconsin exceeded Vermont in the number of cows per farm. In the early 1920s Vermont became the only state in the nation with more cows than people (a proportion many Vermonters preferred) and that ratio existed until 1963, when people finally outnumbered the cows! By 1930 Vermont led all states in the percentage of population which depended on dairy farming for income.

Some urban areas in Vermont grew dramatically in the nineteenth century because local industries prospered. St. Johnsbury tripled in population between 1830 and 1870 as a consequence of the ingenuity of Thaddeus Fairbanks in devising an accurate and simple scale for weighing undressed hemp straw. The growing of hemp was a brief craze in Vermont in 1828–1830 (as was silk later, and countless other farfetched ventures to make the reluctant earth yield undiscovered sources of wealth), and hemp was valued at fifteen dollars per ton. But weighing it was cumbersome until Fairbanks invented the platform scale. He and his brothers manufactured a variety of scales for weighing everything from gold dust to railroad cars. Their scales were sensitive to one one-hundredth of an ounce when minute items were measured, to a fraction of a pound when something weighing several tons was gauged, and the precision of their products made St. Johnsbury famous around the world for its scales. Rutland tripled in population from 1850 to 1880 and became a railroading and manufacturing center, especially after the Howe Scale Company moved there from Brandon in 1877. Barre jumped from 2,060 to 6,812 residents in a single decade, thus experiencing the most dramatic population increase of any town in Vermont's history. At Barre the granite industry used derricks, steam drills, and a railroad with the steepest grade for standard-gauge tracks east of the Rocky Mountains to carry the granite blocks from the quarries to the finishing sheds in the valley below. Burlington shifted from exporting lumber to Canada to importing timber from the north and finishing it into boards and wood products for shipment elsewhere. This traffic was so enormous that Burlington became the third-largest lumber mart in the United States. Springfield prospered because the machine-tool industry, which had its genesis in nearby Windsor, was developed by imaginative pioneers who provided American industry with the machinery to make the cars and airplanes and other mass-produced items which built the American economy.

Immigrants who left other countries to settle in Vermont usually located in these urban areas. The Irish built the railroads and often stayed in towns that grew along the tracks. From the quarries of northern Italy came granite workers and sculptors in such numbers that by 1918 half of Barre's ten thousand residents were Italians. Vermont's quarry towns attracted Scots and Swedes to Barre and Proctor, and Welsh to the slate towns along the Vermont–New York border, and even Spaniards to Montpelier, because all were skilled stonecutters and readily employed. A community of Rusyn-Carpathians from Hungary came to Proctor, and in Springfield a Russian Orthodox Church was built to serve newcomers from Minsk. And coming steadily from the north were French Canadians to work in the mills and till the farms being abandoned by the Yankees. As early as 1832 Burlington had a Roman Catholic Church where French was spoken, and in 1838 Burlington supported the first French newspaper in New England. In 1850 St. Joseph's in Burlington became the first French-Catholic parish in the United States. The town of Winooski, across from Burlington, became known as "the French village" because its mills employed hundreds from Quebec. The French were imported from their impoverished and overpopulated province to do the dirty work that paid little and took long hours; in 1869 a train rolled through St. Albans carrying six hundred men in coaches which were locked to prevent their escape. Today about 9.5 percent of all Vermonters speak French as their mother tongue, and they constitute the largest ethnic element in Vermont.

All these people enlivened Vermont in ways the natives did not always appreciate. The Irish fought with the French and the Welsh, and the Italians had a penchant for radicalism in politics. Anarchists invited Emma Goldman to speak in Barre in 1911, and in 1912 Barre was the first Vermont town to elect a Socialist mayor. Grudgingly the Yankees admired how the Italians spiced Yankee cookery with the herbs they grew in their yards and the mushrooms they knowledgeably picked in the woods. In 1931 the Vermont Commission on Rural Life, a prestigious group of two hundred Vermonters who wanted to invigorate the state, admitted, "Most immigrant farmers bring with them a musical and artistic heritage far richer than that in possession of our native stock." [2] But the newcomers gravitated into the Democratic party because the natives already controlled the Republican party. As a consequence the distinctions in party allegiance in Vermont to this day are largely determined by ethnic identity. Many Democrats do not espouse the urban liberalism which has characterized the Democratic party in most northern and western states since the Roosevelt-Truman era. The result is a seeming anomaly, which permits some lifelong Vermont Democrats to win by big margins in legislative races in Burlington but speak like conservative Republicans when they get to Montpelier.

Efforts were made to induce other immigrants to settle in Vermont but none brought results. A campaign to attract Swedes to Vermont's abandoned farms in the late nineteenth

---

2. Two Hundred Vermonters, *Rural Vermont: A Program for the Future* (Burlington, Vt.: Vermont Commission on Country Life, 1931), p. 21.

century brought only twenty-seven families, and many of them did not stay. A similar effort was made in Finland, and Finnish Hill in Corinth and another hill by the same name in Weston, represent that hope. But only the place names survive. Although a Vermont town might become home for a Jewish peddler who unpacked and became a merchant, or a Lebanese vendor who opened a market, or a young Greek who opened a restaurant, the great influx of European immigration did not affect Vermont as it did New York or the states in southern New England. Many immigrants to America went to live in the manufacturing cities of this nation, and Vermont had few of those. Only 12 percent of all Vermonters were listed as foreign-born in the 1930 census, and today the Roman Catholic population for the state is about 31 percent. The Yankees never lost control of Vermont; they were never seriously threatened. Not until 1972 did Vermont elect a Roman Catholic, Thomas P. Salmon, to the governorship, and not until 1974 did it send a Roman Catholic, Patrick J. Leahy, to Congress. The latecomers were islanders in a Yankee sea.

Ralph Flanders once described Springfield as a center of heavy manufacturing surrounded entirely by cows. The description could be applied to almost all factory towns in Vermont because they are few in number and encircled by broad stretches of pastoral countryside. Furthermore, they aren't as big as centers of heavy industry outside of Vermont. Farm machinery was made in Bellows Falls for decades but this town never grew like Moline, Illinois, where ex-Vermonter John Deere located and built steel plows. At Winooski the American Woolen Company built one of the largest woolen mills in the nation but the Winooski River never nourished the American textile industry the way the Merrimack River fed Manchester, Lowell, Lawrence, and Haverhill, and attracted hordes of Vermont farmgirls (fourteen hundred by 1845) to Lowell to work their looms. Furniture factories arose near timber stands in towns like Orleans and Beecher Falls, but these never grew like the furniture towns in the North Carolina piedmont. For instance, at High Point, North Carolina, a Vermonter named William Henry Snow settled after the Civil War because he liked the looks of the place when he was there as a soldier, and he became the father of the North Carolina furniture industry. Vermont farmers slaughtered lots of pigs but Chicago became hog butcher to the world when Gurdon Saltonstall Hubbard of Windsor, Vermont, settled there in 1835 and started to salt and smoke pork. Most Vermont industries grew because they extracted rocks from the earth, such as marble in Proctor or slate in Poultney and Pawlet, or a mineral such as asbestos from Belvidere Mountain and its environs, which produce 99 percent of all the asbestos mined in the United States. Or they grew because small streams were natural progenitors of small woolen mills in towns such as Johnson, Cavendish, and Quechee. Many grew simply because of the accident of birthplace; Montpelier became an insurance center as well as state capital largely because Dr. Julius Dewey was practicing medicine there when he decided that it was more lucrative instead to sell life insurance. The growth of Springfield's machine tool companies "is a case history in defying the laws of economics," says Wayne Broehl of Dartmouth College in noting that "few towns so disadvantageously situated could have hoped for such industry." [3]

Until the modern surge of economic growth brought firms like International Business Machines to Essex Junction, and spurted the growth of a space-age manufacturer in Vergennes, the Simmons Precision Corporation, the industrial scene in Vermont was meager. More than that, it was somber, too, because the woolen mills in Winooski had emptied when that industry relocated in the South, and the railroad yards in St. Albans left Vermont's most persistent unemployment problem when they closed down. In industrial output Vermont is still pretty much a land of maple syrup a visitor can send as gifts for friends, of wooden toys and Christmas trees, of milk and cider and apples with the tang of the northland in them, and granite for a tombstone, marble for a memorial, and a life insurance policy for a widow. It is where a lot of people came from, except for those who stayed at home to farm or to work in the mills and offices or run ski lodges and cater to tourists.

The ski industry is a recent development in Vermont: the first rope tow in the United States, powered by a Model T engine, was rigged up in Clinton Gilbert's pasture in Woodstock in 1935. By 1975 Vermont had seventy-eight ski areas, eighteen of them with the capability to lift all of Vermont's population to the top of the trails in a single afternoon. But Vermont has also been a warm-weather resort area since George Round, the first owner of the Clarendon Mineral Springs, astutely complied with a dream he had one night in 1776 (when others were dreaming of independence from England, and Ethan Allen was dreaming of freedom for himself), and discovered this bubbling water hole and decided to entice tourists to it. In 1798 he replaced his log structure with a frame hotel with rooms for 100 guests. Visitors acclaimed the health-giving waters, as they did also at Sheldon, Highgate Springs, Brunswick, Middletown, and several other towns in Vermont which thrived on attracting out-of-staters to mineral springs. The most famous of these was at Brattleboro, where Dr. Robert Wesselhoeft, a native of Saxony, built his water-cure in 1845 and attracted such luminaries of the era as Henry Wadsworth Longfellow, Harriet Beecher Stowe, William Dean Howells, James Russell Lowell, and Francis Parkman.

The mineral springs declined in popularity with the Civil War—partly because southerners had been a steady clientele—but resort hotels replaced them in popularity. Visitors would come by railroad to Victorian hostelries like the Pavilion in Montpelier, which was popular with vacationers as well as with legislators attending statehouse sessions, or to quiet and stately towns like Manchester, where Mrs. Abraham Lincoln in 1863 visited with her son, Robert Todd Lincoln. Robert later built an estate in Manchester called Hildene, where he summered, and he died there in 1925. Others, seeking more venturesome diversions, would take the train to Waterbury, ride the trolley to Stowe, and then hire a horse-drawn carriage to take them to the Mount Mansfield House at the summit. Vermonters, with char-

acteristic wariness, were not all convinced that tourism was a
blessing to be sought. Many still feel that way today and echo
Matthew H. Buckham, who was to become president of UVM.
Buckham wrote in 1867:

> Let us do all we can to keep up the notion among our city cousins,
> that to live 'away up in Vermont,' is the American equivalent for
> being exiled to Siberia. Let us tell them that we like to have them
> *visit* us during the few fleeting days in mid-summer when we can
> safely walk about with them in our fields without our buffalo coats
> and bear-skin gowns, but that *they* belong to altogether too delicate
> a race to think of *living through* our severe summers with any
> comfort.
>
> Not that we do not think very highly of our city cousins,
> especially *when we see them in the city*. But when they come with
> their long baggage-train of trunks and band-boxes, and take
> possession of a country village, bringing their livery and their
> minister with them, occupying all the finest building sites, ordering
> all their groceries and toggery from the city, and importing into
> industrious communities the seductive fashion of doing nothing and
> doing it elegantly, they turn the heads of the young, demoralize the
> whole tone of society, convert respectable villages into the likeness
> of suburban Connecticut and New Jersey, and for all these losses do
> not compensate by adding any appreciable amount to the circulating
> capital or to public improvement.[4]

But Vermont hurried the flow of tourism by establishing in
1891 the first state publicity service of any state in the nation. In
1911 this was enlarged into the Bureau of Publicity, and its first
publication, entitled *Vermont, Designed by the Creator for the
Playground of the Continent,* shows that Vermonters knew
tourists had money to spend. The automobile made Vermont
more accessible to vacationers. Shorefront property on a
hundred lakes and ponds filled with cottages and summer camps
for youngsters from the cities and suburbs of the nation, and
Vermonters learned to live with summer people, hunters,

---

4. Matthew H. Buckham, "Burlington as a Place to Live In," in *The Vermont Historical Gazetteer: A Magazine Embracing a History of Each Town, Civil, Ecclesiastical,
Biographical, and Military,* ed. Abby Maria Hemenway (Burlington: Miss A. M. Hemenway, 1867), 1, pp. 723–724.

fishermen, skiers, leafpeepers (the Vermont label for autumn visitors who exclaim at the colors of the turning leaves), and all those genealogists from across the nation searching for their Vermont ancestors who left back when the land seemed hopeless and wasn't even fun to look at.

10

Dissonance in the Hillwinds

*H*EARING the sounds from the Green Mountain playground of today makes one wonder if they echo back in time. The schuss of skis on snow, the clanking of the ski lift gears, the strident blare of a rock and roll band mixing with the clangor of restaurant dishes and bar glasses in an old Vermont house or barn made into a discotheque: these seem incomprehensible in a place where Vermont parents, generations ago, saw their children leave home and spread across the nation because Vermont was too poor to generate much money. The "oh's" and "ah's" of tourists as they go caracoling through the mountains are ironic: those mountains were like prison walls to many nineteenth-century Vermonters, and the world beyond them was more bountiful than the stony soil they enclosed.

"I can never be happy there in among so many mountains," wrote Sally Rice, age eighteen, to her parents in Vermont in 1839, when she explained why she had left to make her way as a hired girl in New York and later as a loom operator in a Connecticut textile mill.[1] The home she left is now one of the ski lodges at Mount Snow in Dover, a huge resort area which has been described as "the Coney Island of Vermont."[2] Robert L.

1. Quoted by Nell W. Kull, " 'I Can Never Be Happy There in Among So Many Mountains'—The Letters of Sally Rice," *Vermont History* 38 (1970): 52.

2. I. William Berry, "He Made a Mountain Out of a Molehill," in *The Young Millionaires*, by Lawrence A. Armour (Chicago: Playboy Press, 1973), p. 114.

Duffus remarks on the same feeling: the mountains shut life in; instead of liberating the spirit of a boy they contributed to what he called the melancholia of Vermont. Vermonters left Vermont by the thousands because it was no playground. To them the sounds of Vermont were the clank of a hoe on a stubborn rock in the soil, of winter winds howling as the snow drifted deeper.

By 1850 the number of Vermonters who had moved to other states was about 145,000. Of the 34,000 Vermonters who served Vermont regiments in the Union army it is estimated that fewer than one-half returned to Vermont as permanent residents after 1865. Time in uniform was credited by the federal government to those who applied for quarter-section homesteads in the West. Many who acted on this opportunity, like Orville Fisk of Moretown, grandfather of the late Supreme Court Justice William Orville Douglas, left towns which had saddled themselves with huge debts because of taxes raised to support the Union cause and settled, as Fisk did, in Minnesota or elsewhere on the frontier. Two of every five Vermonters left the state between 1850 and 1900, and the proportion may actually have been higher because many went to Canada where states of origin were not recorded in census data. Fifty-four percent of all Vermonters were living outside Vermont by 1880; no other state in the nation was losing such a large proportion of its native-born. Vermont's greatest export has been its natives, especially its young people.

They went everywhere in the expanding nation and did everything in advancing its growth. Most remarkable are the many who prospered and became leaders in the rising West and the burgeoning cities. Being Vermonters most of them knew how to work hard, and they were shrewd, practical, and enterprising. The growing nation needed a transportation system, and not surprisingly the Wells of Wells, Fargo was Henry Wells of Thetford; the Adams of Adams Express was Alvin Adams of Andover; and the Russell of Russell, Majors & Waddell was William Hepburn Russell of Burlington, called "the Napoleon of the West." By the score they were the railroad builders, like Frederick Billings of Royalton and Woodstock. He left his name on a major town in Montana through which he built the North-

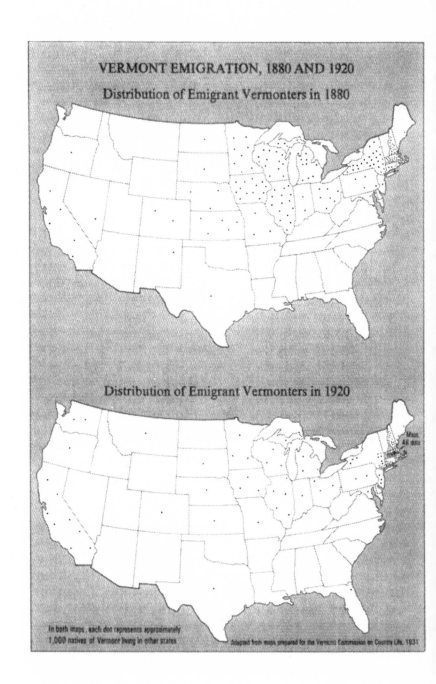

VERMONT EMIGRATION, 1880 AND 1920

Distribution of Emigrant Vermonters in 1880

Distribution of Emigrant Vermonters in 1920

Mass.
46 dots

In both maps, each dot represents approximately
1,000 natives of Vermont living in other states

Adapted from maps prepared for the Vermont Commission on Country Life, 1931 ern Pacific, and he chose Berkeley, in honor of the bishop, as the name for the university city across the bay from San Francisco where he made a fortune during gold rush days as San Francisco's first lawyer. When urban America needed elevators for its skyscrapers the inventor was Elisha Graves Otis, a Vermonter from Halifax. The Pratt of Hartford's Pratt-Whitney was from Woodstock, Harvey P. Hood of the Boston milk firm had come from Chelsea, and the land developer for much of Los Angeles was Moses Sherman of Rupert.

They planted Yankee culture across the Midwest, building churches and schools. Many Vermont women went South after the Civil War to teach the freedmen. There were many wandering the nation, and it is remarkable how their lives intersected: Horace Greeley and George Jones worked as apprentices in the same print shop in East Poultney, and years later in New York one was editor of the *New York Tribune* and the other of the *New York Times*. When Greeley said "Go west, young man, go west," he said it to another Vermonter, Josiah B. Grinnell of New Haven, who went to Iowa, founded the famous college town which bears his name, was elected to Congress, and became Iowa's best and most famous publicist. When Edwin L. Drake of Castleton, Vermont, went prospecting for oil in Pennsylvania he sank his well on land owned by Parcus T. Copeland, a Vermonter whose mother had escaped from the Indians raiding Royalton in 1780.

The two congregational preachers who dreamed of founding a college in Oberlin, Ohio, Philo Penfield Stewart and John Jay Shipherd, had been schoolmates together in Pawlet, Vermont. When John Dewey of Burlington went to Johns Hopkins University to study philosophy he worked under Prof. George Sylvester Morris, a Norwich native and former principal of Royalton Academy. When William G. Wilson formed Alcoholics Anonymous to redeem people like himself from the terrors of alcoholism and asked another sufferer, Robert Holbrook Smith, to be his cofounder, the partnership consisted of an East Dorset native who had gone to Wall Street to make money and a St. Johnsbury physician who was practicing in Akron, Ohio. When it was bedtime in Salt Lake City and Brigham Young was ruminating on which of his seventy wives to sleep with, among them were three from Vermont.

As community builders of all sorts these Vermonters naturally became public leaders. Most remarkable is the extent to which they became prominent in politics. In Wisconsin, as an example, eight of the first eighteen governors were native Vermonters, as were seven of its early senators, and in 1880 every Republican in the top echelon of power in that state had been born in Vermont. Between 1850 and 1900 a total of eighty-eight Vermonters represented eighteen other states in the United States Congress—fifteen in the Senate and seventy-three in the House. "Vermont enjoys the distinction," wrote one observer, "of furnishing more of her sons to other States for Senators and Congressmen than any other State in the Union." [3]

Not just in Congress but in national affairs as a whole it is extraordinary how many ex-Vermonters and their descendants were leaders during the great era of Republican supremacy which began with the Civil War and ended with the depression of the 1930s. Not all of these were Republicans: when Grover Cleveland was in office—the only Democrat to be elected president in the late nineteenth century—he assigned the newly created post of secretary of the interior to William Vilas, a Wisconsin Democrat whose boyhood home in Vermont, a handsome brick structure with a white porch across the front, still faces Chelsea's north green. When Woodrow Wilson went to Washington, he rewarded George Harvey, wealthy publisher of *Harper's Monthly* and a major contributor to his campaign, by sending this Peacham native to England as the United States ambassador to the Court of Saint James. By 1920, however, Harvey was disillusioned with Wilsonian diplomacy and was playing kingmaker in the Warren G. Harding camp of the Republican party. Four years later he was doing the same for another small-town Vermonter, Calvin Coolidge of Plymouth

3. Charles Spooner Forbes, "Vermont's Influence in the Nation," *The Vermonter* 5 (1900): 155.

Notch, when some Republicans mistakenly thought they could beat Coolidge in the primary campaigns of that spring.

It wasn't unusual for pride to pucker in the Green Mountain State when Republicans controlled the presidency and vice-presidency with men who had Vermont connections or antecedents. In 1876, when the GOP elected Rutherford B. Hayes and William A. Wheeler to the top two offices in the nation, the ticket consisted of an Ohio man whose family had migrated from West Brattleboro shortly before Rutherford was born in 1822, and a New Yorker who had been educated in the schools of Franklin County, Vermont, and at the University of Vermont. Four years later, by a strange quirk of fate, both candidates on the Republican ballot had a common Vermont experience to share. The presidential aspirant, James A. Garfield, was from Ohio but had gone to Williams College and then taught penmanship in a small academy maintained in the basement of a church in North Pownal, Vermont. The vice-presidential nominee, Chester A. Arthur, was a genuine Vermonter. He was born in Fairfield in 1829 and had taught in the same academy in North Pownal three years before Garfield was hired to teach there.

Also remarkable is the fact that another Vermonter, Levi P. Morton, had declined the vice-presidential nomination in 1880. If he had accepted he would have become president, as Arthur did, when Garfield died from an assassin's bullet in 1881. Instead of Arthur, a minister's son born in Fairfield, the nation would have received Morton, a minister's son born in Shoreham. Morton did become vice-president when he was nominated and elected with Benjamin Harrison in 1888. In 1892 Harrison replaced Morton with Whitelaw Reid, whose mother had moved from Ryegate, Vermont, to Ohio before this future editor of the *New York Tribune* was born. In 1908, when Theodore Roosevelt anointed William Howard Taft as his successor, he raised this son of a Vermonter to the presidency but disappointed a native Vermonter, Leslie M. Shaw, who also was ambitious for Roosevelt's blessing. Born in Morrisville and raised in Stowe, Shaw had gone to Iowa in 1869, became prominent in banking, served two terms as governor of Iowa, and then in a surprise move by TR was appointed secretary of the treasury. But his prospects for the presidency never developed—probably because his views on international trade were too protectionist for Roosevelt.

Vermont itself provided continuous leadership in the United States Senate because the two Vermont seats, from shortly after the Civil War until the 1890s, were occupied by the same two men. George F. Edmunds was a farm boy who had been raised in Richmond where the Winooski Valley broadens at one of the few lengths in its sixty-mile course to provide some rare flat land in north-central Vermont. Edmunds came in 1866 and stayed until 1891. He was followed by Redfield Proctor, who stayed until 1908. Edmunds's colleague, Justin Smith Morrill from Strafford, came in 1867 and died in 1898. After Morrill's death the seat was held briefly by Jonathan Ross, and then William P. Dillingham of Montpelier held it from 1900 to 1923. Vermonters don't object to long tenure in Congress: Morrill served twelve years in the House before his thirty-one in the Senate, giving him the longest tenure of any American in the U.S. Congress at the time he served. In the twentieth century George Aiken served from 1941 to 1975 and was the Senate's senior member at the time of his retirement. The pattern may hold for the future: Vermont's present junior senator, Patrick J. Leahy, was thirty-four years old when he succeeded George Aiken in 1975.

Edmunds and Morrill, vague figures now in the haze of history, can still be visualized, standing by their Senate desks, as typical of the men Vermont would send to Washington. Edmunds had a flowing white beard and a big bald head; his tongue was so sharp, says one biographer, that he "could blister opponents like sulphuric acid." [4] Morrill was an imposing figure also; he had stern Roman features and fulsome side whiskers, but compared to Edmunds he was more temperate,

4. William A. Robinson, "Edmunds, George Franklin," *Dictionary of American Biography*, ed. Allen Johnson and Dumas Malone, American Council of Learned Societies (New York: Charles Scribner's Sons, 1931), 6:26.

courteous, and even charming. Morrill was characterized as the "Nestor of the Senate," the "Gladstone of America," and the "Grand Old Man of the Republican Party." He stood for good things—such as land grants to help farm boys learn agriculture at colleges, and a tariff that was mildly revenue-making beyond being protectionist, and support for the Library of Congress and the Smithsonian Institution, and better terraces and fountains around the Capitol, and completion of the Washington Monument.

Edmunds was generally recognized as the ablest constitutional lawyer in the Congress, and he supported legislation which guaranteed civil rights and advanced the civil service reforms being advocated by Dorman Eaton of Hardwick and Calais, the tireless champion of that movement. Edmunds proposed the electoral commission which decided the disputed Hayes-Tilden race in 1876 ("Edmunds' Contrivance," his plan was called), and he was a behind-the-scenes author of the Sherman Anti-Trust Act of 1890 because it was directed against the "unnatural and unequal distribution of wealth and power," he wrote years later. He talked of duty, country, and integrity, and shunned patronage-seeking. When he was absent other senators would try to rush through their petty jobbery bills to avoid his scrutiny and sarcasm. One of his colleagues remarked once that if led blindfolded into the Senate he could tell instantly if Edmunds was present because of the tenor of the discussion. Not amiable with his fellows, he was nonetheless urged to run as a presidential candidate in 1880, and he did attract some Republican support. Sen. George F. Hoar of Massachusetts urged him to stay in the race. "But Edmunds," he said, half-facetiously, "just think of the fun you would have vetoing bills." [5]

Morrill had a similar tendency to confine himself to petty matters. Like legendary Yankees who save string too short to save, and put it in a box labeled "string too short to be saved" (and save the box), Morrill habitually saved the red tape—the actual red tape—which was used in that era for wrapping gov-

5. Quoted by H. Wayne Morgan, *From Hayes to McKinley: National Party Politics, 1877–1896* (Syracuse, N.Y.: Syracuse University Press, 1969), p. 73.

ernment papers and packages. He used and reused the same strands scrupulously; the Senate Finance Committee, of which he was chairman, never requisitioned a single yard of red tape, and it was unique in this respect among Senate committees. Vermonters carry frugality with them.

Edmunds was by temperament more picayune than Morrill. One of his colleagues noted, "He can see the knot hole in a barn door, but he can't see the door." [6] Unfortunately, some Vermonters, like Edmunds, carry a frugality of vision, also.

From around the nation they came to Washington, these Vermonters, and served in the House of Representatives in numbers much beyond what such a small state might be expected to provide. Frederick E. Woodbridge of Vergennes, one of Vermont's three Congressmen from 1863 to 1869, remarked at the 1877 commencement of the University of Vermont that he had served in the House with four other UVM alumni, and all five had been students together at UVM at the same time. Woodbridge was in the class of 1841; William Higby, 1840, was elected from Calaveras County in California; Henry J. Raymond, 1840, represented a New York City district; Robert S. Hale, 1842, represented an upstate New York district; and John A. Kasson, 1842, was elected from Des Moines, Iowa.

Woodbridge did not mention William A. Wheeler of Malone, New York, class of 1842, who served from 1861 to 1863 and again from 1869 to 1877 before his term as vice-president during Rutherford B. Hayes's administration. Indeed, by broadening his focus Woodbridge could have included Dudley Chase Denison of Royalton, class of 1840, and Worthington C. Smith of St. Albans, 1843, who represented Vermont districts. Thomas Child, Jr., 1838, also from St. Albans, had been elected from a New York district in 1854 but was unable to attend because of illness. Jason Niles, 1837, had gone south to teach and then to become a lawyer and newspaper editor, and he served one term in 1873–1875 as a Republican from Mississippi during Reconstruction. (Niles was reputed to own the largest private library in all of Mississippi. His son, Henry Niles, mar-

---

6. Quoted by Morgan, *From Hayes to McKinley*, p. 73.

ried Victoria Allen, and her daughter by a previous marriage, a youngster named Estelle Oldham, read extensively in this library. Estelle eventually married her childhood sweetheart, an aspiring young novelist named William Faulkner.)

Thus the University of Vermont produced ten congressmen in the classes which were graduated from 1837 to 1843. Since those seven classes contained a total of only 142 degree recipients, the proportion is amazing. Others matriculated but did not stay for four years, and one of these, Orange Ferris, 1838, became a lawyer in Glens Falls, New York, and served two terms in the House. John Gregory Smith, also of the class of 1838, became governor of Vermont. Another who tried several times to be elected to Congress was Charles G. Eastman, class of 1837, editor of the Democratic newspaper in Montpelier, but he had not learned that being a Democrat in Vermont didn't promise much political success. Most other students at UVM in the 1830s and 1840s were learning very well the art of getting elected to office.

When they went to Washington in the 1860s and 1870s did these Vermonters talk among themselves and with others in the capital who had Vermont roots or connections? During the time President Andrew Johnson was being impeached, did Chief Justice Salmon B. Chase, presiding at that trial, ever chat casually during a recess with Thaddeus Stevens of Danville? Did Chase talk about the schools he had attended in Windsor and Royalton, and Stevens of Peacham Academy, and together did they reminisce about college days at Dartmouth? Did the congressman elected from the Dakota Territory in 1875–1879, a native of Braintree, Vermont, and a former lieutenant governor of Vermont named Jefferson P. Kidder, socialize with the congressman elected from the Arizona Territory, Hiram S. Stevens, formerly of Weston, Vermont, during the two terms they served in the House together? On the senate side, did Jacob Merritt Howard of Michigan introduce himself to Matthew Hale Carpenter of Wisconsin when the latter arrived in 1869 to be inducted into the Senate? Did Howard tell about the schools of Shaftsbury and the academies he attended in Bennington and Brattleboro, while Carpenter told of boyhood pranks in Moretown—some of which caused more than one schoolmaster to abandon teaching because the students were unruly and to flee ignominiously after nightfall from the Mad River Valley?

Those who left Vermont were fond of coming together at occasions which celebrated their Vermont origins. Sometimes these reunions were held back in the hometown and allowed those who stayed to mingle with those who left, to renew acquaintances, and to catch up on gossip about marriages and births and deaths and crops and land sales. Picnic baskets would be spread on the town green, the preacher would declaim during a memorial service in the church, and visitors would wander among the tombstones in the cemetery and look inside the old schoolhouse. Teachers would gasp at the sight of bearded men they remembered as churlish youngsters, and the bearded men would blush and feel those adolescent gaucheries surging forth again. People would speak nostalgically about the old days and old times together, as people do when they come as strangers to familiar places, and try to feel at ease in surroundings which once they knew intimately but must define anew with perspectives which make both them and the old haunts seem wrenched out of time. Everybody would listen during the speechmaking to spiraling grandiloquence about what it meant to be a Vermonter.

Former residents would come from neighboring Vermont towns or from cities in New England and in New York State where enterprising local boys had gone to settle and had persevered and made good in the classic American manner of making lots of money. Sometimes a magnate would come from Chicago or some other distant metropolis to tell the folks at Old Home Day how the Vermont heritage prepared him for success in life. He would describe his loving mother, his stern father, the punctilious teacher, the strict minister who urged no compromise with temptation, and the virtues of early rising, honest toil, and all the other attributes of Vermont life that outfitted him to be manly and excel among his peers.

Around the nation the Vermont expatriates formed themselves into societies and associations for renewing and invigorating their mystic chords of memory which reached back to a common Vermont background. In San Francisco, for example, the Native Sons of Vermont were organized in 1879, and soon their meetings were scheduled for Odd Fellows Hall because it was the largest auditorium in the city. All of its 2,500 seats would be occupied, and ex-Vermonters would still file in and fill all the standing room around the walls. When the Native Sons held a picnic across San Francisco Bay in Berkeley they attracted a crowd of 6,000.

It is interesting now to read the oratory delivered at these assemblages of Vermonters and wonder what the speakers genuinely felt about what they were saying, and what the listeners truly felt about what they were hearing. Emotions must have been mixed. Did speakers praise Vermont knowing in their hearts they were smart to leave it? Did they deliberately idealize it because even nostalgia could soften the flinty life it demanded? Did they urge others to stay in Vermont knowing they wouldn't accept their own advice? Did they urge Vermonters to leave, knowing this would deprive the decaying state of even more vitality at a time when it needed all the talent it could retain? Did listeners applaud while knowing full well "you can't go home again?" Or that they didn't really want to go home again? How many ex-Vermonters admitted as they left these meetings that they had a good time and were glad they came, that Vermont was a good place to visit but they wouldn't want to live there?

The oratory about Vermont at the California Midwinter International Exposition of 1894 revealed these ambivalent feelings. Vermont was the first state to be honored by having a day designated in its honor at this major event, and Gov. Levi K. Fuller and others from Vermont came across the continent to participate with Vermonters who had settled in California and would converge on San Francisco for the festivities. March 4 was chosen as an appropriate day because Vermont had joined the union on March 4, 1791, but because the fourth fell on a Sunday in 1894, Vermont Day was moved ahead to Saturday, March 3. "Friday, March 2nd, found the city full of Vermonters from all parts of the State, many of whom had been here since the days of '49,'' wrote one reporter, ''but who had lost none of that love for their native state which every true Vermonter feels.'' He added that a freakish snowstorm which whitened San Francisco on that day was appropriate ''just to make the Vermonters feel at home.'' [7]

Responding to a toast at a dinner that evening, Col. W. H. Holabird, a native of Shelburne, Vermont, emphasized a theme his Vermont audience—and others like it on other occasions—deeply appreciated. ''I was thinking to-night,'' he said, ''of the comparison between Vermont, the dear old state, and California, and I thought of this great State, apparently without beginning and without end; it is so awful long and so tremendously high that you might just drop Vermont down in the midst of the Sierras somewhere, or in the desert somewhere, and almost lose her; but I will guarantee that if you drop a Vermont Yankee anywhere in California, you will hear from him very soon and very often.'' Here his audience applauded, as it would do frequently as he and other speakers, that Friday and Saturday, described the qualities of Vermonters. Holabird continued: ''If he were dropped in the Mohave Desert, and did not have a compass, and knew nothing about the geography of the State, it would not bother him a bit; he would start a fiber factory out of the yucca plant and go to doing something at once, or if you put him down in the Sierra Nevada Mountains, he would estimate how many matches he could make out of one of those big pine trees and start a match factory.'' Here he drew laughter at his depiction of the endlessly busy Yankee enterpriser. ''In fact, in going up and down the State of California, I am proud to say that, wherever I have found a Vermonter, I have found a thrifty man.'' Later, explaining what he would say to Vermonters back in the Green Mountain State if he could reach them all, he said: ''I would tell them that the cities and the factory towns of New England and of the Middle States are overcrowded, and suggest that they just get hold of the truth concerning California. I

7. Quoted in *Souvenir of "Vermont Day" California Midwinter International Exposition, San Francisco, March 3, 1894* (San Francisco: George W. Hopkins, 1894), p. 8. The description of "Vermont Day" which follows in the text, above, is taken entirely from this *Souvenir.*

would draw a picture for them, a picture of a great empire, the valleys of the Sacramento, and of the San Joaquin, the like of which is not known upon God's footstool; I would tell them of Humboldt County, with its great wealth of timber; and I would like to tell them about the sunny hills of San Jose, the orange groves of the South, the vineyards and orchards of Kings County, and the ninety thousand acres of clover in Kern County, and I should like to show to them the Yankee boys, boys from Vermont, who are planted in California, and making homes that can never be made anywhere else on this green earth.'' This was warmly applauded. Holabird went on to propose that everybody in his audience write to Vermont and tell friends about California and invite them to come and settle. He suggested that California be made into a new Vermont.

The evening continued in the same vein. "There is no State in the Union," asserted R. B. Carpenter, "which has furnished so much brains for the other States; she has furnished the men that the mothers and women of Vermont have taught, and armed, and sent forth to the battle of life. You have a small population because the rest of the world will not let you keep the natives." This prompted laughter. "The rest of the world needs just such men and women. They are all over the country. There is not an industry, there is not an enterprise, there is not a good work going on in any state in the Union, where you will not find Vermonters in the front ranks. And when they are found, they exhibit their training,—they show how they were educated. They have still the same commercial integrity upon which she is founded as upon a rock. A Vermonter believes in his word and in his bond. He believes in living prudently and paying his debts, and they have carried that principle to and through other states." Then he cited the leaders Vermont had produced, noting "no state of similar size has equalled this record."

The audience at the dinner was most responsive to utterances about the virtues inculcated into Vermonters as a part of the growing-up process they experienced as youngsters. "Vermont is not afflicted," said R. B. Carpenter, in a reference to the poor economic conditions which beset the nation following the crash of 1893, "with hard times, strikes, or riots, and she has no army of the unemployed within her borders. The reason for all this is that Vermonters are of old stock; they are Americans to the core. [Applause] They have very few of the paupers and dregs of Europe within their borders. [Applause] Their politics are not controlled by foreigners; they believe in home rule. You know that, because they are unreasonable enough to vote Republican every time. [Great applause] There comes a cyclone; Illinois, Wisconsin, Massachusetts go over. There is Vermont, with her old Republican majority of twenty-seven thousand, just the same. They are born and bred there, and educated there, and the primary education of a Vermonter is, or was when I was a boy, to learn how to work, to do something, and not to go around with his hands in his pockets, idle—to be useful in some way—and they cultivate very largely the education of the physical as well as the intellectual. [Applause] With such training and such culture her sons go all over the world. You cannot find a civilized nation on the face of the globe without a Vermonter. With all his other qualities he is the most migratory creature ever born in the world. And when he goes, he goes for something; he has an object in view. He is not roaming around without a purpose; he has something in his mind, things that he intends to accomplish; and, as a general rule, he gets there [Applause]."

One gets the impression, while reading this oratory, that speakers and listeners alike shared a genuine love for dear old Vermont and the sturdy life it demanded back in the hills and valleys, but also that every person in that auditorium would have agreed with Stephen A. Douglas and all the others who advised that Vermont was a good state to be born in provided a person left while young.

The same thoughts must have occurred to those who stayed behind in Vermont as they listened to speakers orate on Old Home Days and similar occasions. In 1880 in Whitingham, a hilltop community just north of the Massachusetts border, the scene was grisly in a way more eloquent than any speakers could sketch. Whitingham was observing the centennial of its first recorded town meeting, and chairs were arranged around a speakers' stand erected in an open space where the east wall of the Whitingham Town Hall had collapsed. The dilapidated old structure had stood empty except for town meetings for thirty years. Originally built as a church in 1799—the most prosperous year in Whitingham's history, according to one local historian—it crowned the hill along with an academy building which had been erected in 1842 but which rapidly failed to attract enough students. "When they failed to support a school regularly," wrote Leonard Brown, a local historian, about Whitingham's citizens in 1886, "and the inevitable decrease of business in that village became more and more apparent, the Academy building was neglected, and the apparatus therein, of which there was a very well-selected assortment of the value of two hundred dollars or more, was by degrees destroyed or stolen, and the building itself, for want of care or apparent interest to look after and protect it, soon showed signs of decay, and became a prey to vandal hands." [8] The church itself had been shorn of its handsome pulpit, its square pews, its galleries along both sides, its doors and windows and its loose timber by "relic hunters and those too lazy to furnish their own fire wood," wrote another local historian, Clark Jillson.[9] In 1883 the entire structure crumbled when vandals completed their work on the old shell. "For nearly half a century before this," wrote Brown in 1886, "this hill has been the common business center for the whole town, and for many years drew a large share of the trade of adjoining towns. There was a time when this hill was the most central mart for all kinds of merchandise known in this part of the country. The people all took an interest in its progress. A spirit of enterprising emulation pervaded all classes. The common people were of necessity industrious and economical in their habits; the theory of living upon other people's earnings had not yet become popular; few, if any, in this section of the

8. Leonard Brown, *History of Whitingham From Its Organization to the Present Time* (Brattleboro: Frank E. Housh, 1886), pp. 84–85.

9. Clark Jillson, *Green Leaves From Whitingham, Vermont: A History of the Town* (Worcester, Mass.: privately printed, 1894), p. 144. The description of the Whitingham Centennial of 1880 is taken from this book and from Leonard Brown's *Whitingham*.

country adopted that course. Manual labor was no dishonor to any class of citizens; even professional men could work on the farm a portion of the time without detriment to their professional standing. They duly appreciated its invigorating effect on both their physical and mental powers.''

The contrast between Whitingham's past and its desuetude at the end of the nineteenth century continually recurred to these local historians, and must have occurred to those who assembled for the centennial. "From an active, thriving business mart, for every species of merchandise, it has been reduced to a few dilapidated, broken-down, and unoccupied old buildings, that nobody has sufficient interest in to clear off the rubbish that marks the spot where they once stood,'' wrote Brown. Elsewhere he noted: "A careful observation of our own towns shows more than fifty farms that half a century ago were owned and cultivated by thrifty and industrious farmers, that are now abandoned, their buildings mostly demolished, and a large majority of these farms are now comparatively worthless.'' Clark Jillson quoted for his 1894 town history from the report printed not long before in the *New York Evening Post* by a correspondent who had traveled through Whitingham:

> Midway between Williamstown [Mass.] and Brattleboro a few years ago I saw on the summit of a hill against the evening sky what seemed a large cathedral. Driving thither, I found a huge, old-time two-story church, a large academy (which had blended in the distance with the church), a village with a broad street, perhaps 150 feet in its width. I drove on, and found that the church was abandoned, the academy dismantled, the village deserted. Here had been industry, education, religion, comfort and contentment, but there remained only a drear solitude of forsaken homes.

Both Jillson and Brown reflected the narrow and pinched viewpoint so typical of chroniclers of declining villages. Jillson tells of a native son named Horace Roberts, an attorney, postmaster, justice of the peace, and Whitingham's representative in the Vermont Legislature who left town in his thirties to join Gen. Rufus Putnam's colony of New Englanders in Marietta, Ohio, where he established the first academy, planned and superintended the building of the first church, and organized the first Bible society and Sunday school. Then Roberts returned to Whitingham. "He was a lawyer of considerable ability," Jillson added, "and why he should leave the western Eldorado and return to the bleak hills of Whitingham does not now appear of record."

Brown was offended by Jillson (local historians like to quarrel, too) because Jillson, in his 1880 centennial address, included the place and date of Brigham Young's birth in his discourse. "We deem it of little consequence in what locality he was born," Brown remarked acerbly; "it is sufficiently humiliating that Whitingham was his birthplace."

Brown tells how speakers at the centennial occasion emphasized the virtues of farming. The honorable E. T. Butterfield of near-by Wilmington, for example, "entreated the young men to stay at home and cultivate the soil, fully believing it would prove a source of wealth and happiness to them, beyond any other occupation. Farming in this part of the country was the source of all wealth, and young men would find it both honorable and profitable to study it more carefully." A lawyer from North Adams, Massachusetts, the honorable A. W. Preston, was introduced as the "Lion of the Berkshire Bar." Apparently a spellbinder, he offered youngsters in his audience "some very sound reasons for staying on these hills, and setting their aims high, reminding them that their best interests, and their brightest prospects lie in the production of the soil of these hills and valleys; and if they needed help to till their farms, and conduct their households, the best way was to raise it. He urged the young ladies to turn their attention to household duties, and become familiar with domestic endearments, and leave off their trailed dresses. He reminded them of the wisdom of giving their affections to the honest mechanic in preference to the fashionable snob; or to the sunbrowned farmer, not to the white-faced rowdy. He logically denounced the delusions, and artful deceptions of the present day, and most eloquently and earnestly exhorted the young people to follow the precepts and godly examples of their parents and grandparents."

One tries to envision youngsters listening to these hymns

about Vermont. These were lads who had heard about the marvels of California and probably fantasized about crossing the continent to live in that land of spring and summer, of tasty fruits, of vast opportunities to get rich. They must have contrasted the California dream with the decadence they saw all about them. They must have noticed that farmers were not selected to declaim at these community gatherings, and farmers were not addressed as "honorable" and shown obeisance in other ways. It was usually an expatriate who had gone away who beseeched them to stay at home—who glorified farming in his remarks but clearly had himself opted wisely for a softer and more munificent life. Did the youngsters sense the hypocrisy? Did they have feelings like other Americans who would grow up in Sherwood Anderson's Winesburg, Ohio, or in Sinclair Lewis's Gopher Prairie in Minnesota, or in Thomas Wolfe's Altamount in North Carolina, or in countless other villages scattered across the Continent, that the frowzy hometown was a stultifying place, one to escape from? Did they sincerely promise to love the ancestral home but, like those ex-Vermonters in San Francisco, say firmly that they would cast their fates where the money was to be made, where the sunshine was eternal? Did these Vermont youngsters hear a dissonance in the hill winds blowing softly across their upland farms?

What happened to those who chose to stay in Vermont? A lad of ten at the Whitingham centennial of 1880 who accepted E. T. Butterfield's advice to become an "honest mechanic" might have moved in his late teens or 20s to Bennington and worked in the paper mill, or to Springfield to work in the machine shops. His career would have consisted of hard work for paltry wages—and he would have been sixty years old when the Depression of the 1930s set in. His "golden years" wouldn't be any better than his working years.

If he had become a "sunbrowned farmer" he might have worked in the 1930s but not survived the consolidation of small farms into units which were larger and more mechanized. Or he might have sold his house and acreage to "summer people" for use as a country home.

In either case he would be in his 80s when the Vermont

economy started to bustle in the 1950s and the Vermont land-scape started to change dramatically. He might remember the old men of 80 when he was a youth of ten, men born in 1800 who had seen the rise and decline of their hill towns. Now he was witnessing a change in reverse—from decline to rise again. History was tumbling over itself, like a kitten chasing its tail. For years he had heard Vermont's public figures like college presidents and members of the Vermont Commission on Country Life decry that decay and *neglect on the inside* was the major hindrance to Vermont's vitality; now he was hearing that *change from the outside* was threatening Vermont's well-being.

If he lived until 1963 his grandchildren and great-grandchildren would tell him about the IBM plant employing 4,000 workers at Essex Junction and other computer-age industries locating elsewhere in Vermont. They would tell him that the number of people in Vermont finally exceeded the number of cows, and that Vermont was leading the nation in the growth of per capita income. On a pleasant afternoon they might ride to Dover and Wilmington to watch the skiers descending the mountain trails and crowding the huge resorts. They would shake their heads at the number of vacation homes being built on the steep hillsides. At home that night, after watching the evening news on television, they might discuss the handsome young Democratic governor, Philip H. Hoff, who talked of growth, and federal grants, and social programs, and the need to reapportion the Legislature. Everybody would remark on the changes the old man had seen in his lifetime, and the old man would agree.

Did he feel cheated because Vermont's prosperity in the final days of his life excluded a lot of hard-working Vermonters like himself? The Vermont heritage taught the virtues of hard work, but the rewards seemed to come to those who had time to play. That didn't seem to fit the heritage he had absorbed, or the one he wanted to pass along to his descendants.

Part III

Heritage

11

The Message Was Marrow in Their Bones

ERMONTERS have a heritage as distinctive as their history. Individuality is a major part of it because people had to work hard and be self-providing to eke out their livings from this contrary country. Also, they had to be resourceful to the extreme of being ingenious and frugal about their resources. Vermont is a demanding state to live in.

Vermont also demands acquiescence in how the earth and the skies defy human effort to affect destiny. It is the perfect environment for all the Calvinism which poured into New England and persisted in the Puritan tradition which was carried to the uplands and implanted here: man must work hard, but his fate is beyond his power to decide. Many Vermonters knew what Calvin Coolidge intended in 1927 when he issued his famous and mystifying statement, "I do not choose to run for President in nineteen hundred and twenty-eight." Others may have deduced a deliberate ambiguity in that phraseology—a coyness inviting a draft from the Republican party for renomination for another term—but not so among Vermonters. In Vermont everybody knows there is ample work to do, and the problem is to choose which tasks have priority over others. Of all the options open to Coolidge he chose among them not to run again. Naturally he chose to say it in the genteel language of upcountry New Englanders who know by experience and inheritance that it is important to work even if the choice, in the larger design of things, doesn't have much consequence when the outcome is revealed. That choice lies with God.

The effort Vermont demanded from its earliest settlers is difficult to imagine. Often the father of a family would come by himself to erect a shelter and clear some land, go home when winter set in, and then return with his family. In 1769 this is what Bartholomew Durkee of Pomfret, Connecticut, did to prepare a new home for his wife and five children in Pomfret, Vermont. Early in 1770 they were on their way. Henry Hobart Vail describes the journey:

> There was a usable road for horses and sleighs as far as Fort No. Four; but northward from that point the ice on the river furnished the only road. Goods and children were packed on hand sleds, which were hauled by the two parents, each wearing snowshoes. A clearly marked trail led to the house of Jonathan Burch in Hartford, near the Queechy River. This was the nearest habitation toward Pomfret. This pioneer couple threaded the woods northward ten miles with their loads. They reached their log hut on March 6th, 1770. It was only partially roofed and had neither door nor window. Digging out the snow from the corner beneath the roofed part made a space for their beds. A fire was soon started in the rude chimney. There was no scarcity of wood, and food had been brought along. Warmth, food and shelter made the children comfortable and the daily labors of the parents soon created a home. At first a large stump served as a table. The earthen floor was covered with saplings split in two, laid with the flat side up. This puncheon floor served until a saw-mill was in operation to provide boards. Spring came, and seeds were sown in the newly cleared land.[1]

Not all adjusted to pioneer life as smoothly as the Durkee family. Elias Smith was thirteen years old in 1782 when he and his father walked from Lyme, Connecticut, to South Woodstock, Vermont, a distance of 180 miles, which they covered in thirteen days. The father had prepared a homesite on one hundred acres in South Woodstock during the previous year. Thirty-four years later Elias recalled the final part of the journey and their approach to that hut:

1. Henry H. Vail, *Pomfret, Vermont*, 2 vols. (Boston: Cockayne, 1930), 1:102.

We had about two miles to go; the first mile we went without much difficulty; this brought us to the foot of a hill which we were to ascend to get to the house. A considerable part of this mile, a cart had never been. It took us till sometime in the afternoon, to cut away the logs and stumps so that the team could pass along. After many sweats and hard pulls, my father pointed us to the house, about forty rods ahead, the sight of which struck a damp on my spirits, as it appeared to me only an abode of wretchedness. After going to it and taking a general view of the house and land around, before the team came up, I determined within myself to return to Connecticut; thinking it better to be there to dig clams for my living, than to be in such a place. . . . Though I was some over thirteen years, I cried; part of the time because I was disappointed, and sometimes for madness. With this fixed determination to return, I went down to the team, and passed by the team down the steep and dismal hill as fast as possible. My father, observing my rapid course, called after me, asking me where I was going; and commanded me to return to him. I feared to disobey him and returned. He asked me where I was going; my reply was, to *Connecticut.* He ordered me to return. This order I obeyed, though with great reluctance, as it appeared to me better to die than be confined to such a place.[2]

Of all the accounts of hardship the most moving was written by Seth Hubbell in 1824, when he was sixty-five years old. "Seth Hubbell must have been a veritable Samson," wrote Walter Teller when he reprinted Hubbell's memoir. In the latter part of February, 1789, Hubbell set out from Norwalk, Connecticut, for Wolcott, Vermont. After recounting an arduous trip to Wolcott, Hubbell wrote:

I had now got to the end of my journey, and I may say almost to the end of my property, for I had not a mouthful of meat or kernel of grain for my family, nor had I a cent of money to buy with, or property that I could apply to that purpose. I however had the good luck to catch a sable. The skin I carried fifty miles, and exchanged for half a bushel of wheat, and backed it home. We had now lived three weeks without bread; though in the time I had bought a moose

2. Elias Smith, *The Life, Conversion, Preaching, Travels, and Sufferings of Elias Smith* (Portsmouth, N.H.: Beck and Foster, 1816), pp. 35–36.

of an Indian, which I paid for by selling the shirt off my back, and backed the meat five miles, which answered to subsist upon. I would here remark that it was my fate to move on my family at that memorable time called the "scarce season," which was generally felt through the state, especially in the northern parts in the infant settlements: no grain or provision of any kind, of consequence, was to be had on the river Lamoille. I had to go into New-Hampshire, sixty miles, for the little I had for my family, till harvest, and this was so scanty a pittance that we were under the painful necessity of allowancing the children till we had a supply. The three remaining children that I left in Hydepark, I brought one at a time on my back on snow-shoes as also the whole of my goods.[3]

For the next sixteen years Seth struggled tenaciously to establish himself and his family on a farm in the northern wilderness, but hardship continued to afflict his life. The final catastrophe was illness in 1806 which took his wife and one daughter and weakened Seth so much he was unable to work for a year. The result was a pile of debts which caused him to lose his farm—"my little all," he called it. "Though I have been doomed to hard fortune," he wrote in concluding his memoir, "I have been blest with a numerous offspring; have had by my two wives seventeen children, thirteen of them daughters; have had fifty-one grand-children, and six great grand-children, making my posterity seventy-four souls."[4]

One of Seth's great-grandsons, Carroll Hubbell, was ninety-four years old in 1976 and lived in Kirby, Vermont. Although born in Elmore, not far from the farm Seth Hubbell cleared in Wolcott, he went to Connecticut to work (reversing the direction of his great-grandfather's trek) and a half-century later came back to Vermont to retire. "I farmed a little in my younger days before getting married," he says. "Me and my wife left Vermont like a lot of folk—went right back down to the area where my great-grandfather Seth Hubbell moved from.

---

3. *A Narrative of the Sufferings of Seth Hubbell & Family in His Beginning a Settlement in the Town of Wolcott, in the State of Vermont* (Danville, Vt.: E. & W. Eaton, Printers, 1829), reprinted in *Twelve Works of Naive Genius*, ed. Walter Teller (New York: Harcourt Brace Jovanovich, 1972), pp. 3–6.

4. Hubbell's *Narrative*, in Teller's *Twelve Works*, p. 15.

Got into the train business there and worked with the New Haven Railroad as a locomotive engineer for almost fifty years."

The oral historian who interviewed Carroll Hubbell was Ethan Hubbard of Craftsbury, and to augment his tape-recording he took photographs of Carroll inside the blacksmith shop he had moved onto his land and remodeled into a home, and outside where they strolled over his acreage. "This piece of land here was a forest when I began clearing it at the age of eighty-two," Carroll commented. "The whole area was choked with big logs and brush and stones. I had to clear it just like my great-grandfather cleared the land when he first came up." [5] Seth Hubbell's legacy of hard work persisted among his descendants.

It is regrettable that Seth Hubbell died before a camera could record his features; posterity deserves the chance to peer into the eyes of a person who could endure such a lifetime in Vermont. But Seth Hubbell's generation didn't have cameras and tape-recorders for preserving its history, and for that we are the losers. Fortunately the late nineteenth century had Abby Hemenway, an eccentric but indefatigable spinster from Ludlow who labored for thirty years to record all the details of Vermont's history she could possibly assemble. The result embraces five thick volumes, totalling six thousand pages, an estimated four million words. Her *Vermont Historical Gazetteer* is a monument to her fanatic dedication, and also a monument to Vermont itself. Her practice was to goad local historians in each community to glean all the minutiae of town history, and it was this technique which induced Seth Hubbell to tell the story of his life. Others distilled their experiences into a few words. Nathen Capen, the Goshen contributor to Abby's *Gazetteer*, was able to query an early settler, a Mrs. Gale, about pioneering in Vermont. "When I asked old Mrs. Gale what were the hardships," he wrote, "she answered, very significantly, *'it was all hardship.'* " [6]

5. Quoted in *News and Notes*, newsletter of the Vermont Historical Society 27 (1976): 11–12.

6. Nathan Capen, "Goshen," in Hemenway's *Vermont Historical Gazetteer*, 1:36.

There is space on the statehouse walls for Mrs. Gale's pithy recollection.

Time has always been important to Vermonters, even today when tourists exclaim how history has slowed to a walk in this pastoral haven and cars must stop at a cattle crossing to wait until all the cows have ambled across the road. But tourists don't get up early in the morning to milk those cows, seven mornings each week, and then hustle all day to finish other tasks before they are milked again, seven late-afternoons each week. Tourists on vacation don't realize that farmers work continuously and rarely take vacations. Vermont is inexorable: it is where trees must be tapped when the sap runs, and hay must be mowed and baled and stacked in the barn before rain falls, and crops must be harvested before the frost strikes, and where the garden must be prepared in the fall for the peas to come in the spring. Time demands that wood must be cut before winter comes, and then stacked to dry a whole year because it will burn better during the winter after the one fast approaching. "It pays to keep a wigglin' " is how a Vermont saying puts it; weather is no excuse to sit in the sun on the first warm day in the spring, or on what might be the last hazy-lazy day of Indian summer. "People ask what's the best time of year for pruning apple trees," said Sen. George Aiken, who would rather talk about trees and plants and flowers than politics. "I say 'when the saw is sharp.' " [7]

Throughout Vermont's history the emphasis on hard work has persisted. During the War of 1812, as incredible as it sounds, Lt. Thomas Macdonough was able to build his fleet on the banks of Otter Creek near Vergennes in a span of forty days. Timber that stood uncut when men began to fell trees was shaped into the ships within six weeks, and these ships defeated the British at the decisive Battle of Plattsburgh. That victory assured American dominance of Lake Champlain.

Evidence of the will to work turns up in the everyday items

7. Quoted in "Senatorial Spotlight: Senator from Vermont," *City East* 1 (1968): unpaged, in Aiken Papers, Crate 79, Box 3, University of Vermont, Burlington.

Vermonters read and the workaday squibs they wrote about their daily efforts. As a historian who reads these fragments, I am impressed by the constant exhortations to be busy and avoid idleness. Specimens of these admonitions recur in the pocket-sized almanacs the farmers valued for their advice on how to be productive, and which today are still curled from having been carried in hip pockets generations ago. One example is in *The Farmer's Guide, or Practical Hints for Every Day Life,* published in Manchester in 1893: "When morning comes, chores can be done while breakfast is in progress. After breakfast let all hands go to work, especially the head of the family. Instead of telling about your rheumatism and 'business to town,' go to work. Exercise is what you need. What can be more disgusting to the feminine occupant of the house than an old pair of boots around and the very head of the family in them?" [8] A Mrs. Williamson in Hartland, who was seventy-eight years old in 1888, demonstrated that she didn't need the female equivalent of prodding like this. In a diary entry she wrote: "One Morning's Work. Made a fire, mended pants, set the breakfast going, skimmed ten pans of milk, washed the pans, ate breakfast, went to the barn and milked two cows, brought the cream out of the cellar, churned fifteen pounds of butter, made four apple pies, two mince pies, and one custard pie, done up the sink, all done at nine o'clock." [9]

Children learned early that time was too precious to be squandered. Many didn't even have time for childhood because they needed to provide incomes for their families—as Dorothea Dix, the future penal reformer, did for hours each day, binding her father's religious tracts in Barnard. "I never knew childhood," she said later in life. Luke Poland, recalling his youth in Waterville, said, "I was brought up and educated in a sawmill," and Justin Morrill said he strode through childhood "with long strides." Unable to continue his schooling after he was fifteen years old, Morrill championed education when he served in the

8. N. P. Hulett, *The Farmer's Guide, Or Practical Hints for Every Day* (Manchester, Vt.: Manchester Journal Job Office, 1893), pp. 7–8.

9. *Vermont History* 37 (1969): 93.

U.S. House and Senate; he wanted other youngsters to have the opportunities he missed because he had to work while still a lad.

Vermonters did not hesitate to make their children work; into the 1930s the proposed child-labor amendment to the U.S. Constitution never had much chance of ratification by the rural-dominated legislature in Montpelier. Many Vermonters have memories from childhood of being imbued with the virtues of hard work. Walter Needham of Guilford recalled that his grandfather's favorite story was Aesop's fable about two frogs who fell one night into a milkpail; one gave up because the predicament seemed hopeless, but the other kicked all night, trying to get out, and in the morning was found sitting atop a pad of butter. In Fairfield the sons of Darius Smith recalled how he worried about time escaping as he pounded on the stovepipe to wake up his boys and set them on their prebreakfast chores. "Get up," he would shout. "Today is Monday, tomorrow is Tuesday, the next day is Wednesday, the week is half over and not a lick of work done yet." [10]

But Vermonters valued education as highly as Morrill valued it by being deprived of it, and often education and work were squeezed together so time could do double duty in promoting both. The Reverend Aaron Hutchinson of Pomfret, who delivered the sermon in Windsor at the outset of the Constitutional Convention of 1777, usually labored in his fields with a pupil he had accepted for tutoring. "Tradition says," Henry Hobart Vail tells us in his Pomfret history, "that even while plowing, or milking the cows, conversation was carried on with his pupil in the classic tongues." [11] Paul Harris, the founder of Rotary International, was raised by his grandfather in Wallingford, and on hot summer afternoons his grandfather would take him to the barn and drill him on words in ancient spelling books.

Hard work and schoolwork were equally cherished by parents, if not by children, and schools were built as soon as

10. Quoted by Marjorie Little Napoli, *The Smith Genealogy* (n.p., n.d. [1974?]), p. 166.

11. Vail, *Pomfret*, 2:354.

communities were settled. The aftermath of the passion for education is evident today in Vermont: this small state has eleven four-year colleges and an assortment of other institutions of learning—junior colleges for women, Catholic colleges, business colleges, a school for international training, and a newly founded law school on its own campus in South Royalton. The diversity is noteworthy, too, from Norwich University, a private military university at Northfield where the cadets march in uniform, to offbeat colleges like Bennington and Goddard, and small but earnest liberal arts colleges like Middlebury and cosy Marlboro. The respect for learning is evident in the presence of community libraries in the smallest of towns since the first one was established at Brookfield in 1791; it is still in service not far from the floating bridge. "Old books for sale" is on roadside signs back on twisting hill roads. Luke Poland and Justin Morrill were men of broad classical training, despite educational limitations, because they impelled themselves to learn. Once at a large dinner I sat next to Ralph Flanders, then retired from the U.S. Senate, and I asked him what he was reading at that time. Although he never went to college I knew Flanders was a constant reader and lover of books because he had published eight of his own. I expected him to say he was reading such-and-such a book. Instead he said, "I am reading history, religion, and philosophy."

Parents inculcated their children with the seriousness of work and education. In 1857 George B. Green of Windsor gave a small account book to his daughter, Ann Elizabeth Green, in which she could record her income and expenses. Inside the front cover, in an even script, George Green inscribed this advice:

> Be *particular* to make it an *invariable* rule, to put down *every* cent you receive—of *whom* and *when* and *every cent* you pay out— to *whom* and *when*—*be sure* to date every writing—*Never* sign a writing without *reading* and *understanding* it *perfectly*—*always count* and *reckon* your money *yourself*—*never* trust to other peoples count, but see for yourself—mind your *own* business, and let others mind theirs—never be a *Meddler*—*Be careful how, who,* and *what*

you *hear* and *believe—Never* delay the work of today for tomorrow—it may never come—and be at *all times conscious* that the *eye of God* is watching *every action, word,* and thought.[12]

Youngsters got the message, and the heritage was like marrow in their bones. On faded blue paper a Panton girl, Harriet A. Tappan, in 1854 wrote a school essay she titled "The Advantages of Industry," which distilled this virtue:

> It is of great importance that we should be industrious. Our time labor and ingenuity should be employed to the best advantage. Both body and mind were made to labor. Some persons are constantly wishing to be rich, thousands have become so but they had to be industrious and have patience and economy while others are wishing for knowledge when they might have become learned if they had employed their time in study and reflection. A person that performs no labor is not as healthy as one that earns his living by the sweat of his brow. He cannot be proud of his own usefulness neither can he enjoy himself as well although he may be surrounded with luxury and ease. What would become of this world if it were not for industry almost every thing would cease to exist. We should therefore improve the present time as the old saying is, 'Take care of the minutes and the hours will take care of themselves.' [13]

Harriet's earnestness would have pleased Marshall Hapgood, the country storekeeper in Peru, Vermont, in the late nineteenth century. He would have considered her a well-trained Vermont girl. These are the instructions he issued to his store clerks about 1880:

> Never on any account run this store for a day unless you have had eight full hours sleep on the night previous. This will necessitate you to be in bed by ten at the latest. I will have no person undertake to run my store who has had only a half rest the night previous. Saturday and Sunday nights are yours—do what you please with them. But if upon the other nights, you fail to be in bed by ten o'clock, you are positively forbidden to unlock the store the next

---

12. Reprinted on rear cover of *Vermont History* 39 (1971).

13. Quoted by Helen Tappan Utterback, "A Schoolgirl of the Fifties—A Daughter of Old Vermont," unpub. typescript, Vermont Historical Society Library, pp. 59–60. Quoted with permission.

day. This of course does not apply to cases of illness or necessity but due to sitting up with any healthy young lady.

Put your whole mind, during business hours, upon business and business—only business alone. Tell no stories, listen to no stories. Talk about nothing but business in business hours. There will be enough to keep you fully employed if things are kept perfectly straight. When folks detain you to tell you a long story, leave them. Consider every moment as worth something and you will just hit the mark. Waste no time upon fooling with customers,—and let me repeat, talk nothing but business in the store and be hindered in nothing by listening to anything but business talk.[14]

The store opened at 6:30 in the morning and didn't close until the last customer had been served. Since the clerk lived upstairs over the store, where his lamp or candle would shine through the window, he probably was tired enough to douse his light at 10:00 P.M. rather than run the risk of having Hapgood see his light burning beyond the curfew.

Vermonters took this tradition with them in their migrations across the nation, and generations of Americans were influenced by it in schoolrooms and churches and working places where the expatriates from Vermont preached that diligence is dutiful, and practiced what they preached. A cabinetmaker's daughter from Arlington, Viola Knapp Ruffner, played a crucial role in Booker T. Washington's rise to eminence as the foremost Negro leader of the late nineteenth and early twentieth century. "He learned *how* to work under the tutelage of a remarkable New England woman," Louis R. Harlan wrote of this Vermont teacher who went south and married Gen. Lewis Ruffner. Booker Washington was one in a line of houseboys who suffered under Mrs. Ruffner's sharply issued requirements. More than once young Washington ran away from the Ruffner homestead, but gradually a bond of affection and trust grew between the lad and the strict Vermont lady, and she taught him how to read. "She was the first person," wrote Harlan, "to teach him the Puritan ethic of hard work, cleanliness, and thrift on which his later social philosophy was based." Washington later re-

14. Quoted by Ruth Mansfield, "The Country Store," *Vermont Life* 9 (1955): 58.

called of her: "I soon began to learn that, first of all, she
wanted everything kept clean about her, that she wanted things
done promptly and systematically, and that at the bottom of everything she wanted absolute honesty and frankness." Washington learned so well from Mrs. Ruffner, Harlan added, that "for
the rest of his life he could never see bits of paper strewn in a
house or in the street without wanting to pick them up at once.
He could never see a yard cluttered with trash without a restless
urge to clean it, a paling off a fence without wanting to hammer
it back on, a button off or a grease spot on clothes without
wanting to attend to it." Years later, after delivering a speech in
Rutland, Washington visited the house in Arlington where Viola
Knapp was born. "For me it is a shrine," he said, removing his
hat and bowing his head.[15]

The versatility of these Vermonters is as noteworthy as their
industriousness and self-sufficiency. The women, as described
in Abby Hemenway's *Gazetteer,* "picked their own wool,
carded their own rolls, spun their own yarn, drove their own
looms, made their own cloth, cut, made and mended their own
garments, dipped their own candles, made their own soap, bot-
tomed their own chairs, braided their own baskets, wove their
own carpets, quilts and coverlets, picked their own geese,
milked their own cows, fed their own calves, and went visiting
or to meeting on their own feet." [16] Women in Vermont have
done everything that men have done since Ann Story, widowed
with children, farmed in Salisbury during the Revolution and
dug a cave into the bank on Otter Creek to hide her family when
Indians had burned her cabin. Vermont demands resource-
fulness from all its people. Carl Zuckmayer, the German dramatist who lived as a poultry farmer in Barnard during World War
Two, has remarked on how the ordeal of living in a 1783 farmhouse made his spouse learn skills that society has traditionally
reserved for men. "My wife became a specialist in plumbing

15. Louis R. Harlan, *Booker T. Washington: The Making of a Black Leader
1856–1891* (New York: Oxford University Press, 1972), pp. 28, 42, 43.
16. Quoted by Ralph Nading Hill, *Yankee Kingdom: Vermont and New Hampshire,*
ed. Carl Carmer (New York: Harper and Brothers, 1960), p. 138.

repairs," he has written (and Vermont women can understand how easily that would happen), "and even later on, especially during the early postwar years in Germany, she always carried a small box of tools in her baggage. She used them one Easter Sunday in Hamburg's best hotel, to the horror of the chambermaid. Standing on the toilet seat, she repaired the incessantly gurgling tank." [17]

Male or female, it is understandable why Ralph Waldo Emerson, when he was writing his essay on "Self Reliance," looked to the countryside of northern New England for his ideal embodiment of American virtues instead of looking towards the cities. "A sturdy lad from New Hampshire or Vermont," Emerson wrote, "who in turn tries all the professions, who teams it, farms it, peddles, keeps a school, preaches, edits a newspaper, goes to Congress, buys a township, and so forth, in successive years, and always like a cat falls on his feet, is worth a hundred of these city dolls." [18] Emerson was exaggerating, but not too much. In the early twentieth century it turned out that there were more native Vermonters listed in *Who's Who* in proportion to state population than from any other state. Native Vermonters exceeded the national average for all the states by a four-to-one ratio.

Their inventiveness was also uncommon. "They are all farmers," Ira Allen wrote in a letter he added as an appendix to his *History*, "and again every farmer is a mechanic in some line or other, as inclination leads or necessity requires. The hand that guides the plough frequently constructs it, and the labors of the axe and the plane often evince a degree of genius and dexterity that would really amaze you." [19] Curious to know how things work, and eager to make their labor more productive, these restless Yankees couldn't keep their hands from fussing

17. Carl Zuckmayer, *A Part of Myself: Portrait of an Epoch* (New York: Harcourt Brace Jovanovich, 1970), p. 366.

18. Ralph Waldo Emerson, "Self Reliance," in *Ralph Waldo Emerson*, ed. Frederic I. Carpenter (New York: American Book Co., 1934), p. 106.

19. Ira Allen, *The Natural and Political History of the State of Vermont*, (London: J. W. Myers, 1798), publ. in *Collections of the Vermont Historical Society*, p. 476.

with tools and leftover remnants from something or other which might be made useful again if by assiduous trial and error they could adapt familiar items for new purposes or find new sources of energy. Back in the shed or out in the barn, when time allowed their imagination and their fingers to experiment, they pursued these dreamy visions of perfecting some improvement or mechanical device which, they believed, was not beyond their innate shrewdness and practicality to contrive. When daylight had faded they would putter, and when the earth was covered with snow they would give time to perfecting the contraptions which would make life more efficient and less arduous. Handy fellows, without formal training in science, they taught themselves and motivated themselves steadfastly in their rural isolation. From these hinterlands came some amazing advances in technology.

Two blacksmiths in Brandon, Thomas Davenport and Orange A. Smalley, in 1834 devised an electric motor, and two years later a farmer, Wareham Chase, who had never been more than thirty miles away from his Calais home, rigged up a similar machine. None of these men profited from their breakthroughs because they were at least a generation ahead of the time when electricity replaced steam as a major source of power. Davenport's neighbors scoffed at the electricity his experiments were producing and thought he would be wiser to work steadily at his forge instead of fidgeting with make-believe projects that kept his family impoverished. In fact Davenport became dispirited because he demonstrated his electric telegraph to Samuel F. B. Morse, who at that time was a struggling portrait painter, and it was Morse who capitalized on this invention by embodying the ideas of several people, including Davenport, in his 1837 patent. Many of these dreamy upcountry contrivers were better with their hands than with their heads; Samuel Morey of steamboat fame was another of this group who sadly lacked the business acumen to translate their ideas into wealth. On the shores of Lake Morey in Fairlee, when the nights are still and mist is rising off the water in the moonlight, summer people in the cottages tell guests to watch for a ghostly vessel slipping through the opaqueness because Samuel sunk his last steamboat to the bottom of that lake believing Robert Fulton, whose *Clermont* steamed up the Hudson River in 1807, had stolen his invention.

At Windsor, and nearby at Springfield, these tinkering Yankees left bustling communities as their memorials instead of the obscurity which veils Davenport and Morey and the others. It started when Asahel Hubbard shrewdly got himself appointed warden of the Vermont State Prison at Windsor and paid inmates twenty-five cents per hour to manufacture the hydraulic pump he had patented in 1828. In 1835 he turned to making rifles. These were designed by his son-in-law, Nicanor Kendall, who figured out how a safety device could prevent accidental firings like the one that almost killed Hubbard's daughter. Kendall, who was engaged to marry the girl, was riding with her one day when he spied a squirrel he wanted to shoot, and while reaching under the lap robe for his rifle the gun fired and the bullet grazed the hair of his future bride. Three years later in Windsor, Richard Smith Lawrence devised a way to make firearms on an assembly line with interchangeable parts, and possibly the first major application of this basic industrial process was implemented in this Connecticut Valley town. Rifles made in Windsor were shipped to the Republic of Texas for use in its war with Mexico, to the British for use in the Crimean War, and to Union soldiers fighting Confederates. Windsor hummed during the Civil War; some 5,000 men were employed in its gunshops. Springfield started to hum in the late nineteenth century as it supplied the nation's major manufacturers with the machines necessary to fill the American cornucopia with mass-produced goods—milling machines, turret lathes, thread grinders, chucking grinders, gear shapers, spindle automatics, and more.

These mechanical wizards seemed to specialize in products which sprung from a compulsion to serve the New England ethic of efficiency, thoroughness, and exactness. Thus they found ways to fireproof a safe, to punch a time clock, to wring a wet mop, to refrigerate a railroad car, and, in the case of Thaddeus Fairbanks, to make scales which were incredibly precise.

Their persistence was as unwavering as Fairbanks was tireless; he sat up all night, unable to sleep, when he was mentally evolving the concept of the platform scale.

Most persistent of all was James Wilson, the Bradford farmer who was the first American to make geographic globes for commercial sale. While visiting downriver at Dartmouth College in 1796 he saw two globes that fascinated him intently. He decided to duplicate them. On his farm he used a wood-turning lathe to smooth two solid spheres of wood, to which he glued paper on which he had sketched the meridian lines and the outline of the continents. Realizing his knowledge of astronomy and geography was meager, he sold some of his livestock in order to buy the third edition of the *Encyclopaedia Britannica* for $130 from a Ryegate book dealer. Then he decided to learn copper engraving, and after hiking to Boston and then to Newburyport, unable to find an instructor he could afford, he walked to New Haven, Connecticut, where Amos Doolittle taught him.

Back in Bradford, Wilson improved his skill, made his own presses and lathes by drawing on the blacksmithing he had learned as a youngster, produced his own inks, glues, and varnishes, designed his own maps, and did his own printing. When he was unable to determine the true proportion of meridians on a globular surface he walked to Charlestown, Massachusetts, to ask Jedediah Morse, the famous geographer, to show him how. After fourteen years of effort he sold two globes for $50 a pair. On his farm he made the wooden supports for the globes, their brass quadrants, and even the boxes in which he shipped them. Business was good, and in 1815 he moved his factory to Albany, New York. Not only could he undersell globes imported from England, but his were acknowledged to be more accurate. Not one to rest from tinkering, Wilson continued to work on science-teaching devices. At the age of eighty-three he made all the parts of a planetarium which demonstrated the motions of the heavenly bodies and the seasons, and the procession of the equinoxes, all of which he synchronized by a hand-turned crank.

These inventors were frugal, just as all Vermonters learned that thrift is a way of life. When Thomas Davenport needed silk to insulate the copper magnets for his electric motor he tore his wife's wedding dress into strips. When Silas Hawes of Shaftsbury had a couple of old and broken saw blades he didn't want to throw away he devised the carpenter's square by welding the two together at right angles. From this the Eagle Square Manufacturing Company of South Shaftsbury was started in 1817. Previously the squares had been made of wood and when used by blacksmiths on hot iron they would burn.

Vermonters learned to hoard their resources, regardless of wealth. Thomas Emerson Ripley of Rutland was getting started as a lumberman in Tacoma, Washington, and wanted to impress his father when the senior Ripley visited the Pacific Northwest. The father was a banker who was called "The General" because he had commanded a regiment in the Civil War. Young Ripley planned that one of his partners would be slitting envelopes when "The General" arrived so these blank scraps of paper could be used on their reverse sides for writing memos. "Waste not, want not," the partner sang out on showing the elder Ripley what he was doing, and "The General" nodded his approval of this economical practice. When his son was growing up, "The General" repeatedly reminded his offspring that "Life is Real! Life is Earnest!" and was not hesitant to add, young Ripley recalled, "a discouraging reference to the sweat of my brow." Young Ripley went to college at Yale, and when vacationing at home in Rutland his father would review with him the money he was spending in New Haven. "The auditing of my cash account was an unmixed horror," the son remembered, "for his eye unerringly caught the signs of forced balances. With rapid pencil he computed the inordinate sums I had spent for postage stamps." Suspecting this expenditure was inflated, "The General" once did some quick figuring on a scratchpad and calmly announced, "Tom, during the last term you have written six letters a day and ten on Sundays." [20]

Those who do not know Vermonters are continually befud-

20. Thomas Emerson Ripley, *Green Timber: On The Flood Tide to Fortune in the Great Northwest* (Palo Alto, Calif.: American West Publishing Co., in collaboration with the Washington State Historical Society, 1968), as quoted in *News and Notes* 20 (1969): 2–3.

dled by this trait. On August 27, 1929, Gov. Franklin D. Roosevelt of New York met with Gov. John Weeks of Vermont to dedicate the bridge connecting Crown Point with Chimney Point across Lake Champlain. The two states had jointly built the bridge. The governor of New York exclaimed about the beauty of the steel span and its achievement as a feat of civil engineering. The rejoinder from the governor of Vermont, riding with Roosevelt in an open car, was a grumpy lament that Vermont had to pay $5,000 to purchase the land on its side of the lake where the bridge abutments were placed. Weeks thought that price for that land was exorbitant, and FDR afterward liked to tell the story of how the governor of Vermont was unable to enjoy the dedication of a million-dollar bridge because he begrudged that $5,000 expenditure.

Another story often told by Vermont humorists illustrates how Vermonters can deprive themselves willingly of the common things of life. A Vermonter wandered down Washington Street in Boston and decided to look at merchandise inside Jordan Marsh and Company, New England's largest store. A salesman asked if he could help, but the Vermonter said he was just looking. The salesman tried to be more helpful by suggesting specific items. "These are pajamas, sir—you know, pajamas," he said, detecting uncertainty in the eyes of the Vermonter. "You wear these at night." The Vermonter was unimpressed. "I don't need those," he replied firmly, and added: "I don't go anywhere at night except to bed."

The persistence of Calvinism may be a great virtue, of benefit for the nation as well as for Vermont, even if the image of tight-lipped, tight-fisted Vermonters in the money-mad affluence of modern America makes them look like comic figures, country bumpkins, "green as the green mountains from whence they came," as Herman Melville described them shipping out of New Bedford in the 1840s in his great American allegory, *Moby Dick*. The tradition itself may be jeopardized as more Vermonters define their lives in terms of what the Barre-Montpelier Road and other places like it can provide. The juxtaposition of old and new, and the uncertainty about who will cause what values to prevail, are visible in Royalton and aptly summarized by Hope Nash in her superb history of that community:

> No family in town was too poor to have a television set, and this had something to do with a rapid change in ideas about the conduct of life. Many people still liked well-kept old houses and gardens, preferred to can (and now freeze) their own fruit and vegetables, dig their own potatoes, and perhaps keep chickens or even a pig; liked their old kitchen stove for warmth and good baking; kept family furniture and put what was not in use, in the attic, along with spare parts for mending; laid by bits of iron, leather, and boards; straightened nails; believed in saving money; and would do anything on earth to keep from coming on the town. Right alongside them, often in the same family, were people who longed to live in a mobile home or a tiny pre-fab with no attic or cellar, plastic furniture, automatic gas; to eat pre-cooked meals and commute to work; to buy on credit a camper, two cars with trailers for two snowmobiles, a fiberglass boat, and a riding mower for the tiny yard. This was not just an age difference; many older people wished for the simple life in the trailer, and some young people wished to get back to the simple life on the farm.[21]

21. *Royalton*, by Hope Nash (Lunenburg, Vt.: Stinehour Press, for the Town of Royalton, the South Royalton Woman's Club, and the Royalton Historical Society, 1975), p. 70.

12

Voices from Killington and Mansfield

$\mathcal{A}$S a state which demanded effort from all its citizens, the prospect that Vermont would develop an aristocracy of wealth or rank was unlikely from the outset. The Vermont heritage is full of examples of snobbish people being put in their place by the sturdy yeomen of the Green Mountains. Gov. Thomas Chittenden enjoyed seating prestigious guests at his noontime table with the hired men called in from the fields for their dinners. Once the governor was splitting firewood in his dooryard when a well-dressed stranger rode up, dismounted, and asked the woodchopper to hold the reins while he inquired for the governor. Chittenden cheerfully complied with this request, and then watched the stranger as he learned at the door, after polite bows and inquiries, that the governor of Vermont was the person standing behind him, holding his horse. On another occasion the governor was riding his horse to Newbury, to attend a meeting of the legislature, and in the town of Washington he stopped at the home of Capt. Eleazer Bartholomew to ask if he could spend the night. The captain did not recognize the governor and said his house was crowded but the traveller could sleep on the floor if that was acceptable. The governor accepted. During the night a noisy rainstorm prompted an old sow with her piglets to push open the door and the pigs nestled around the governor to sleep warmly. In the morning the pigs were put outside and the governor was on his way. The captain went also to Newbury that day, and when he realized his overnight guest had been Governor Chittenden, and he remembered how the pigs had bedded with the governor, he was chagrined. But he resolved his embarrassment by mumbling, "Well, if he don't say anything, I won't."

Neither British royalty nor a president of the United States were impressive figures to egalitarian Vermonters. Two anecdotes illustrate how Vermonters refuse to be obsequious. The first is best repeated as Abby Hemenway included it in her *Gazetteer:*

> During the visit of the Prince of Wales to this country, not many years after the close of the Revolution, that bigoted scion of royalty passed through Vermont, on his way to Canada. In the northern part of Brookfield resided Abner Pride, a shoemaker by trade, and, as his house was a long way from any other, it was frequently made a stopping place by travelers. The Prince called here for refreshment, on his journey, and, when about to take his leave, stepped up to Mrs. Pride, with saucy freedom, and kissed her. Observing that she showed signs of resentment, he remarked, soothingly, "Oh, never mind; you can now tell your people that you had the honor of being kissed by an English Prince." Mr. Pride, from his work at his bench, had witnessed the scene and, hearing these words, rose indignantly, and, with a kick, more forcible than graceful, ejected the impertinent prince from the door, sending after him this mocking farewell, "O, never mind; you can now go home and tell your people that you have had the honor of being kicked out of doors by an American cobbler." [1]

The anecdote about an American president concerns James Monroe, and what would happen should he visit Shaftsbury, Vermont. Signed simply "A Farmer," and dated June 20, 1817, in Shaftsbury, a letter to the editor of the *New Hampshire Sentinel* was printed on July 12, 1817. The letter reads:

> Mr. Clark—I have seen in the papers a great account of the reception of President Monroe in Baltimore, Philadelphia and New York. They turned out the military to escort him; fired guns, and

---

1. E. P. Wild, "Brookfield," in Abby Maria Hemenway, ed., *Vermont Historical Gazetteer* (Burlington: Miss A. M. Hemenway, 1867), 2:865.

had great dinners. Now if President Monroe comes along, thro, Shaftsbury, (where our Governor lives) I will tell you what we will do, and what we will not do.

We will not escort him into town; he will ride along alone.

We will not present him any written formal address.

We will not fire any cannon, and none will be fired unless our nine pounder goes off itself out of pure joy.

Our innkeeper in the middle of the town shall give his horses some hay and oats.

About a hundred of us will call and shake hands with him, and converse with him familiarly while he stays with us.

He shall have a good dinner of bread, pork, beef, and potatoes, with a clean plate, and sharp knife and fork; the whole without ceremony; no wine unless he brings it along with him. When he goes away, if we are pleased with him we will bid him a good bye, and wish him a good journey, and pray that his life and health may be preserved as long as he conducts himself properly—That is all.[2]

Among themselves Vermonters learned that a man's word is the token of his integrity, and to this day many genuine Vermonters prefer staunchly to transact business on the basis of an oral agreement instead of the legalese of a written contract. It is hard to be anonymous in Vermont—everybody is watching you—and the uncaring and insensitive character of business transactions in larger and depersonalized societies is not common here. Vermont is where a garage mechanic will estimate the cost of repairing your car, and then fix it for less than the estimate.

Fierce equality has characterized Vermonters in their relations among themselves for two centuries. This spirit is embodied in the Vermont Constitution adopted at Windsor in 1777. The present language is virtually the same as the initial version; few revisions have been made in it since 1777. It is a liberal document, drawing thirteen of its nineteen articles from the Pennsylvania Constitution of 1776, which was formulated under Benjamin Franklin's chairmanship immediately after the Declaration of Independence was approved at Philadelphia. It also continued

2. Quoted in *News and Notes,* newsletter of the Vermont Historical Society, 14 (1962): 17.

some of the liberal features of William Penn's royal charter of 1681. Since many Vermonters were transplants from Connecticut there are Connecticut influences in this document, such as the Freeman's Oath which requires a voter or office-holder to act in accordance with his conscience. Although Vermont's constitution is the shortest of all fifty state constitutions it outdid its predecessors in the business of enlarging freedom by becoming the first state constitution to abolish slavery. It also made Vermont the first state in North America to provide universal manhood suffrage. It affirmed from the Pennsylvania Constitution such rights as freedom of speech and of the press, the right of assembly, prompt and impartial justice, trial by jury, free elections, protection from search and seizure, and the right to govern the state's own internal police. In addition the Vermonters added restraints on writs of attachment and a prohibition against transferring to courtrooms outside Vermont the trials of citizens charged with committing crimes within the state. It is easy to imagine how some delegates at Windsor who had been Green Mountain Boys and had scuffled with Yorkers in some of those encounters before the Revolution were insistent on assuring that Vermont would have complete jurisdiction over its internal affairs. Memories of the attempt to kidnap Remember Baker were still fresh; they were not about to let those Yorker intrusions occur again.

The Constitution stated that a citizen could not be deprived of his civil rights because of religious convictions. In 1783, however, the Legislature authorized each Vermont town to tax its residents for support of a minister and a meeting house if two-thirds or more of the voters were "of similar sentiments with respect to the mode of worship." This act was repealed in 1807, after the legislature in 1801 allowed any Vermont taxpayer who demurred from paying for this support to be excused. All he had to do was visit his town clerk and sign an affidavit which asserted: "I, the subscriber, do not agree in the Religious opinion with a majority of the inhabitants of the town." Quoting that right to be contrary, the distinguished historian Edward Chase Kirkland exclaimed "There spoke Vermont. If loyal to the Vermont heritage we should remember that individual convictions are more important than cooperation, that personal independence has more merit than being bulled or high-hatted into uniformity . . . When Henry D. Thoreau announced that he belonged to 'the party of one' he might have been echoing a voice from Killington or Mansfield.''[3]

The right to be contrary has allowed many Vermonters to speak from moral grounds also as high as Killington or Mansfield; the state has often viewed national issues from the lofty elevation of righteousness. As Dana Doten expressed it, "No Vermonter would wish to deny that the State has, from the outset, carried particularism to the verge of intransigence; the motives only are in dispute. Vermont apologists have defended this attitude as the very essence of liberty. Outside observers have considered it as a consistent manifestation of unenlightened perversity." [4] Instances of it vary from stern support of abolitionism before the Civil War to ideological opposition towards a Connecticut Valley Authority, modeled on the Tennessee Valley Authority, which public power advocates in Franklin D. Roosevelt's New Deal proposed in the 1930s but Vermonters wouldn't accept. To their credit or disgrace Vermonters can be doggedly stubborn. John Ingersoll Gilbert, a Pittsford native who went to UVM and was headmaster at Royalton Academy before settling in Malone, New York, and becoming a lawyer, was elected to the New York Legislature at the same time Theodore Roosevelt was serving there. Of Gilbert it was said, during his time at Albany, that "his influence for the right was strong." He explained his stance quite simply: "They talk about temptations at Albany. I was never tempted by anyone. When a man's position is known to be beyond the reach of corruption there are no more temptations at Albany, than there are in a Sunday school." Roosevelt told him many years later: "I have always thought of you as embodied conscience, and when I have had important questions before me, I have sometimes

---

3. *North Country Journal* (Woodsville, N.H.), August 27, 1970.

4. Workers of the Federal Writers' Project of the Works Progress Administration for the State of Vermont, *Vermont: A Guide to the Green Mountain State* (Boston: Houghton Mifflin Co., 1937), p. ix.

asked myself whether or not you would approve my decisions and actions. I have tried to do what you would consider right, and I think I have done it." [5]

But not all who watch steadfast Vermonters are convinced that "embodied conscience" is their major motive. Some see the stubbornness they express in terms of right versus wrong as actually a mask for a reactionary position on issues. While reading a copy of John Gardner's *Self-Renewal*, which I had borrowed from Montpelier's Kellogg-Hubbard Library, I was amused to see "!Vermont" penciled into the margin opposite this passage: "A common strategem of those who wish to escape the swirling currents of change is to stand on high moral ground. They assert that the old way is intimately bound up in moral and spiritual considerations that will be threatened by any change." [6]

Ethical pretensions are as likely to be punctured in Vermont as readily as the arrogance of self-appointed guardians of public taste or political wisdom. On the front porch of a store in Weston a few years ago I paused to read a wordy notice the owner had posted about being closed on Sundays because it is the Lord's Day, but not content to let the matter rest at that point he elaborated some opinions about the need of religion in this troubled world. Underneath somebody had scribbled in pencil: "Didn't see you in church last Sunday."

Actually many are less troubled by the self-righteousness of Vermonters than by their dismaying inability to understand the world's frightening problems and the fact that Vermont is not aloof from them. In their approach to state problems some Vermonters are still living in the era of more cows than people. It is a provincialism which is easily mocked, although the humor can turn quickly to a serious discussion of how long Vermont can retain its pleasant characteristics while around it the world is becoming increasingly polluted and overpopulated. An ex-

5. Evelyn M. Wood Lovejoy, *History of Royalton, Vermont, with Family Genealogies 1769–1911* (Burlington: Free Press Printing Co., 1911), pp. 330–331.

6. John Gardner, *Self-Renewal: The Individual and the Innovative Society* (New York: Harper & Row, 1964), p. 49.

change between two farmers in Corinth exemplifies this problem of cautious perspective: they were talking across a pasture fence at twilight, as the moon rose slowly above them. One said to the other, nodding towards the moon, "Looks as big as a plate, don't it?" The other showed himself to be a Vermonter of greater vision by replying: "Wal, prob'ly if you was right up thar where 'tis, t'would be as big as a cart wheel." [7]

The same point about the need among Vermonters to broaden their perspectives on the state's beauty, and protect it from developers who would ruin it in the process of peddling it, is conveyed by another story. It concerns a Vermont farmer who finally tired of trying to squeeze his living from his rocky soil and telephoned the real estate agent in town to put his farm up for sale. The agent was delighted and asked the farmer to describe the place. The farmer kept detailing its layout as an operating farm while the agent kept asking questions that summer people would raise when they came to inspect the property. It was clear that the farmer and the businessman had two different visions of the future of the farm—one saw it still covered with cows, the other saw it as a vacation home, or the site of several homes. Trying to get the conversation onto his course the real estate agent asked: "What can you see from the living room windows?" The farmer still didn't sense the agent was basically interested in knowing about vistas. "From the living room windows you can see the barn real well," said the farmer. "Otherwise there's nothing to see but a great big pile of mountains."

Although many Vermonters have lived high in the hills and far back in the valleys the rural isolation which fosters self-sufficiency has not deterred co-operative efforts among them. Work bees and communal barn-raisings were necessary from the outset for these rural people, and electric co-ops and food co-ops are common in the Green Mountains today. The separate towns of Randolph and Bethel were the first in the nation to agree to hire one town manager for both communities. Perhaps

---

7. Town of Corinth History Committee, compilers and editors, *History of Corinth, Vermont, 1764–1964*, 2nd ed. (West Topsham, Vt.: Gibby Press, for the Town of Corinth, 1974), p. 230.

the sense of community pervading Vermont as a whole is one reason that Vermonters are willing to tax themselves heavily and provide welfare benefits and other social programs. Paul F. Douglass, a former Vermonter who became president of American University in Washington, D.C., has noted that Vermonters view their state with the same neighborly outlook as people who belong to a local improvement association and want to better their community. This perspective may explain why every New Deal program which respected state and local autonomy was approved in Vermont even if Vermont never voted for Franklin D. Roosevelt. "Vermonters will do nothing that you tell them to," runs an anonymous expression, "but most anything that you ask them to." A higher percentage of Vermonters voluntarily designated one dollar of their federal income taxes for the presidential election campaign funds in 1976 than did Americans in any other state. In Vermont the proportion was 35 percent; nationally the average was 28 percent.

Nonetheless, as inner-directed persons in David Riesman's nation of other-directed people, Vermonters make it clear that concessions for the general good are decisions to be self-willed and not assumed or elbowed ahead by some implied but murky mystique, especially a false one contrived by the media hucksters or the political smooth-talkers. In this regard Vermont is like Missouri, where they still quote Willard D. Vandiver's famous boast of 1899: "I am from Missouri. You have got to show me." Vermont is a "show me" state. Peter Jennison, a native of Swanton who now is a publisher in Taftsville, used to introduce himself as a Vermonter by saying it is "like being from Missouri, only more so." This obduracy is illustrated by the worst of all Vermont jokes, so stale and wormy that it should be allowed to mold in a compost heap. I wince at telling it:

> Out-of-stater: "Hey mister, does it make any difference which road I take to White River Junction?"
> Native Vermonter: "Not to me it don't."

For Vermonters to concede, moreover, on some matter of public good is not to concede the right to rescind whatever was freely authorized. Early legislative sessions adopted the habit of solemnly re-enacting the approval of the state constitution, not bothered by the fact that the legislature's existence was dependent on the constitution as its foundation, as if this reaffirmation was necessary to fertilize the government of a free people.

The tendency is also evident in squabbles among church-goers. Another anecdote illustrates the point: "How many churches do you have in this town?" a visitor once asked a native. "Waal," replied the Vermonter, "we used to have two, but they united." After a pause, he added: "Now we have three."

The truth of this story is not exaggerated. In Richmond between 1812 and 1814 the "Old Round Church" was built by five denominations—Baptists, Congregationalists, Methodists, Universalists, and Christians—for use on a prearranged basis by all. The church, which is a sixteen-sided polygon with an octagonal belfry, is a handsome wooden building and has been called the first community church in America. But soon the various sects began arguing with each other and withdrew to separate buildings they constructed. In 1880 the Old Round Church became Richmond's town hall. Henry Ford wanted to buy it and move it to Sudbury, Massachusetts, where he was assembling buildings near the Wayside Inn, or to the Dearborn Museum in Michigan. The town refused to sell.

One can imagine Richmond citizens arguing about Ford's offer because Vermonters love to argue. Argument ranks with storytelling, gossip, and sighting deer in the woods and fields by the roadsides as a popular Vermont pastime. One old-timer in East Poultney was quizzed by an architect about the design of a weathervane on a church spire which had blown down in a storm in 1898, when the elderly Vermonter was a youngster. The old-timer said his recollection would be improved if some of his boyhood chums were still alive. "I could have done better if I had someone to argue with," he said regretfully. [8]

Vermont lore is amply studded with examples of feuds waged furiously—of the Congregational minister who wouldn't cross

8. Quoted by Charles T. Morrissey, "On Books," *Vermont Life* 29 (1974): 13.

the town green while the Episcopal bells were tolling; of the two owners of a sawmill who split with each other during the anti-Masonic excitement and could no longer work together as partners and arranged that one would be in the mill only in the morning, the other in the afternoon; of friends of the deceased at a Danville funeral who lined up on opposite sides of the open grave, Masons on one side of the coffin and Anti-Masons on the other, each contingent refusing to acknowledge the other. In Ludlow in 1845 a Mr. Franklin Riggs installed a bar in his home, and the frivolity which occurred there was disgraceful in the opinion of the Reverend Watsos Warren, a Congregational clergyman. One day Mr. Riggs was preparing to paint his house, and as a friendly gesture he asked the Reverend, who was passing by, what color the minister thought would be suitable. The minister suggested with acerbity that the color of West India rum would be appropriate for Mr. Riggs's house. With an epithet Mr. Riggs retorted that he would paint it the color of Mr. Warren's character, and he proceeded to cover his house with a coat of black paint.

The tendency to quarrel may float in the shifting currents of the mountain air, even if Dr. Jarvis did not comment on this trait when he discussed Vermont as a dizzy place. Newcomers adopt the habit, often with alacrity. Rudyard Kipling came to Vermont to live in 1892 because his bride, Carrie Balestier, had summered in the Brattleboro area in her girlhood. For four years the Kiplings lived in Dummerston, and here he wrote two of the *Jungle Books* and *Captains Courageous* and developed the glimmerings of *Kim*, which appeared in 1899. The Kiplings were happy in Vermont except for one drawback; Beatty Balestier, the great author's brother-in-law, lived down the road, and he was an improvident and intemperate man who liked to argue. The contentiousness got so fierce that they dragged their family dispute into public by going to court to the great entertainment of their Windham County neighbors. Kipling was distraught at the whole unpleasant business; in 1896 he took his wife and two Vermont-born children to England and said goodbye to Vermont forever. It is curious to ruminate on what would have happened to his literary career, and to Vermont's modest amount of well-written literature about itself, if he had stayed permanently in Vermont. Probably his own output would not have varied, since his imagination was able to reach to torrid India while Naulakha, his house in Dummerston, was swept by winter winds and snow. But Vermont would have been the big gainer, since the pieces he wrote about Vermont weather and scenes are excellent.

Matthew Lyon is another who came to Vermont and thrived on argumentation—so much so that he and Roger Griswold of Connecticut engaged in the first fisticuffs between Congressmen on the floor of the House. Lyon was arrested under the Alien and Sedition Acts of 1798 for criticizing President John Adams, but while cooling his passions in the Vergennes jail he ran for re-election to Congress and his Vermont constituents voted him back into office. That says something about the way Vermonters can tolerate disputation.

"Freedom and Unity" is appropriate as the state motto. When Alger Hiss was being tried for perjury in New York in 1948 he contemplated a request to move his trial to Vermont; he felt the press had prejudiced the jury in New York whereas in Vermont he would receive fair-minded justice from impartial jurors. When his lawyers considered a change of venue to Vermont they were told that Hiss would probably get a conviction or acquittal in Vermont but not a hung jury. Vermonters, they were told, like to argue cases until they are resolved. The request to move the trial was denied so this hypothesis was not tested.

Vermonters speak crisply, and their candor can pierce like a wintry wind off Killington or Mansfield. Rarely is there shilly-shallying or beating around the bush in Vermont. Isaac Tichenor, who succeeded Thomas Chittenden as governor, was travelling in a section of Vermont far from his home in Bennington when he stopped to admire a stone wall being built by a farmer. The governor examined the wall on both sides and then exclaimed "Bless me, friend, what a beautiful and noble wall you are building—I don't believe there is another equal to it in the state." The farmer appreciated the compliment but wasn't seduced by it. "Yes, governor," he replied, "it's a very good wall to be sure, but I can't vote for you this year." [9]

In our own time the direct and unadorned speech of Vermonters catches the unwary by surprise. A vehement Republican went into the Montpelier Post Office one day to buy some stamps. The clerk behind the counter gave him a recent issue with the jut-jaw profile of Franklin D. Roosevelt. The old Vermonter looked at FDR on the stamps and then glared at the postal clerk. In a slow voice, holding the stamps gently by his fingertips so the clerk could see FDR too, the old fellow said very deliberately: "you really don't expect me to lick the backside of these stamps, do you?"

The late Beatrice Vaughan of East Thetford told a similar story to illustrate how summer people can be difficult when they attend a country supper. One city fellow seated himself at a long table and was asked by the chairlady of the supper committee, who also served as his waitress, "Do you like baked beans?" He said he couldn't stand baked beans. "Do you like brown bread?" she asked. He said he disliked brown bread. "Do you like rhubarb pie?" she asked. He said he couldn't tolerate the thought of eating rhubarb pie. "In that case," she said, "you'd better call it that you've already eaten," and with that she gathered up his plate and utensils and went off to the kitchen.

At town meetings the words can fly. But they can be effective, too, because people do listen. Dorothy Canfield Fisher has described how one of Arlington's meetings debated the need to repair bridges as opposed to building a new grade school. The town could afford one or the other but not both, and advocates of repairing the bridges were clearly winning more support until the village grocer, Patrick Thompson, got to his feet and in words she remembered as "intense as the flame of a blowtorch," spoke his mind:

"I say 'If we have to choose, let the bridges fall down!' What kind of a town would we rather have, fifty years from now—a place

9. Hiland Hall, "Bennington," in Hemenway's *Vermont Historical Gazetteer*, 1:177.

where nit-wit folks go back and forth over good bridges? Or a town
which has always given its children a fair chance, and prepares
them to hold their own in modern life? If they've had a fair chance,
they can build their own bridges. You know which of these two is
really wanted by every one of us here. I say 'If we have to choose,
let the bridges fall down!' '' [10]

Thereupon Arlington voted for the new grade school.

A similar turn-around in a Thetford town meeting in the
1960s resulted in the preservation of the covered bridge at Thetford Center. Article 12 on the agenda for the town meeting
posed the question: Should the bridge be repaired, or should it
be replaced by a concrete span? The lone businessman in Thetford Center wanted a bigger bridge so his trucks could cross it
safely, and the selectmen seemed sympathetic to his viewpoint.
Most townspeople figured the old covered bridge would be the
loser. Noel Perrin, a Dartmouth College professor of English,
described the fate of Article 12 with particular interest because
he lived next to that covered bridge and was attending his town
meeting that year:

> We got through the first eleven articles in less than an hour. Then
> we spent the rest of the morning arguing—"debating" is too
> elevated a term for town meeting style—Article 12. Sentiment
> gradually mounted for keeping the covered bridge, chiefly because
> of the brilliant fight put up by an old man who had been our rural
> mail carrier for fifty-one years—had taken the mail through that
> bridge in a horse and sleigh, then a 1911 Cadillac, and finally a Jeep
> station wagon. It came near time to vote. Then one of the
> proponents of the new concrete bridge got up, holding a formidable
> list in his hand. He is a leader in town. He told us he liked the old
> wooden bridge as well as anyone—but he wasn't sure we realized
> how much it would cost to repair it. And he began reading
> specifications and prices from his list: the number of new 12″ X
> 12″ bridge timbers required, and what each would cost; numbers
> and prices for joists, and so on. The total kept mounting; we
> taxpayers began having second thoughts.
>
> Then a young fellow in back stood up, a workingman with a

---

10. Dorothy Canfield Fisher, *Memories of My Home Town* (Arlington, Vt.: Arlington
Historical Society, 1955), p. 101.

lumberjack's shirt on and a three-day growth of beard. "I don't know where he got them prices from," he said, "but I know this. I work up to the mill in Ely, and we can sell you all that stuff a hell of a lot cheaper than what he said." Every head turned to stare. Undeterred, he went from memory through each item the other man had mentioned, repeating the figures and then quoting the lowest price his mill could offer.

After that we voted. Usually we have voice votes to save time, but this was an important decision, and the selectmen passed out slips of paper. "We wrote "Yes" if we wanted a new bridge, "No" if we didn't. We filed by the ballot box and dropped the slips in, and when we finished the selectmen counted them. It took fifteen minutes. The first Selectman then walked to the microphone. "Guess we're keepin' it," he said. "Twenty-one 'Yes,' hundred and twenty-one 'No.' " There was a brief roar of triumph. Then we had lunch.[11]

Town meeting oratory is most memorable for its humor, and with everybody in town assembled for socializing after a long seige of winter isolation it is understandable why Vermonters are not reluctant to speak out. And townspeople listen because a sudden gaffe is good entertainment, providing hearty laughter and much guffawing afterwards when the episode is recalled and retold. Ruth Rasey tells how Rupert voters, assembled in their town hall, had voted for various town officials when 'Bijah Dean stood up and called out, "Mr. Moderator, we need some cuspidors." Since they had just voted for "first selectman," "first constable," and the like, a newcomer who was impressed by the titles and unfamiliar with all the terminology stood up and proudly announced, "Mr. Moderator, I nominate Dan Meehan for First Cuspidor." After the hilarity died down, the cuspidors were duly sworn in. Robert L. Duffus tells about a fellow who lacked an elementary grasp of arithmetic but sensed a movement in the discussion of the school budget toward reducing the allocation. He got to his feet and proposed that the town's proportion of a state-supported program be lowered from three-fifths to three-fourths.

11. Sonja Bullaty and Angelo Lomeo, photographers, with text by Noel Perrin, *Vermont in All Weathers* (New York: Viking Press, 1973), pp. 18–19.

But Vermonters welcome participation in public discourse from anybody who feels impelled to speak, and those who speak are not hesitant to volunteer their judgments even if their schooling was rudimentary and their voices do not bear traces of an Ivy League education. Lawyers and judges, especially, are targets for barbs since typical Vermonters are not necessarily enthralled by the reasoning or eloquence of attorneys. In Vermont courtrooms the judges in their robes sit flanked by two judges in street clothes. These side judges are elected biennially by the voters, and their function is to advise the judges on local circumstances about plaintiffs and defendants and witnesses, in order to assist in reaching equitable verdicts. For this they receive thirty-nine dollars each day the court is in session. The two side judges are authorized to offer more than local scuttlebutt about cases and principals; they are empowered to overrule a judge if they believe he has erred, and there have been instances when side judges have been sustained by a higher court when decisions have been appealed.

Vermonters prize common sense as a superior virtue. Samuel Read Hall, an educational innovator who founded the first normal school in America, at Concord, Vermont, in 1823, put great emphasis on common sense in his *Lectures on School-Keeping:*

> It is not every one of those, even, who possess the requisite
> literary attainments, who is qualified to assume the direction of a
> school. Many entirely fail of usefulness, though possessed of highly
> cultivated minds. Other ingredients enter into the composition of a
> good schoolmaster. Among these *common sense* is the first. This is
> a qualification exceedingly important, as in teaching school one has
> constant occasion for its exercise. Many, by no means deficient in
> intellect, are not persons of common sense. I mean by the term, that
> faculty by which things are seen as they are. It implies judgment
> and discrimination, and a proper sense of propriety in regard to the
> common affairs of life. It leads us to form judicious plans of action,
> and to be governed by our circumstances, in such a way as men in
> general will approve. It is the exercise of reason, uninfluenced by
> passion or prejudice. It is in man nearly what instinct is in brutes. It
> is very different from genius or talent, as they are commonly

defined, but is better than either. It never blazes forth with the splendour of noon, but shines with a constant and useful light.[12]

To compliment a person for having common sense is among the highest accolades Vermonters can bestow. Time after time in the literature Vermonters created about themselves the emphasis given to it by Samuel Read Hall is reaffirmed. People who are new to Vermont's political folkways soon learn that "common sense" is the best premise on which to rest an argument. The premise holds whether the issue is as local as the cost of mowing the grass in the village cemetery or as statewide as the omnibus appropriation bill in the legislature. To favor something because it is "liberal," or "conservative," or "innovative" or even "traditional" is often enough to make it fail; liberals and conservatives will be suspicious of it from their opposing viewpoints, as will innovators and traditionalists. In spite of the fact that many innovations may be traditional, and liberals and conservatives often act differently than they philosophize, the guiding principle in Vermont is simply this: never phrase in ideological terms what it is you wish to accomplish. Instead refer to it as the "common sense" way to solve a problem. For synonyms use words like *sensible, wise,* and *normal.* Do this even when your common sense solution is imaginative, pioneering, untried, and will totally disrupt the status quo. The most conservative member of the Vermont Senate worked to secure state ownership of the St. Johnsbury and Lamoille County Railroad when he put aside his ideology and convinced himself, and his colleagues, that purchase of the railroad was the common sense solution to the problem of keeping it in operation. The Legislature approved radical land use controls when it passed Act 250, but every supporter from Deane C. Davis, the centrist governor who had been board chairman of the National Life Insurance Company, to members of the House and Senate preferred not to verbalize it that way. If Vermonters ever feel impelled to form a modern version of the Green Mountain Boys, in order to exert authority over land they

12. Samuel Read Hall, *Lectures in School-Keeping* (Boston: Richardson, Lord and Holbrook, 1829), pp. 30–31.

probably don't have proper titles to, the twentieth century nomenclature would probably not be "Green Mountain Boys" for such a vigilante group. Instead they would call themselves the Common Sense Associates (as did one group of real estate agents and developers who formed to undo many of Vermont's environmental regulations). History would call it the Common Sense Movement. Thomas Paine would be relegated to lesser stature as that other fellow, a friend of Thomas Young's in Pennsylvania, who wrote that other stuff about common sense.

It is understandable why common sense should run through Vermont's history as a major value. Making a state of this terrain, and making a living in it, forced a person to use his wits. John Dewey, born in Burlington in 1859, drew from this tradition of his home state to influence American education everywhere. "John Dewey's brand of instrumental pragmatism is nothing other than the Yankee's common sense, practical way of looking at every day situations and problems in terms of getting things done," [13] commented Paul F. Douglass and Jacob B. Abbott.

In the late 1960s a political scientist, Charles H. Sheldon of Southampton College of Long Island University, surveyed judges in Nevada, Utah, and Vermont to ascertain variations in philosophic outlook, legal competency, and social background. Sheldon listed "common sense" as one of seven choices in a questionnaire about factors influencing judicial decisions. Exactly 35.7 percent of the Nevada judges marked "common sense"; 47.3 percent of the Utah judges did the same; and 72.2 percent of the Vermont judges did likewise. The Vermonters, in other words, cited "common sense" twice as often as the Nevada judges.[14] Perhaps "Common Sense Under Law" should be inscribed in the granite over the front door to the State Library Building, where the Vermont Supreme Court meets, next to the statehouse in Montpelier.

13. Paul F. Douglass and Jacob B. Abbott, *The Yankee Tradition* (Burlington: Free Press Printing Co., 1941), p. 74.

14. Charles H. Sheldon, "The Uniqueness of State Legal Systems: Nevada, Utah, and Vermont," *Judicature* 53 (1970): 333–337.

Vermonters live in the land where good fences make good neighbors, as Robert Frost wrote in "Mending Wall." Good fences require prodigious effort to build and constant effort to repair. Hunters beat them down, snowmobilers snip wires so their trails can run unimpeded, and frost tumbles stones onto the ground. The poet said he would prefer to know what he was walling in or walling out before he built a wall, but most Vermonters simply walk the property line on an appointed day repairing the wall as they go believing that good fences do indeed make good neighbors.

The walls Vermonters erect between themselves are like the walls traversing their rock-strewn landscape. When emotion does erupt it is more often like a frost heave than a bubbling geyser. Many Vermonters simply choose not to emote. Calvin Coolidge recalled that his father showed emotion only on two occasions: the first was when young Calvin's mother died; the second was when the Colonel climbed the midnight stairs in the Plymouth farmhouse on that sweltering August night in 1923 and in a trembling voice told his son that Warren Harding had died in San Francisco and Calvin was now president of the United States.

Samuel Clemens (Mark Twain) discovered the same characteristic for himself when he lectured once in Brattleboro and couldn't induce any substantial laughter from his audience of stone-faced Vermonters. Wondering why his humor was so ineffectual that night he walked around to the front of the theater afterwards and heard a Vermonter helping his wife into their buggy say "B'golly, that fellow was so funny tonight I could hardly keep from laughing."

When Vermonters marry the walls do not necessarily come tumbling down. Generally they stand unbreached, enduring the vicissitudes of matrimony just as they withstand the onslaught of wind-driven snowstorms. Connubial bliss does not depend on fervid passions; more often than not Vermont marriages seem like business alliances between silent partners. One elderly Vermont farmer, so a story is told, was seated with his wife by the fireplace one evening, as he finished reading the day's issue of the *Brattleboro Daily Reformer,* and she sat mending in the opposite chair. (This is not an unusual scene: "a barn, a fence, and a woman always need mending," states a Vermont proverb.) He looked at her several times with stealthy glances, and finally couldn't restrain himself from speaking. "Rebecca Jane," he said, speaking her full name as was his custom in the privacy of their home (unlike his public speech, when he did not refer to her by her first name but by her title of "Mrs."), and then repeating her name again, "Rebecca Jane," with rare solicitation and a tremor in his voice. "When I think of all you have meant to me," he said slowly, "the bearing of the children and the raising of 'em, the keeping of the house, the cooking, the mending, the cleaning, the nursing when we were sick— when I think of all these things for all these years," and he paused, "I can hardly keep from telling you."

Probably Rebecca Jane said nothing in reply but smiled demurely with her eyes fastened on her needle and thread. Vermonters were taught early, Dorothy Canfield Fisher recalled, that

> Praise to the face
> Is open disgrace.[15]

Marriage was duty, they also learned, and marriage to a Vermonter might be a lifelong testing of stamina. Thomas Ainsworth of Windsor impressed his bride, Hannah Burnham, when he swam across the Connecticut River in the 1780s to marry her on the New Hampshire side, because the first thing they did as newlyweds was swim together back to Windsor. Stewart Holbrook tells in *Yankee Exodus* how a Montpelier lawyer left his home to walk to his office one morning, but instead of tending to his substantial practice he decided to walk on, beyond the Green Mountains, arriving ultimately in Louisiana where he quietly began a new life with a new wife. Twenty-two years later, he arrived back in Montpelier, walked into his home, put his hat on a rack, and asked if supper were ready. Even in the

---

15. Dorothy Canfield Fisher, "Introduction" in Earle Newton, *The Vermont Story: A History of the People of the Green Mountain State* (Montpelier: Vermont Historical Society, 1949), p. vi.

course of an ordinary marriage, spared of normal doses of male heedlessness, life for these women could be a continuous ordeal. One wonders about the private thoughts of a Cornwall woman who bore twenty-two children in her life, twenty-one of whom did not survive infancy. Her husband, Dr. Frederic Ford, says Beulah Sanford in *Two Centuries of Cornwall Life,* was "a very social man, with many pleasant anecdotes to relate. His laugh—peculiar both for its manner and its heartiness—cannot be forgotten by those who were favored to hear it." [16]

From a masculine viewpoint, in the endless contesting of wills before the concept of open marriage became fashionable, Vermont males also knew the anguish and frustration of an unhappy marriage. One reason that Ethan Allen was available to lead the Green Mountain Boys was that he had made the dreadful error of marrying a shrew, Mary Brownson. Some pranksters tried to scare Ethan, after he had been tippling one night in a tavern, by hiding behind some tombstones he would pass on his way home, and rising up with ominous cries that they were Satan and his henchmen and were going to capture him and take him away. "You don't scare me," Ethan shouted at Satan, "I married your sister."

In modern times the war continues: A divorce counselor told how a midwesterner named Joel ended his marriage of eighteen years to a Vermont girl: "She was what some people might think of as the typical New England woman: Hard-working, taciturn, not very demonstrative or emotional. Somehow she always managed to rig things so that I would feel guilty. Nothing I ever did was good enough for her, although she never came out and said so." [17]

For people from other parts of the nation, where affection is not restrained by taciturnity, the glacial disposition of Vermonters can be upsetting. When Gladys Baker came from Alabama to Burlington as the wife of Roy L. Patrick she felt Ver-

16. Beulah M. Sanford, *Two Centuries of Cornwall Life* (Rutland, Vt.: Sharp Printing, 1962), p. 83.

17. Mel Krantzler, *Creative Divorce: A New Opportunity for Personal Growth* (New York: M. Evans & Co., 1974), p. 249.

monters were intentionally giving her the silent treatment, and
after a year of emotional starvation she turned to a psychiatrist.
He pronounced her to be in fine shape. But she wasn't satisfied.
"What about a woman's need of *hearing* some of these nice
things occasionally? Just a word to make her feel liked and
wanted?" He brushed that aside. "Nonsense!" he said. "Up
here in Vermont we take such things for granted—haven't paid
my wife a compliment in twenty years." At that she exploded
with a comment that afterwards made the rounds and became
classic specimen of Vermontiana: "In order to get a compliment
out of a Vermonter you'd have to go around with a horse-
whip!" [18]

The countryman's self-restraint is typified in a story George
Aiken told. A superb humorist, who can salt his speech with
straight-faced whimsy as well as Robert Frost did in the verses
of his final years, Aiken prefers quips to stories, and his anecdotes often feature the smartness of animals rather than
human idiosyncrasies. But to illustrate how Vermonters can
sublimate their passions he recounts how a farmer came out
of his barn one night, milkpails in hand, and smelled the first
scents of spring. There was a warmish breeze in the air, leaves
were budding, and all that was written in the Song of Solomon
about springtime was also in his Vermont world that night. He
could feel himself respond to the life-giving forces being renewed right then on his farm. Walking into his house he set
down his milkpails. "Wife," he said, "it's too beautiful a night
to stay in the house; I think I'll go out and kill a hog." [19]

Some outlanders have a difficult time adjusting to Vermont
terseness and understatement. They say about Vermonters what
Alice Roosevelt Longworth heard about Calvin Coolidge in a
doctor's office and passed along—that the president must have
been weaned on a pickle. Another explanation is that all Vermont youngsters, in the era before indoor plumbing, dreaded a

18. Gladys Baker (Mrs. Roy L. Patrick), "Converted Southerner," in "What and
Why Is a Vermonter?", *Vermont Life* 2 (1948): 8.

19. As told by Jonathan Daniels, *A Southerner Discovers New England* (New York:
Macmillan Co., 1940), p. 253.

cold and drafty outhouse on chilly days, and as a result Vermonters as a whole grew up constipated and carried irritability into adulthood as part of their heritage. But Vermonters explain it matter-of-factly, in terms of accepting the world with its limitations and not solely for self-indulgence and the pleasures that can be exploited from it. The Calvinism which came as puritanism to this Old Testament land, where Seth Hubbell and the others were tested with the afflictions of Job, is a continuing tradition. Much of the strength of Vermont is rooted in it.

Vermont is the state which gave to the world George Perkins Marsh—the first American to question the mindless way mankind was transforming the global environment and to predict a tragic destiny for humanity if exploitation of finite resources was continued. In Burlington in 1860 he began his classic, *Man and Nature; or Physical Geography as Modified by Human Action*, the book which became, in Lewis Mumford's phrase, "the fountain-head of the conservation movement" [20] when it was published in 1864. In it Marsh focused on "the great question," as he called it: "whether man is of nature or above her." His answer was not assuring: "Man is everywhere a disturbing agent. Wherever he plants his foot, the harmonies of nature are turned to discord." There was no doubt in his mind that man had to make peace with nature. He wanted to title his book *Man the Disturber of Nature's Harmonies*, but his publisher, Charles Scribner, talked him out of that. As Marsh's biographer has put it: "Anyone with a hoe or an axe knows what he is doing, but before Marsh no one had seen the total effects of all the axes and hoes. Once Marsh made this general observation, the conclusion was, for him, inescapable." His book, "must be considered the origin of a revolution in American thought."

For Marsh the ideas in *Man and Nature* began in his childhood in Woodstock. His home was on the lower slope of Mount Tom, where Frederick Billings later built his estate, and after

---

20. Quoted by David Lowenthal, *George Perkins Marsh: Versatile Vermonter* (New York: Columbia University Press, 1958), p. 246. The account of Marsh in the text, above, is taken from Lowenthal's *Marsh.*

him Laurance Rockefeller. Young Marsh went often to the tree-less summit of Mount Tom and surveyed the village of Wood-stock below and the fields and pastures in the valley of the Ot-tauquechee. He also saw how men were abusing the landscape; hillsides denuded of timber allowed water to run rapidly into the Ottauquechee and cause more frequent flooding—three in one decade washing out the bridge his father built across the river at the foot of the hill. Summers with dry spells caused the river to dry up almost completely because the rainwater had not perco-lated through the soil. He and his father, Charles Marsh, would ride in a two-wheeled chaise along the hilltop roads around Woodstock to look at the landscape, especially the trees along the roads. "To my mind," young Marsh recalled afterwards, "the whole earth lay spread out before me. My father pointed out the most striking trees as we passed them, and told me how to distinguish their varieties. I do not think I ever afterward failed to know one forest-tree from another." Charles Marsh was eager for his son to learn about the environment; George remembered once how his father "stopped his horse on the top of a steep hill, bade me notice how the water there flowed in different directions, and told me that such a point was called a *watershed.*"

Other things he learned well, too. Following his two brothers to Dartmouth, he became a teacher at Norwich University, then a manufacturer, lawyer, editor, legislator in Montpelier and in the U.S. Congress, and a long-time diplomat in Turkey and Italy. He was conversant in twenty languages, learning to speak them as quickly as he could read them. He was America's foremost authority on English and Scandinavian linguistics, a compara-tive philologist, and probably America's broadest scholar in the nineteenth century. He helped to found the Smithsonian Institu-tion and was urged to be its secretary. He was an influence for improved public taste in art and architecture, and by es-tablishing principles of railroad regulation he tried to tame the technology which his nation glorified. This versatility was rooted in his background: "Omnicompetence," wrote his biog-rapher, "had been a marked trait of the American from the start, and was surely characteristic of nineteenth-century Vermont, which required and fostered talents as diverse as those of any Western frontier community.''

As a Vermonter he was solemn and reserved and had a low estimate of his achievements as a scholar. He viewed himself as a professional in no field but one, linguistics, and only partially in that. New England Calvinism was in him; his wife, Caroline, called him "the last of the Puritans." He was at his desk habitually at 5:00 A.M. and when he married Caroline he suggested 6:00 A.M. as an appropriate hour for the wedding, and she agreed.

People said he looked more like a farmer than a lawyer or businessman or congressman. Thus you can picture him attending an agricultural fair at Rutland in September 1847 to judge pigs and oxen and maple sugar. Later that day he gave a talk to the Agricultural Society of Rutland County, and for the first time outlined publicly the ideas which *Man and Nature* contained seventeen years later:

> The suddenness and violence of our freshets increases in proportion as the soil is cleared; bridges are washed away, meadows swept of their crops and fences, and covered with barren sand, or themselves abraded by the fury of the current. There is reason to fear that the valleys of many of our streams will soon be converted from smiling meadows into broad wastes of shingle and gravel and pebbles, deserts in summer, and seas in autumn and spring.
>
> The changes which these causes have wrought in the physical geography of Vermont within a single generation are too striking to have escaped the attention of any observing person. Every middle-aged man who revisits his birth-place after a few years of absence looks upon another landscape than that which formed the theatre of his youthful toils and pleasures. The signs of artificial improvement are mingled with the tokens of improvident waste, and the bald and barren hills, the dry beds of the smaller streams, the ravines furrowed out by the torrents of spring and the diminished thread of intervale that skirts the widened channel of the rivers, seem sad substitutes for the pleasant groves and brooks and broad meadows of his ancient paternal domain. If the present value of timber and land will not justify the artificial re-planting of grounds

injudiciously cleared, at least nature ought to be allowed to reclothe them with a spontaneous growth of wood.[21]

Marsh was developing a big idea, bigger than he and those Rutland County farmers realized in 1847. As it played in his mind in the years ahead he developed it further. Caroline pestered him to write the book that became *Man and Nature,* and she deserves thanks for that; it is the most consequential message ever delivered by any Vermonter.

As Marsh loved trees so George Aiken loved wildflowers when he was a boy in Putney at the turn of this century. This was not an exotic interest; Vermont has more than twelve hundred varieties of wildflowers—more than any other New England state. Aiken has recalled how his interest grew:

> In the farthest corner of my father's pasture was a small woodlot of sugar maples, birches, hop hornbeam and pignut hickory, growing on rocky, ledgy ground. The cows were usually turned out to pasture the last of April and it was my work and that of old Shep to get them down to the barns in time for milking every night. Usually their bovine obstinacy would prompt them to linger in this small woodlot in the far end of the pasture to make Shep and me as much work as possible in getting them. But in this little grove of hardwoods there were quantities of Springbeauties, Hepaticas, Bloodroot, Violets, Squirrelcorn and Dutchmans-breeches, which so entranced the young man of eight years that it was occasionally necessary for some older member of the family to not only come after the cows, but Shep and me as well.[22]

Unable to afford a college education, Aiken became a horticulturist and orchardist. Putney made him a politician when it sent him to the Vermont House of Representatives in 1931; soon he was rising up the ladder—speaker, lieutenant governor, and governor. In January 1941 he went to Washington as a U.S. senator (although he is still addressed as "Governor" in Ver-

21. George Perkins Marsh, "Address Delivered Before the Agricultural Society of Rutland County," in Barbara Gutmann Rosenkrantz and William A. Koelsch, *American Habitat: A Historical Perspective* (New York: Free Press, 1973), p. 357.

22. George D. Aiken, *Pioneering With Wildflowers,* 4th. ed. (Englewood Cliffs, N.J.: Prentice-Hall, 1968), p. 1.

mont), and in January 1975 he came home to Vermont to stay. He authored three books during those years in politics and has issued a forth since his retirement. One is *Pioneering With Wildflowers,* a classic in its own way, which he dedicated to Peter Rabbit "in the hope that flattery will accomplish what traps and guns have failed to do and that the little rascal will let our plants alone from this time on." [23] His wife, Lola, wants him to write another book—this one for children about the squirrels and pigeons he fed daily in Washington, but he prefers to experiment with growing a disease-free raspberry plant. Vermont sends people like this to Washington; Sen. Warren Austin was an orchardist who loved to talk about his trees as well as politics.

In Washington, Aiken was known as a modest and shrewd country man, as befits a U.S. senator whose Putney home is on a road still not paved. The Washington social whirl didn't excite him, even when presidents invited him for evening entertainments. "When you go to the White House," he once advised, "get a seat near the door, so that when they dim the lights, you can sneak out." His colleague and close friend, Sen. Mike Mansfield of Montana, described him as "neither a hawk nor dove but a wise old owl." [24] His common-sense solution to American entanglement in the Vietnam War was termed "the Aiken formula": declare "victory" in accordance with a modest definition of American aims in Vietnam and reduce our commitment proportionately. That puckish advice, defining the problem to fit realities, was a voice echoing from Killington or Mount Mansfield. If accepted it would have reduced the greatest misfortune of recent American history to a lesser tragedy.

They still have much to say in the modern world, these Vermonters, even if they economize in language. Ice and granite may be in the walls they construct around themselves, but that isn't the whole of it. Dilys Laing of Norwich conveyed the es-

---

23. Aiken, *Pioneering With Wildflowers,* p. v.
24. Quoted by Charles T. Morrissey, "George Aiken: Citizen," *Vermont Life* 29 (1974): 24.

sence of their heritage in a 1940 poem she entitled, simply and succinctly, "Vermonters":

> These are the people living in this land:
> proud and narrow, with their eyes on the hills.
> They ask no favors. Their lips defend
> with speech close rationed their hoarded souls.
>
> You cannot love them or know them at all
> unless you know how a hardwood tree
> can pour blond sugar in a pegged-up pail
> in the grudging thaw of a February day.[25]

Vermonters have a rich heritage to draw upon—or discard if they do not choose to preserve it. Rarely have they edged towards speaking lyrically about it, but a century ago Charles C. Parker allowed himself a few flourishes and a resonance from the Book of Psalms in his gentle summing-up:

> Amid countless hardships and privations the first settlers laid the foundations of this community. It was not all done as we could have wished—nor all with the wisest forecast of the future. But they did, nevertheless, a great and stern work; into that work we have entered. They sowed, often in sadness; we reap in joy. Their work is done; ours is yet on our hands. These hills and these valleys, the fertile soil of which they laid open to the sun with the river that winds among them and the grand settings of the mountains, were beautiful to them. They are beautiful, exceedingly beautiful to us. Verily the lines are fallen to us in pleasant places. We have a goodly heritage.[26]

25. *Vermont History* 38 (1970): 157.
26. Charles C. Parker, "Waterbury," in Hemenway's *Vermont Historical Gazetteer*, 4:823.

13

What Happened to the Goodly Heritage?

T is an omnipresent heritage, too. Travelling through Vermont is like visiting a vast outdoor museum, a countryman's Williamsburg, a Walt Disney world where elderly Vermont farmers and their wives go strolling like Mickey Mouse and Minnie Mouse against a stage set of white frame houses and village greens. Not only is it full of antique shops but taken as a whole it is like one huge antique shop. Half of Vermont's residents seem employed in selling old chairs, or spinning wheels, or wooden sap buckets, while the other half is peddling maple syrup, or honey made by genuine Vermont bees (recently honored by the Vermont legislature as the official state insect), or native-grown corn, or rabbits, or homemade soap and candles, or old post cards, or whatever. It is a wonder that a descendant of one of America's great robber baron families hasn't tried to preserve Vermont in toto, or that the National Park Service hasn't persuaded the Congress to buy it. For history hunters it is an excellent game preserve.

Heritage is important to the natives. It brings them together in groups like the Vermont Old Cemetery Association, which urges people to neaten the burial grounds scattered everywhere, and the Vermont Folklore Society, which meets to exchange riddles and aphorisms which have been handed down from generation to generation as family lore. Other groups discuss old tools which aren't in use any longer, or the cancellations of

191

Vermont post offices which Washington suspended decades ago when crossroad settlements lost their general stores. The biggest of all is the 251 Club, which has about five thousand members and draws huge crowds to its annual dinner each summer at the National Life Insurance Company cafeteria in Montpelier, after which slides of covered bridges are shown, or some similar program features what club members like to see through their windshields as they drive through Vermont. Anybody can join the 251 Club, but after paying annual dues a person will be categorized as a "plus member" or as a "minus member." A "plus member" has visited all of Vermont's 246 towns and five gores. (Gores are unorganized parcels of land which lie outside the boundaries of neighboring towns; they exist because the early surveyors left these odd-shaped pieces unattached to other jurisdictions, and many gores have remained mostly uninhabited since the first surveys were done.) A "minus member" aspires to visit all 251 localities, and this can be challenging because the uninhabited town of Lewis, near the Canadian border, has an abandoned road leading into it, and visitors must climb over fallen tree limbs and through the underbrush to get to Lewis and return to say afterward they have been there. At the 251 Club dinners the "plus members" are asked to stand up, and they do so proudly while the rest of us, seated with our shame, applaud them for winning their merit badges. The scene is like a banquet for Boy Scouts or Girl Scouts except that these scouts have aged considerably. The similarity may not be coincidental: interestingly the first Boy Scout troop in America was organized in Barre in 1911.

The heritage lovers gather each year for the "pilgrimage" to the Rockingham Meeting House, where on a sweltering Sunday afternoon in August they sit in dress-up clothes on hard bench pews in that spare wooden temple of New England Congregationalism and peer up at a speaker proclaiming the virtues of the Vermont heritage from the high-boxed pulpit near the ceiling, where the heat is more intense. In Calais the Old West Church Association conducts services on four summer afternoons, and members stand to sing hymns beneath an inscription across the wall behind the pulpit which emits a scent of brimstone for those who ignore its injunction: "Remove Not The Ancient Landmark Which Thy Fathers Have Set." To Brownington they come on an August Sunday from all the towns of Orleans County to meet at the Old Stone House, a massive stone structure which Alexander Twilight built almost single-handedly from 1827 to 1829 as an "Athenian Hall" to educate the youngsters of these upland farms. But the hilltops were abandoned by the farm families and the academy closed; now it is a museum run by the Orleans County Historical Society. To Ferrisburg they come to honor Rowland Robinson, the blind Quaker author of nineteenth-century local color in rural Vermont—dialect and all—whose stories are richly revealing of Vermont folkways a century ago and deserve more readers than they receive. To meetings of the Genealogical Society of Vermont and of their local historical societies they come to reminisce about old times or boast of family roots. Vermont has more than one hundred-twenty-eight locally-based historical societies. For loyalty to local history that must rival Essex County, Massachusetts, which Walter Muir Whitehill once estimated had the highest ratio of historical societies to land surface of any part of the United States—when the tide was in.

The Vermont heritage is in the faces of these people, and in their voices when they speak with a Yankee twang. Most of them are elderly. In their meetings, when they lament the modest amount of government money for preserving a local landmark or providing some other history-related program, and suggest somebody get in touch with their representative in the Vermont Legislature, or the governor, or a senator in Washington, one notes the irony of the suggestion. The local representative these days may well be a Democrat, a young fellow who might have settled in the district less than a decade ago; more often than not the governor since the early 1960s has been a Democrat; and the senator in Washington might be Democrat Patrick Leahy, a champion of historic preservation. Has the heritage of Republicanism moved away from upcountry New England and been transformed to serve a different outlook in the sunbelt and the Far West? Mention the Watergate scandals in Vermont and the old-line Republicans don't argue that Richard Nixon was treated unfairly or victimized by the media. In Vermont, Richard Nixon is remembered in dour silence. Nobody apologizes for voting Republican and getting him into the presidency; nobody excuses what he did there. The heritage of decency in public life is still in them, together with the desire to do good things and help the community, even if the party of their inheritance loses as many elections as it wins these days.

These Vermonters move daily among heirlooms in their homes. Family portraits are on the walls, maybe with a sampler, done by grandmother in her girlhood, proclaiming lines from the Book of Ecclesiastes. Inherited china is in the glass-doored cabinet, looking as if it had been a wedding gift for a young couple off on a honeymoon trip to one of the great expositions in Philadelphia in 1876, or Chicago in 1893, or Saint Louis in 1904. Ancient clocks tick solemnly as if they were measuring the dwindling moments left before mortal time expires, and high-back rocking chairs also swing to a deliberate cadence. Lace doilies are pinned to the arms of Victorian sofas. Books like Dorothy Canfield Fisher's *Vermont Tradition*, and Perry Merrill's *Vermont Under Four Flags* are on the bed table, together with a copy of *Vermont Life* and *Yankee Magazine*. A wooden chest is at the foot of the bed, containing heavy blankets for cold winter nights, and grandma's multicolored quilt is a fluffy bedspread. Old bedsteads represent unspoken memories of those who were born there, or died there, or were conceived there.

It is a goodly heritage, ubiquitous, and a comfortable article of faith in the credo of all Vermonters who are proud of their ancestry. But if the heritage is so revered, an outsider might ask, why have Vermonters been so laggard about preserving what they venerate? Why haven't they broadened the understanding of their distinctive heritage? The paradox is similar to what Stewart Holbrook wrote about Ethan Allen: most Vermonters had heard of him, but few actually knew much about him. Historical consciousness in Vermont, surprisingly, is more rhetoric and ritual than deeds.

For travelers the Vermont landscape bespeaks history without much help from interpretive techniques to enrich the experience. The state historic markers program is in disarray at the very time some might expect these roadside signs to be more plentiful and more informative. Actually there are fewer markers today than there were a few years ago because existing ones aren't being replaced. Drivers hit them and vandals steal or mutilate them, despite their heft and the firm way they are anchored in concrete.

Other markers are erected close to the shoulders of the roads, and for motorists to slow their cars or tarry to read entire inscriptions is to risk a collision from the rear. Some markers are simple misstatements of history. One on State Street, in front of the Vermont Statehouse, declares in its first sentence that Montpelier became the capital of Vermont in 1808. Actually the Vermont Legislature chose Montpelier to be the state capital in 1805, and the first legislative session was held in the first statehouse in 1808. Perhaps this is a minor correction, but a state which values its heritage shouldn't put erroneous information on historical markers in front of its statehouse.

The same problem besets the historic sites program in Vermont. The most curious of these sites is one which purports to be a replica of the parsonage in Fairfield where Chester A. Arthur was born in 1830. But research published in *Vermont History* in 1970 by Prof. Thomas C. Reeves of the University of Wisconsin shows that Arthur was born elsewhere in Fairfield a year earlier, in a log cabin the family was occupying until the new parsonage was completed during the summer of 1830. To date the evidence Reeves assembled has been ignored by the Vermont Division of Historic Preservation.

At Plymouth Notch is Vermont's other presidential birthplace, and here visitors can see where Calvin Coolidge was born in a structure attached to the rear of the general store and the post office, and where he was raised in the family homestead across the road. The cluster of buildings include the church where the Coolidges worshipped, a cheese factory, an old stone schoolhouse, and a barn full of antique tools and carriages. Down the road is the village cemetery where the president was buried near his kin. He visited here often and loved the Notch—as does his son, John, who runs the cheese factory and lives in a white house on a knoll a few hundred yards behind the homestead. Few presidential birthplaces in the nation convey a sense of the man in terms of his early surroundings as keenly as Plymouth Notch does for Coolidge. Still one feels that the interpretation of Plymouth and of Coolidge is not all it could be. Every president from Coolidge's successor, Herbert Hoover, to Gerald Ford has had or is having a presidential library built.

The Presidential Libraries Act of 1955 was retroactive, at Herbert Hoover's request, and Vermont could have capitalized on the act for obtaining a bigger building than the reception center opened at Plymouth in 1972, one with many more documents and artifacts to display and safeguard for research use, but the state did not choose to do so. The Coolidge papers are the last of the presidential collections to be deposited in the Library of Congress, and although a microfilm of that collection can be purchased for $1,610, there wasn't a set at Plymouth or anywhere else in Vermont in 1980. Every president since Herbert Hoover has had an oral history project launched to tape-record interviews with people who knew the president or dealt with him, but only in 1975 was a modest program begun to interview residents of Plymouth Notch and others who could describe the Coolidges and Plymouth's history since the 1890s. At Plymouth Notch there is not a film or slide show about Calvin Coolidge that can be shown as tourists gather in the small auditorium in the reception building, nor are there cassette tapes and recorders to rent and carry through the village in order to hear about the history which exudes from those buildings. Recordings of Coolidge's voice were made on discs and have been preserved, but none are available at Plymouth. A visitor comes and goes without hearing that dry twang so characteristic of the Vermonters raised in a settlement like this.

The absence of good aural and visual resources about Vermont is surprising—the lack of films, particularly, since sometimes the state seems populated by shaggy filmmakers looking for patrons to finance movies about disappearing aspects of Vermontiana. Recently some Vermont films have been well made, such as one about preservation of the Old Red Mill in Jericho, but Vermont still doesn't have a single good film about Vermont itself.

Nor are tape-recordings available to tourists who want to walk around Mount Independence across from Fort Ticonderoga, or at the Constitution House in Windsor or the statehouse in Montpelier. "Travel tapes" could be rented to motorists on Vermont's interstate highways and describe the countryside as a car moves along (at a speed of 55 miles per hour or less, in order not to get ahead of the taped narrative). These tapes could explain the rocks and trees, the vistas, the architecture of visible structures, the history of the towns along the way, and even include examples of the Vermont folksongs collected by Mrs. Helen Hartness Flanders and the verses of Robert Frost which were inspired by the Vermont landscape. "Travel tapes" could be used on backroads, too, to tell about overgrown farms and cellar holes and abandoned orchards and towns which slid downhill to the valleys when the railroads were built.

Vermont museums present bits and pieces of the Vermont story, and artful collections are exhibited at the Bennington Museum and the Shelburne Museum, but an overview of Vermont's genesis and role as an American state isn't available even at the museum of the Vermont Historical Society, often called the State Museum, in the Pavilion Building near the statehouse green. Museum curators haven't mounted exhibits which explain what tourists often want to know and schoolchildren ask about—why villages have greens, why bridges were covered, why sap rises in the maple trees in the spring, why leaves turn bright colors in the fall. Reconstructions have not been made to show vividly how early settlers like Seth Hubbell made their pitches. Vermont's fourteen years as an independent republic are rarely portrayed in museum environments, although Reuben Harmon's mint, where Vermont coins were struck, could be used since the structure survives in 1980 as a shed on a farm in Rupert.

Themes of regional importance have not been embodied in museum displays, an omission that presents an opportunity to local historians. Addison County would be the ideal location of a museum depiction of one-crop devotion to sheep-raising in the 1830s, and Franklin County for Vermont's rise to eminence as a dairy state. Any number of Vermont hill towns stand as visible evidence of the great migrations westward and cityward in the nineteenth century, yet no American museum has yet been built to depict the theme that Frederick Jackson Turner emphasized as one of the most important in American history. Vermont would be an ideal place for such a museum because one of Turner's forebears left Tinmouth, Vermont, after the War of 1812 and was part of the westward movement.

Tourists to Vermont have discovered the Vermont heritage even if Vermonters take it for granted. In the mid-1960s, the Vermont Development Department took a survey among visitors to Vermont to ascertain what attracted them here. When the questionnaires were tabulated the most frequent response was "scenery"; tourists like to look at the beauty of the hills and valleys. The second most frequent response was a category labeled "history, museums." Indeed, the percentage of respondents citing this attraction equaled the combined percentage of all who marked hunting, fishing, and skiing. The Development Department was dubious about the findings of its survey; a recheck that quizzed respondents to an advertisement about Vermont in the *Philadelphia Inquirer* produced the same percentages.

But Vermont has not organized its history-related programs in any systematic fashion for preserving its heritage and interpreting it to residents and visitors alike. A person driving to Montpelier to get advice about historical projects might think his task would be as simple as maneuvering his car into a parking space in front of the statehouse, but he may shuffle among several different offices around the statehouse green before his day is done. The number of disparate agencies concerned with state history is remarkable for such a small state. The Vermont Historical Society has many manuscripts and related holdings in its library in the Pavilion Building, but gubernatorial and other official papers are in the custody of the editor of state papers, who is employed by the secretary of state. The Division of Vital Statistics, a rich treasure-trove for family historians, is also in the secretary of state's office. The records of state agencies are in the Public Records Division of the Department of Administration. The Division of Historic Preservation is in the Department of Development and Community Affairs, but maintenance of highway markers is a function of the Department of Transportation. Old Vermont newspapers are in the custody of the Vermont Department of Libraries.

The Vermont Department of Education oversees the teaching of Vermont history in the schools, and it also included the Vermont Arts and Crafts Service from 1941 to 1976 until the legislature refused to finance it any longer—an unfortunate curtailment in the bicentennial year. The Vermont Council on the Arts provides history-related services, but it has its own office. So does the Vermont Council on Humanities and Public Issues, also history-minded, but it operates from Hyde Park, an hour's drive north of Montpelier. UVM is Vermont's principal depository for manuscript materials—the papers of Warren Austin and Dorothy Canfield Fisher are two of its major collections—but the Vermont folk songs collected by Helen Hartness Flanders are in the Abernathy Library of Middlebury College. A student of George Perkins Marsh would have to use the Baker Library at Dartmouth College as well as the Bailey-Howe Library at UVM for Marsh manuscripts.

Dispersal is a manageable part of the situation; more serious is the number of sources which weren't preserved at all or allowed to go to out-of-state depositories. Apparently the papers of Gov. Carroll Page have been lost forever, and George Edmunds destroyed his files after leaving the Senate. Ralph Flanders gave his papers to the Syracuse University Library except for the voluminous correspondence induced by his censure of Sen. Joseph R. McCarthy; these papers he donated to the Wisconsin State Historical Society. The photographic plates of snowdrops made ingeniously by Wilson "Snowflake" Bentley of Jericho were given to the Buffalo Museum of Science, in New York.

One reason for this lack of interest in collecting Vermont materials is that scholars concerned with Vermont topics have not been numerous or productive, and they have not generated efforts to acquire the sources from which history is written. At UVM the faculty is not pushed to publish; the university will hire a young historian who hasn't written a book and promote him all the way to a tenured professorship—still without a book to show for his research time and long vacations. Every other college in Vermont, except for Middlebury, demands even less publishable scholarship from its faculty. No institution in Vermont offers a doctorate in history or in any of its related social sciences like political science and sociology. Unlike other states Vermont is not strewn with graduate students looking for fresh dissertation topics and unexamined manuscript materials to exploit. The University of Vermont awards only a handful of master's degrees in history each year, and usually only three or four of these students write theses in Vermont history. Serious research about Vermont is more often done outside of Vermont than within. There is historical irony in the fact that Charles A. Jellison, who reconstructed Vermont's independent course as a republic in his excellent biography, *Ethan Allen: Frontier Rebel,* published in 1969, is a professor at the University of New Hampshire and his publisher was the Syracuse University Press in New York. People from New Hampshire and New York are telling Vermonters about Ethan Allen. In scholarship Vermont remains a land in-between. Its history is still untravelled terrain.

As with the escapades of the Green Mountain Boys, so too with Vermont historiography in general: the tendency has been to focus on episodes instead of continuities and neglect the major social forces which influenced the larger segments of its population. From the Civil War to World War Two the historiography of Vermont pretty much followed the same course: Vermont's role in the fighting of the war on the southern battlefields is followed by the details of the St. Albans raid (1864); the futile efforts of the Irish Fenians to invade Canada from northern Vermont (1866; 1870); the sending of troops to quell a riot in the Ely copper mines (1883); the visit of Vice-president Theodore Roosevelt at Isle La Motte, where he learned that

President William McKinley had been shot in Buffalo (1901); the scene in the Coolidge parlor when Calvin took the presidential oath from his father (1923); the great flood (1927); and the defeat of the Green Mountain Parkway (1936). We need to know much more about the ordinary lives of typical Vermonters through those decades—who stayed and who left, how people earned their livings, and why—to pose just one political question—Vermont farmers voted stolidly Republican while the governors they elected were mostly businessmen of great personal wealth. Vermont's history is full of tantalizing questions which haven't been answered yet. They haven't been asked yet.

Local history provides an excellent microcosm for studying distinctive features in Vermont's past, but to date most local historians have not pursued these opportunities. When town histories are published they tend to focus almost totally on the people who stayed in the towns, ignoring the paramount significance of the emigrations which caused some towns to lose more than half their populations in the nineteenth century. What did the migrants carry away with them? Merle Curti and his associates compared eleven Vermont towns in the Winooski Valley with Trempeleau County, Wisconsin, where many Vermonters settled in the mid-nineteenth century, but no Vermont historians have followed this model since it was put forward in 1959.[1] Holman D. Jordan, Jr., in a doctoral dissertation done at the University of Alabama in 1966, used federal census data imaginatively to point out that the farmer is the "forgotten man" in Vermont's town histories. Some of these towns were dependent on farmers for their economic vigor, but this truth isn't evident in the published histories of these towns. As Jordan says about these volumes:

> All but the men and women of prominence are neglected for little or no information about them comes from the usual sources. Men who were not lawyers or doctors, who did not serve in government, or who were not prominent in the affairs of a local church are rarely included in these histories. At best, the authors include some of the

1. Merle Curti and others, *The Making of an American Community: A Case Study of Democracy in a Frontier County* (Stanford, Calif.: Stanford University Press, 1959).

less conspicuous people in occupational catalogs. The history of a
town or county must be more than a fabric of interwoven
descriptions of the lives of a few individuals.[2]

Curti suggested that many letters must have been written between the Vermonters who migrated to Wisconsin and their relatives who stayed at home in Vermont, but few of these letters
have come to light and been preserved in Vermont. States like
Wisconsin, where many ex-Vermonters settled, have collected
many letters of this type, and they deserve to be microfilmed
and made available to Vermont researchers because many describe Vermont conditions in order to bring the western relatives
up-to-date about family news and local events in the old home
towns. Vermonters were remarkably literate; those district
schools taught well. One who went from Ludlow to Indiana,
Calvin Fletcher, kept diaries all his life (1798–1866), and Hubert Hawkins of the Indiana Historical Society wrote, "He is
the nearest thing to a Samuel Pepys that we had in early Indian-
apolis." [3] Frank Haskell, a Tunbridge native, wrote a classic of
Civil War literature, a letter of 110 pages describing the battle
of Gettysburg.[4] Other writers of equal talent may lie undiscovered. Richard G. Winslow, a Ph.D. candidate at Pennsylvania State University, discovered one in the forgotten pages of
a Montpelier newspaper, the *Green Mountain Freeman*. His
name is Wilbur Fisk, and he enlisted from Tunbridge to join the
Second Vermont Regiment in the Civil War. His commander
was Gen. John Sedgwick, the subject of Winslow's dissertation.
Letters by Fisk which described army life were published in the
Green Mountain Freeman. "After examining many diaries, letters, items of this nature," commented Winslow, "I judge the
Fisk collection to be undoubtedly the finest of its type I have
ever seen. Written with insight, humor, and intelligence, Fisk

2. Quoted in "Is the Farmer the 'Forgotten Man' in Vermont History?", *News and Notes,* newsletter of the Vermont Historical Society, 18 (1967): 69.

3. Quoted in *News and Notes* 22 (1970): unpaged.

4. Franklin A. Haskell, *Haskell of Gettysburg: His Life and Civil War Papers,* ed. Frank L. Byrne and Andrew T. Weaver (Madison, Wis.: State Historical Society of Wisconsin, 1970).

gives a most human and accurate description of the battles, camp life, rumors, furloughs to Vermont, and so forth. It's the type of item I wish I had discovered during my first day of research rather than in the sixth month." [5]

Primary sources of this nature are valuable also because Vermonters have not produced volumes containing state and local history of the type Hubert Howe Bancroft assembled in California and Lyman Draper did in Wisconsin. Even knowledge about Vermonters who fought in the Civil War is not as ample as historians and others might assume. Elliot W. Hoffman, a UVM graduate student who wrote his M.A. thesis on William Wells, a Vermont general who received a medal of honor for gallantry at Gettysburg, has commented on the absence of this information. "After the Civil War," Hoffman noted,

> Vermont was one of the few Northern states that did not indulge in an orgy of publications about the service of units and soldiers. The military and political contributions of the State were significant, yet the veterans recorded few of their deeds, perhaps feeling that their actions needed little embellishment or finding that they were not as adept with the pen as with the sword. Unlike most Northern states, Vermont regiments (*sic*) published few histories, and still fewer individuals recorded their reminiscences. While Vermont had the usual active veterans' organizations, the Grand Army of the Republic and the Loyal Legion, they did little to alter this laconic attitude towards the literature of the Civil War.

"When the Civil War generation passed," Hoffman concluded, "much of the story passed with it." [6]

Scholarly research about Vermont does not have to be an esoteric pursuit solely for the edification of professional historians. It can also be a dialogue between lay adults who want to inform themselves about Vermont's distinctive past. More than adults are involved, actually, because the teaching of Vermont history in Vermont schools is shamefully inept, and scholarly literature would help teachers improve their presentation of Vermont in

---

5. Quoted in *News and Notes* 22 (1970): unpaged.

6. Elliot W. Hoffman, "Vermont General: The Military Development of William Wells, 1861–1865, M.A. thesis, University of Vermont, 1974.

their classrooms. Teachers prepared in other states find themselves teaching Vermont history in Vermont schools and rightfully feel totally unprepared for the task. Teachers trained at Vermont colleges are no better prepared. The problem has persisted for so long that most people who lament it have lost their zest to fight it.

But some signs of reversing the deplorable situation are heartening. The University of Vermont has obtained George Aiken's voluminous senatorial files, and efforts to collect the papers of other Vermonters are now underway. The Aiken papers have been enriched by oral history interviews with the senator and others involved in his career; these interviews are a beachhead for more oral history in a state which cries for preservation of this kind to document its uniqueness and to compensate for the absence of written sources. A young and imaginative Montpelier teacher from Seattle via Oberlin College, Amy Davis, has successfully applied the "Foxfire concept" of oral history to Vermont by sending out her eighth-grade students to interview old-timers about their experiences, and Howard Shapiro of Putney has helped to spread this teaching device throughout the state. The Eva Gebhard-Gourgaud Foundation and the Cecil Howard Charitable Trust, both under the capable direction of Robert Sincerbeaux of Woodstock, have compensated for Vermont's paltry number of state-oriented private foundations by providing seed money for several architectural preservation projects throughout Vermont, and demonstrated in the process that small foundations, compared to the philanthropic giants, can be immensely effective.

Other efforts include the hiring of a professional archeologist, Giovanna Neudorfer, by the state in order to inventory prehistoric sites and to protect them. The quarterly magazine of the Vermont Historical Society, *Vermont History,* publishes scholarly research and could be a major force in acquainting Vermonters with reliable interpretations of their past if it could be more assertive in commissioning articles on unaddressed subjects instead of passively waiting for contributions through the mail. The University Press of New England, founded a decade ago and a consortium to which UVM belongs, finally provides a scholarly outlet for monographs about the Vermont story.

For support these efforts require money. The costs of research fellowships for generating publishable monographs on significant aspects of the Vermont story is not cheap, nor is the expense of oral history interviews to capture the Vermont history in the words of the people who have lived it, complete with the north-country accent which the homogenizing influences of America's mass media will probably erase in Vermont within a generation. But the money exists: Vermont is populated by wealthy people who continually sing praises of the Green Mountain State but haven't been educated yet to the opportunity to direct their personal philanthropy to the state they love. Most summer people spend their philanthropic dollars in Greenwich or Princeton or the other towns where they live in the winter. This opportunity may be the most fertile of all. As an example of its potential, the Vermont Historical Society in the 1960s was averaging only about $250 annually in gifts; in 1970–1971 it raised $128,000 to install its new museum inside the reconstructed Pavilion Building. The sum of $128,000 isn't impressive in these days of extraordinary costs, but to rise to that level from $250 yearly is noteworthy.

The time has come for Vermont to honor its heritage by saving the sources which are the raw materials of history, by preserving the buildings of historic character, by recording the oral history interviews, by inspiring the literature which explains Vermont to Vermonters, by improving the teaching of Vermont in our schools, and by doing all the related chores which need doing. On a rainy weekend in 1926, J. Cheney Wells came to Vermont to poke around antique shops, and from that excursion came the inspiration for Old Sturbridge Village in Massachusetts. Wells was a wealthy man because he and his family had fostered the growth of the American Optical Company in Southbridge, Massachusetts, just south of Sturbridge. Vermont needs a man like him, or many like him, today. But unlike Wells, who was inspired in Vermont and took his zeal home to Massachusetts, Vermont deserves people who will encourage

Vermonters to keep the Vermont heritage in Vermont. Since Old Sturbridge Village was started in 1947, it has moved a covered bridge to its village from Dummerston, Vermont, and also the Asa Knight Store, which operated on the Dummerston Green from 1827 to 1851.

The days when that type of cultural exportation could happen should be ended forever. Curators at Old Sturbridge cannot be faulted for seeing a good thing and guaranteeing preservation of two structures which might have languished if left on their own sites in Vermont. But Vermonters should ask themselves why the tavern sign from the old Hayes Tavern in West Brattleboro is now exhibited in the Rutherford B. Hayes Library in Ohio, when in Vermont the Hayes Tavern was demolished to make room for a parking lot at a state liquor store. Vermonters who visit the Fenimore House at Cooperstown, New York, should ask why a huge wood carving of Abraham Lincoln done by Frank W. Moran of Bakersfield, Vermont, an excellent piece of American folk art, was not retained in Moran's Vermont. Vermonters who visit the Smithsonian Institution in Washington and inspect the gunboat *Philadelphia*, sunk at the Battle of Valcour Island in Lake Champlain on October 11, 1776, and raised in 1935, should ask why it was taken to Washington. It is the only surviving original war vessel of the American Revolution, and it should have remained in the Champlain Valley.

Vermonters can be faulted if they don't raise their vision of their own history to equal the high estimate that outsiders have of Vermont history. Likewise, they can be faulted if they don't absorb the lessons their own history offers about the need to preserve the resources of their own state. They need to contemplate what George Perkins Marsh saw about him in Woodstock in the early nineteenth century—that Vermonters were being heedless of their resources and turning the harmonies of nature to discords. Just as a state can ignore the ecological bonds uniting man with nature, so too can it thoughtlessly lose its cultural heritage linking past with present.

A goodly heritage deserves more than rhetoric and ritual from the natives, and more than prattle from nostalgia-seekers who come to Vermont from other states. Vermont deserves a host of

Abby Hemenways to act on behalf of the Vermont heritage so it will be preserved and interpreted in a variety of ways. And Abby deserves a marker by her gravesite in Ludlow, bearing a well-composed inscription about her single-minded devotion to preserving Vermont's first century of history. The marker should be well-positioned so it can be read unhurriedly by those who pass by, and sturdily implanted and safeguarded so it doesn't disappear some night in the darkness. The same is true of the heritage she did so much to preserve.

Part IV

Reckonings

14

Fantasy and Solace from the Hills of View

IS it possible to anticipate what Vermont will look like several decades hence? Historians are amused by efforts to answer that type of query. It is hard enough to be a historian without being a seer, and since history itself is full of the contingent and unforeseen it is a humbling enterprise to trace our background without venturing even gingerly onto the unsteady foreground. Besides, people who are unwilling to comprehend dispassionately the experiences they have lived are hardly qualified to anticipate what the days ahead may bring. It is fallacious, also, to commemorate events which transpired two hundred years ago without emphasizing the tentativeness and uncertainty of occurrences which in retrospect appear inevitable—as if the outcomes were ordained and delivered on tablets to Moses or Ethan Allen and carried down from the mountaintops for our edification. When news of the British encounters with Minutemen at Lexington and Concord came to the Green Mountain Boys they gathered at Jonas Fay's tavern in Bennington to explore "futurity," as they termed it, but they found it "unfathomable."

Accordingly, if the world is warming up and the icecaps start to melt Vermont can expect refugees from the seacoast cities to evacuate to the safety of its hills. They would become the latest wave of those who have sought sanctuary in the upcountry. If the world is getting colder Vermont can expect an emigration to less frigid places. Ice has been known before to be a factor in the shaping of Vermont.

If an earthquake ripples along the San Andreas Fault and tumbles a hunk of California into shambles, we can expect a sudden influx of those handsome suntanned blondes with the winsome smiles, good teeth, and easy mores. At last the West Coast will discover Vermont. Likewise, if business firms flee bankrupt cities with high tax rates and intolerable living conditions, we can visualize a Vermont which looks like the newly sprouted cities of the sunbelt, with glass-walled high-rise office buildings, freeways for the endless flow of cars, smog, congestion, crime, and all the other noxious products of modern America. That would be progress in the eyes of some who feel that progress, by current definitions, is long overdue in Vermont. They are pleased that Burlington at present is booming; Chittenden County is the second fastest-growing county in New England.

But a more realistic prognostication is that prosperity will continue to bypass Vermont. Energy may become much more expensive in New England in the years ahead—now it is as costly as anywhere in the nation—and the lure of the sunbelt will be as enticing as the lure of the West in the nineteenth century. Transportation to urban markets will still be a drawback. Taxes will remain high. Jobs will still be scarce and pay poorly, although the outlook for attracting small firms running clean industries and offering specialized services seems more promising and sensible than trying to sweet-talk the big manufacturers into locating here. It is discouraging to realize that probably Vermont will still be unable to provide enough jobs for its homegrown citizens; ambitious youngsters will still bid farewell to the old hometown and head for the big corporations and the big cities. If ways can be devised for keeping family farms in operation while agribusiness continues to revolutionize farming, we can expect much of future Vermont to look like today's Vermont—rural and scenic, and a place where the hard-working can find a hardscrabble existence. Otherwise Vermont will be wooded, not pastoral, and barns will continue to crumble. It is difficult to think of Vermont without farms to syncopate the rhythm of its rolling landscape, but once this state was 80 percent clear of its timber; now it is at least 76 percent covered again. The trend may continue more rapidly than we anticipate.

Like it or not, Vermont will become more of a recreational state. Harold A. Meeks, a geographer at UVM, sees this trend as overwhelming: "The resource of Vermont," he has declared, "is not asbestos in Belvidere, nor milk in Franklin, nor granite in Barre, but is recreation for the millions of people confined to the urbanized areas both to the north and south of the state." [1] But tourist-trap jobs are mostly seasonal and servile, and not as numerous as assumed. Primarily the recreation business in Vermont is financed by out-of-state people who hire out-of-state people to entertain out-of-state people. One wonders if the tension between natives and newcomers will become more bitter, hardening into open discord as outsiders try to preserve the environment the old-timers see as increasingly difficult to exploit for earning enough to pay for food, fuel, adequate housing, and other basic needs. Sheaf Satterthwaite, an environmentalist who lives in Bennington County, has asserted that natives and outsiders are already lining up against each other and staring across a social chasm, as unpleasant as it is to recognize this divide. "We find in Vermont two nations," he wrote, "one of natives working the land and the other of seasonal players passively looking at the land. The first is represented by that dwindling group of people actually pushing, pulling, and working the soil of their own landholdings and the second by both Vermonters and outsiders skimming greater distances over vaster surfaces, whether on highways or ski slopes." [2] Encounters between outsiders and insiders have pretty much been a matter of humor—how the native deflated the uppity city person, or how the summer people joked about the laconic sayings of the local handyman. These are like town-gown tensions in a college community—irritating to the point of being abrasive, but always

1. Harold A. Meeks, *The Geographic Regions of Vermont: A Study in Maps* (Hanover, N.H.: Geography Publications at Dartmouth No. 10, 1975), p. 162.

2. Sheafe Satterthwaite, "Puckerbrush, Cellar Holes, Rubble: Observations on Abandonment in Vermont," in *Vermont Landscape Images, 1776–1976*, ed. William C. Lipke and Philip N. Grime (Burlington, Vt.: Robert Hull Fleming Museum, 1976), p. 31.

surmountable if tolerated patiently and enjoyed as the topic of good stories afterwards. But they could become more serious, just as college towns became serious places of conflict in the 1960s. It seems incredible, and an observer wants to borrow again from Sinclair Lewis and say, "It can't happen here."

It seems ludicrous, too. While seated on the top floor of the library tower at Memphis State University in early 1975, reading oral history transcripts, my mind flashed back to Vermont and how its social problems seem so minor and manageable. The Memphis transcripts were detailed reminiscences about the bitter strike of sanitation workers in 1968 which culminated in the assassination of Martin Luther King, Jr., America's most effective advocate of social justice in the twentieth century, in that city on April 4, 1968. The South and all its historic problems were embodied in these memories of the Memphis tragedy—the enslavement of blacks, and of whites, too, by the system they enforced; the sharecropping that developed after the Civil War; the mechanization which drove poor and illiterate blacks from the cotton fields of Mississippi, Arkansas, and Tennessee into Memphis; the growth of the city with its urban aspirations and needs; the impatience of unskilled blacks for decent income and human dignity; the violence. Vermonters don't bear any of that heavy burden of history. In the most rural state of the nation, 99.5 percent white, sanitation is simply a matter of agreeing on where to dump the garbage. What Martin Luther King, Jr., knew about Vermont was pretty much limited to the fact that the two theologians he studied for his doctoral dissertation, "A Comparison of the Conceptions of God in the Thinking of Paul Tillich and Henry Nelson Wieman," had spent ten days at a religious retreat at the Fletcher Farm in Proctorsville, Vermont, in 1935 and had argued for strongly divergent concepts of God. Tillich was a transcendental monist, Wieman was an exponent of behaviorism in theology. King was the first scholar to explore formally the differences expressed at Proctorsville eighteen years after that exchange had occurred. He never had to come to Vermont to lead a civil rights march like the one which brought him to Memphis and to his death.

In view of what black Americans and white Americans have

gone through to undo the injustices of centuries, perhaps Vermonters can get over their hangup about nativity and lay to rest the most frequent question in contemporary Vermont: "Were you born here?" The Windsor Constitution of 1777 stated that a Vermont resident could serve in the legislature two years after settling in the state and beginning his citizenship. That period of probation seems as ample now as then.

It could become as insignificant as an academic issue in an academic town simply because the newcomers may overrun the natives just as the Americans overwhelmed the true natives, the Indians, in the great American story celebrated by the bicentennial. Matthew Buckham's fears that Vermont's respectable villages might be converted into the likeness of suburban Connecticut and New Jersey may have been understated. A geographer at Dartmouth College, Vincent H. Malmstrom, was not hesitant to project his analysis of demographic trends. "Geographically, then," he wrote,

> there is little doubt as to what the future holds for Vermont. A generation hence, when twice as many people crowd this planet as at present, the super-cities which bracket Vermont both to the north and south will find in this still, semi-isolated oasis of beauty what will then be the equivalent of a 'high-class residential district.' In the year 2000 business and professional people (few of whom will be Vermonters) will be commuting to the centers of Megalopolis from their villas on Lake Champlain or their chalets in the Green Mountains as easily as they now do from Westchester or Chevy Chase.[3]

The land in-between won't be in-between any more.

The prospect is an unhappy one. But if the nation itself adjusts its values to fit the austere times which seem to lie ahead, when the postindustrial and postconsumptive era of depleted resources demands an end to our throwaway culture, then perceptions of Vermont as a place to live may contain more than visual nostalgia for a Currier and Ives America. If moneymaking loses its zest as America's dominant cultural value, and

3. Vincent H. Malmstrom, "Vermont: A Geographic Appraisal," *Middlebury College News Letter* 41 (1967): 11.

if a return to simple living becomes popular as the major life-
style of the American future, then Americans may look to Vermont for guidance. Vermont will be the pacesetter, the symbol
of the new way of life.

If a new ethic and sensibility spreads in this country, rejecting
all that spawned the Vietnam morass, the Watergate scandals,
business briberies and political corruption, and the lies and violence and inanity that beset our lives, and if we reaffirm the
ideals that made the United States the noblest venture ever
created by mankind, then Vermont could be the place where the
turnaround is least difficult. When work is measured by the
honesty and quality which motivates it, and the workman does
not feel demeaned by what he does all day, a hardy Vermont
value will no longer be lamented for its rarity. When food is nu-
tritious and naturally tasty, and not adulterated by the chain
stores to fit or further contrive the consumer habits of a nation
beguiled by what the advertisers say is good for us, Vermont
can demonstrate how local farmers can work with local distribu-
tors through co-operative agreements which once were common
in these hill towns. If timber resources can be utilized for creating energy, Vermont has ample woodlands to develop. If crafts-
men can become economically self-supporting, the re-emergence
of home industries and small manufacturers would be a way to
vitalize a feature of Vermont's worklife which persisted well
into the early years of this century. If individuality can be respected and rewarded, the cantankerous Vermonter, fiercely independent, will be a new folk hero for all who want to break the
mold of the technocratic culture which constantly is sorting people, and classifying them, and measuring them by numbers fed
into or spewed out of computers. If America wants government
that is responsive and democratic, Montpelier can show how it
operates. If America wants clean air and water, Vermont can
show how to safeguard these resources. If America still wants to
see beauty, Vermont still has an eyeful. If America wants to see
humans make peace with their environment, relating themselves
to the earth and the passage of days and seasons in all kinds of
weather, the land of George Perkins Marsh offers a place which
is ideal to try.

It may be futile for Vermont to try to revive these practices of an earlier society and economy which were doomed one hundred and fifty years ago when hill farmers had to compete with more productive farmers elsewhere in America, and agrarianism succumbed to industrialism, and Vermont's terrain wasn't suitable for either. Forward-thinking may be wistfulness. Viewing the world with common sense, Vermonters may have to choose among alternatives which are not pleasing, separately or collectively. One is to become a new suburbia; another is to be the playground of rich city people; the third is to concentrate further in little islands of commerce, manufacturing, and bureaucracy, and acquiesce in all the Barre-Montpelier Road represents.

These options mean that much of Vermont will survive like a forgotten country churchyard, where the grass grows unattended, the gravestones tilt, and dry leaves blow aimlessly among the rows where bearded old Vermonters were laid to rest, together with their worn-out wives and the youngsters who didn't migrate away with their brothers and sisters. One wonders if the values Vermont needs most today are also buried in the churchyard, and if they too live only in history.

One thinks about the old Vermonters while walking among their tombstones and cellarholes, and along their stone walls and through their covered bridges over the streams of time. Their villages are clusters of memories; their surrendered farmsteads, now marked by lonely lilac bushes in purple splendor, are memorials to toil. They left behind many remnants which cause us to marvel at their perseverance: the wooden sled exhibited inside the Stowe Town Hall on which the first settler dragged his worldly goods to that winter outpost; an etching of Andersonville Prison on the wall of the Bethel Library as terrifying as if Dante's *Inferno* were the inspiration for the suffering perpetrated on Vermont soldiers by their Confederate capturers.

My own Vermont experience has memories which bridge the chasm between the present and the recent past. One is a recurring scene in which I hasten from my office in the Pavilion Building at noon to drive with Dan Neary to a secluded pond, beautifully framed by the Worcester Mountains, and after a lunch-hour dip and a barefooted walk along the quiet dirt road to Dan's house we eat sandwiches and chew on celery and raw carrots while dressing. Then a quick ride back to Montpelier, feeling rejuvenated by that swim and gloating all afternoon about the pleasure of it. Not even the wealthiest New Yorker can belong to a club which provides a lunch-hour treat as refreshing as that; with swimming holes nearby who needs a three-martini lunch? Well into the crisp days of autumn Dan and I keep plunging into that pond, daring each other and the ice-cold water to tell us it's time to quit, and finally we surrender with proud talk about "setting a new record" for late-season swimming—but next year we'll try to break it.

In Vermont the friendships are plentiful. We sing and dance and carouse and laugh when neighbors appear on stage in amateur theatricals. We also commiserate as marriages break up and other things come undone, and help the afflicted to endure the hard days. Lord, what solace Vermont provides! Friendships nourish like ripened berries and vegetables, and sweeten life like maple syrup.

With my son, Mike, I can go to football games at tiny Norwich University, and for two-dollar tickets we sit on creaky bleachers at the fifty-yard line and watch visiting teams from little colleges like Bates, Tufts, and Worcester Polytechnical Institute play with as much verve as Michigan and Ohio State can muster against each other. But we are glad not to be sitting in those huge stadiums where the football factories strive for national ranking. At Norwich we can watch the clouds play with autumn foliage on a distant hillside, where a red barn stands next to a green clearing. By neck-craning while watching a punt spiral downfield we can see another good show overhead: Canadian geese, in their V-formations, heading southward as the earth turns and signals the coming of winter.

With friends there is joshing about the imagery *Vermont Life* magazine projects about Vermont, and we twit Brian Vachon, its editor, for publishing a "moonlight and magnolia" version of Vermont. Is the world so naive that it believes we are picture-postcard people up here? That we still go around in winter in horse-drawn sleighs? Yet we remember a delicious picnic supper one twilight on some land four of us bought in Greensboro, with the most delectable stuffed eggs, cheese, home-preserved pickles, homemade bread, and other Vermont pleasures. As we ate we watched the farmer who cuts our hayfield, Everett Young, work with his son as a full moon rose over the Youngs' red barn, and that moon was as gorgeous as any ever pictured in *Vermont Life*. Afterwards we went down the road to hear a concert by the Craftsbury Chamber Players, and our spirits soared with their strings.

Similarly, I remember a blustery Christmas Day in Greensboro, enjoying good talk as always with Bill and Helen Maier by the warming fire in their broadboarded house built before the Civil War, while the snow swirled outside in the fierce wind. Suddenly through the living room window we saw a sleigh go up the hill between the snowbanks outside. A real horse-drawn sleigh—and on Christmas Day! Norman Rockwell could have posed that scene. My daughter, Susan, was seven then, and she quickly put on her coat and snowboots and scarf and mittens and ran outside in the subzero weather to wave down the driver on his return. Sure, he would give her a ride in his sleigh, and with harness bells ringing he took her all the way down the hill to the frozen lake and then all the way back. Her cheeks glowed as brightly as her eyes when she came in and warmed herself by the fireplace while describing her adventure.

Every Vermonter has personal memories and private places—be they quiet streams for canoeing or self-made cross country ski trails back where a field gives way to a copse of trees and the cold winter wind sounds like a whispered conversation. Most of my memories focus on shadowy places where I have rummaged for the history of Vermont—in attics and cellars. Once I descended through a trap door into the narrow crawl space underneath the Barnes House at Chimney Point in Addison, looking for the foundation walls which were built by that Dutchman, Jacobus Ten Warm, in 1690 and survive as probably the oldest remnants of a man-made structure in Vermont. But I have also climbed the hills of view and perched against a rock for most of a sunny afternoon, surveying the Vermont landscape and trying to drink up the scene like rich milk.

Life steers us most often through the valleys, not onto the hilltops, and yielding with grace to reason it is inevitable that all of us must descend and go with the drift of things. But life is richer if Vermont has seeped into a person's sinews, and if it is cherished as an experience to live as well as a state to live in.

A parting hope is that Vermont can still be different, and show America how to be different.

Suggestions For Further Reading

Whenever people ask me to recommend one book about Vermont, I usually respond by suggesting six. These six cover the chronology and main themes of Vermont's history since the state was settled.

The first is Charles A. Jellison, *Ethan Allen: Frontier Rebel* (Syracuse, N.Y.: Syracuse University Press, 1969; paperback edition, Taftsville, Vt.: Countryman Press, 1974) because it portrays Ethan's life against the backdrop of events which shaped Vermont. The second book is David M. Ludlum's classic study, *Social Ferment in Vermont, 1791–1850* (New York: Columbia University Press, 1939; republished, Montpelier: Vermont Historical Society, 1948; republished, New York: AMS Press, 1966) because it describes Vermont's vibrant growth to its ebb by the mid-nineteenth century. The third is Harold F. Wilson, *The Hill Country of Northern New England: Its Social and Economic History 1790–1930* (New York: Columbia University Press, 1936; republished, New York: AMS Press, 1967), which concerns Maine, New Hampshire, and Vermont but gives as much space to Vermont as it does to both the other states and explains why Vermont was a rural oasis by the onset of the Great Depression. The fourth covers Vermont politics in the 1930s and '40s, Richard M. Judd, *The New Deal in Vermont: Its Impact and Aftermath* (New York: Garland Publishing, Inc., 1979). The fifth is a sophisticated interpretation of Vermont politics from the 1930s to the 1970s, Frank M. Bryan, *Yankee Politics in Rural Vermont* (Hanover, N.H.: University Press of New England, 1974). The sixth can be either Lewis D. Stilwell, *Migration From Vermont* (Montpelier: Vermont Historical Society, 1948), or Stewart H. Holbrook, *The Yankee Exodus: An Account of Migration from New England* (New York: Macmillan Co., 1950; paperback edition, Seattle: University of Washington Press, 1968).

For a more detailed knowledge of Vermont's early history one can profitably consult Matt Bushnell Jones, *Vermont in the Making 1750–1777* (Cambridge, Mass.: Harvard University Press, 1939; reprint, Hamden, Conn.: Archon Books, 1968), and Chilton Williamson, *Vermont in Quandary 1763–1825* (Montpelier: Vermont Historical Society, 1949). Ira Allen's *Autobiography* is included in volume one of James B. Wilbur, *Ira Allen: Founder of Vermont, 1751–1814*, 2 vols. (Boston and New York: Houghton Mifflin Co., 1928). Frederic F. Van de Water, *The Reluctant Republic: Vermont 1724–1791* (New York: John Day Co., 1941; paperback edition, Taftsville, Vt.: Countryman Press, 1974) is probably the best-written account of early Vermont although its research is "candidly parasitic," as Van de Water admits. But the paperback edition is valuable because of the excellent introductory essay written for it by H. Nicholas Muller III. Two other essays by Muller provide the most informed analysis of Vermont politics in its formative years: "Myth and Reality: The Politics of Independence in Vermont 1760–1777" in *Perspectives '76* (Hanover, N.H.: Regional Center for Educational Training, 1975), and "Ira Allen's Vermont," which is chapter four (pp. 213–240) in *Early Nationalist Historians,* volume four of Lawrence H. Leder, *The Colonial Legacy* (New York: Harper and Row, 1973). Muller appended a chronology of Vermont, 1724–1791, to the paperback edition of Van de Water's *Reluctant Republic,* and readers may find it helpful as they explore the confusion of Vermont's history prior to statehood. A chronology of Vermont to 1872 was compiled by Esther Monroe Swift and published in Brenda C. Morrissey, ed., *Abby Hemenway's Vermont: Unique Portrait of a State* (Brattleboro, Vt.: Stephen Greene Press, 1972).

Another way to become acquainted with Vermont is to read books which describe its character. A brief but excellent text by Noel Perrin accompanies the photographs by Sonja Bullaty and Angelo Lomeo in *Vermont* (New York: Viking Press, 1973). Further observations by Perrin are in his *First Person Rural: Essays of a Sometimes Farmer* (Boston: David R. Godine, 1978), and *Second Person Rural* (Boston: Godine, 1980). Views from the past and present are in T. D. Seymour Bassett, compiler and editor, *Outsiders Inside Vermont: Travelers' Tales Over 358 Years* (Brattleboro, Vt.: Stephen Greene Press, 1967; 2nd edition, Canaan, N.H.: Phoenix Publishing, 1976). Specimens of Vermont writing are anthologized in Arthur W. Biddle and Paul A. Eschholz, eds., *The Literature of Vermont: A Sampler* (Hanover, N.H.: University Press of New England, 1973). Several of the thirteen books written to date by Ralph Nading Hill are informative, most notably *Contrary Country: A Chronicle of Vermont* (New York: Rinehart and Co., 1950; 2nd edition, Brattleboro, Vt.: 1961), and *Yankee Kingdom: Vermont and New Hampshire* (New York: Harper and Row, 1960; updated edition, 1973). Contrasts between Vermont and New Hampshire are examined by Eric P. Veblen in *The Manchester Union Leader in New Hampshire Elections* (Hanover, N.H.: University Press of New England, 1975).

Vermont is a work of art as well as a distinctive culture, and the photographed beauty of Vermont is most vividly conveyed in Ralph Nading Hill, Murray Hoyt, and Walter R. Hard, Jr., eds., *Vermont: A Special World* (Montpelier: *Vermont Life* magazine, 1969), itself a book so beautiful it has sold almost 60,000 copies. Coming in 1980 from Vermont Life is its sequel, *Vermont for Every Season*. William C. Lipke and Philip N. Grime, *Vermont Landscape Images 1776–1976* (Burlington, Vt.: Robert Hull Fleming Museum, 1976, distributed by Stephen Greene Press) succeeds admirably in relating Vermont's terrain to its rendition in art. Others interested in Vermont's artistic heritage should look at Robert L. McGrath, *Early Vermont Wall Paintings 1790–1850* (Hanover, N.H.: University Press of New England, 1972), and Adele Godchaux Dawson's handsome biography, *James Franklin Gilman, Nineteenth Century Painter* (Canaan, N.H.: Phoenix Publishing, 1975). Old photographs as art and history are in Ralph Nading Hill, ed., *Vermont Album: A Collection of Early Vermont Photographs* (Brattleboro, Vt.: Stephen Greene Press, in association with *Vermont Life* magazine and the Vermont Historical Society, 1974).

Exploring specific sections of Vermont is a good way to absorb its variety, and an introduction is best obtained by consulting Harold A. Meeks, *The Geographic Regions of Vermont: A Study in Maps* (Hanover, N.H.: Geography Publications at Dartmouth No. 10, 1975). Likewise, a look into Esther Monroe Swift's *Vermont Place-Names: Footprints of History* (Brattleboro, Vt.: Stephen Greene Press, 1977) provides a ready orientation because she divides her massive compilation into chapters covering sections of the state. Ralph Nading Hill's *Lake Champlain: Key to Liberty* (Taftsville, Vt.: Countryman Press, in association with the Burlington *Free Press*, 1976) depicts the entire Champlain Valley. Robert E. Pike, *Drama on the Connecticut* (Eatontown, N.J.: H-H Press, 1975), achieves a similar goal in describing the Connecticut River Valley from its headwaters to the Massachusetts border. Bennington County is fortunate in having its history adeptly rendered in text and photographs by Tyler Resch in *The Shires of Bennington: A Sampler of Green Mountain Heritage* (Bennington, Vt.: published by the *Bennington Banner* for the Bennington Museum, 1975).

Vermont communities often have excellent books describing local history. Ernest L. Bogart, *Peacham: The Story of a Vermont Hill Town* (Montpelier: Vermont Historical Society, 1948), is one of the best town histories ever published in the United States. Visitors to Burlington and its vicinity should know about Lilian Baker Carlisle, ed., *Look Around Chittenden County, Vermont* (Burlington, Vt.: Chittenden County Historical Society, 1976), because it pictures and describes sites and structures of architectural and historical interest. Glen M. Andres, *A Walking History of Middlebury* (Middlebury, Vt.: Middlebury Bicentennial Committee, 1975) is one of several booklets for history-seekers on foot. Two similar guides, *A Walk Through Montpelier: Buildings to Discover* (Montpelier: Montpelier Heritage Group, 1974) and *A Second Walk Through Montpelier* (Montpelier: Montpelier Heritage Group, 1976), describe the visual history of Vermont's capital city. Robert L. Hagerman, *Mansfield: The Story of Vermont's Loftiest Mountain* (Essex Junction, Vt.: Essex Publishing Co., 1971; reissued, Canaan, N.H.: Phoenix Publishing, 1975) is comprehensive for anyone who wants to see Vermont from its top. Everybody who pursues a curiosity about some portion of Vermont will sooner or later pick up at least one of the five heavy tomes of Abby Maria Hemenway, *The Vermont Historical Gazetteer,* (Burlington, Vt., Claremont, N.H., Montpelier, Vt., and Brandon, Vt., 1868–1891), a rich treasure of detail, much of it fascinating and flavorful, about Vermont.

Lighter books are readily available for those who want to explore Vermont athletically—Roioli Schweiker, *Canoe Camping—Vermont and New Hampshire Rivers* (Somersworth, N.H.: New Hampshire Publishing Co., 1977); Ruth and Paul Sadlier, *Fifty Hikes in Vermont: Walks, Day Hikes, and Backpacking Trips in the Green Mountain State* (Somersworth, N.H.: New Hampshire Publishing Co., 1974); and *Bicycle Touring in Vermont* (Montpelier: Vermont Recreation and Park Society, 1973). Less strenuous but equally rewarding are strolls through Vermont graveyards, and twenty-five are described in Andrew Kull, *New England Cemeteries: A Collector's Guide* (Brattleboro, Vt.: Stephen Greene Press, 1975). Families travelling in Vermont in search of their roots should carry Gilbert H. Doane, *Searching for Your Ancestors: The How and Why of Genealogy* (Minneapolis: University of Minnesota Press, 4th rev. ed., 1973), because this native of Fairfield, Vermont, sprinkles his narrative with examples of Vermont problems encountered while sleuthing for Vermont forebears. Travellers who are intrigued by Vermont's covered bridges will benefit from Herbert Wheaton Congdon, *The Covered Bridge: An Old American Landmark* (Brattleboro, Vt.: Stephen Daye Press, 1941; reissued, Middlebury, Vt.: Vermont Books, 1970), or Richard Sanders Allen, *Covered Bridges of the Northeast* (Brattleboro, Vt.: Stephen Greene Press, 1957; rev. ed., 1974).

Anyone exploring the Vermont countryside will enjoy Charles W. Johnson, *The Nature of Vermont: Introduction and Guide to a New England Environment* (Hanover, N.H.: University Press of New England, 1980). The same is true of David Lowenthal, *George Perkins Marsh: Versatile Vermonter* (New York: Columbia University Press, 1958) because Marsh developed his pioneer ideas about ecology while observing man's relationship to his environment in his Vermont travels. Other biographies which show the Vermont influences in their subjects are George Dykhuizen, *The Life and Mind of John Dewey* (Carbondale and Edwardsville, Ill.: Southern Illinois University Press, 1973), and Donald R. McCoy, *Calvin Coolidge: The Quiet President* (New York: Macmillan Co., 1967), although Ishbel Ross, *Grace Coolidge and Her Era: The Story of a President's Wife* (New York: Dodd, Mead and Co., 1962), also does well. Coolidge is most fairly represented by Edward Connery Lathem in two books he has edited: *Meet Calvin Coolidge: The Man Behind the Myth* (Brattleboro, Vt.: Stephen Greene Press, 1960), and *Your Son, Calvin Coolidge: A Selection of Letters From Calvin Coolidge to His Father* (Montpelier: Vermont Historical Society, 1968).

Vermonters have spoken for themselves in memoirs they have written, and these are often sprightly as well as informative. For two political leaders who earned wide respect see Ralph E. Flanders, *Senator From Vermont* (Boston: Little, Brown, 1961), and George D. Aiken,

Aiken: Senate Diary, January 1972–January 1975 (Brattleboro, Vt.: Stephen Greene Press, 1976). An engaging autobiography focusing mainly on the 1920s and 1930s is by former Vermont Governor (1969–1973) Deane C. Davis, *Justice in the Mountains: Stories and Tales by a Vermont Country Lawyer* (Shelburne, Vt.: New England Press, 1980). Another is Marshall E. Dimock, *The Center of My World* (Taftsville, Vt.: Countryman Press, 1980), in which one of the great founders of public administration as a modern profession advocates a deliberate return to agrarian values in Vermont similar to what is espoused in Chapter 14 of this book as "fantasy and solace." The first woman in the United States to become lieutenant governor of a state, Consuelo Northrop Bailey, has recounted her life in *Leaves Before the Wind: The Autobiography of Vermont's Own Daughter* (Burlington, Vt.: George Little Press, 1976). Life in the Vermont Senate is entertainingly described by a professor of political science who was elected to represent Windsor County, Frank Smallwood, in *Free and Independent* (Brattleboro, Vt.: Stephen Greene Press, 1976). Robert L. Duffus has conveyed the essence of his Vermont upbringing in two books, *Williamstown Branch: Impersonal Memories of a Vermont Boyhood* (New York: W. W. Norton and Co., 1958), and *The Waterbury Record: More Vermont Memories* (New York: W. W. Norton and Co., 1959). Dorothy Canfield Fisher wrote warmly of her community in *Memories of Arlington, Vermont* (New York: Duell, Sloan and Pearce, 1957; originally published as *Memories of My Home Town* by the Arlington Historical Society, 1955), and Zephine Humphrey wrote a personalized version of her town's history in *The Story of Dorset* (Rutland, Vt.: Tuttle Company, 1924; reprint, 1971). Other first-person narratives which transmit the tenor of life in Vermont are Walter Needham, as told to Barrows Mussey, *A Book of Country Things* (Brattleboro, Vt.: Stephen Greene Press, 1965) about farm life in Guilford, and Russell H. Farnsworth, *Over Cram Hill* (Burlington, Vt.: Queen City Printers, 1967) about Braintree in central Vermont.

Some essayists are excellent in portraying Vermont as a place to live; my favorites are Edward Hoagland's pieces about Vermont's Northeast Kingdom in *The Courage of Turtles* (New York: Random House, 1970), *Walking the Dead Diamond River* (New York: Random House, 1973), and *Red Wolves and Black Bears* (New York: Random House, 1976), together with Harold F. Blaisdell, *The Philosophical*

Fisherman (Boston: Houghton Mifflin, 1969). Contemporary novelists have set their fiction in Vermont—most notably John C. Gardner in *October Light* (New York: Alfred A. Knopf, 1976), and Nicholas Delbanco in his trilogy *Possession* (New York: William Morrow and Co., 1977), *Sherbrookes* (Morrow, 1978), and *Stillness* (Morrow, 1980), which is admittedly set in a mansion like the Park-McCullough House in North Bennington (a public museum, open to visitors). North Bennington was also the home of Shirley Jackson, whose disquieting short story of New England town life, "The Lottery," first published in 1948 in the *New Yorker*, is still a shocker and can be found in *The Magic of Shirley Jackson*, ed. Stanley Edgar Hyman (New York: Farrar, Straus and Giroux, 1966).

The most recent study of Vermont's sociopolitical life is Neal R. Peirce, "Vermont: The Beloved State," pp. 233–284 in his book, *The New England States: People, Politics and Power in the Six New England States* (New York: W. W. Norton and Co., 1976). Basic data about Vermont is available in the *Vermont Year Book*, a directory published annually since 1930 by the National Survey of Chester, Vermont. The last general compilation of *Vermont Facts and Figures* was issued in 1975 by the Office of Statistical Coordination of the Vermont Department of Budget and Management, but Graham M. Bright, ed., *The Vermont Economic Almanac 1980* (Bellows Falls, Vt.: Vermont Business World) contains updated information. The *Vermont Legislative Directory and State Manual* is issued by the office of the Vermont secretary of state in the first year of each biennial session of the Vermont General Assembly. Guidebooks to all of Vermont are rapidly dated, but the two best at this writing are Madeleine Kunin and Marilyn Stout, *The Big Green Book, A Four-Season Guide to Vermont* (Barre, Mass.: Barre Publishing, 1976), and David DeLorme, *The Vermont Atlas and Gazetteer* (Yarmouth, Maine: David DeLorme and Co., 1978). Just issued is Daniel Robbins, *The Vermont Statehouse: A History and Guide* (Montpelier, Vt.: Statehouse Preservation Committee of the Vermont General Assembly and the Vermont Council on the Arts, 1980), a thorough historical narrative augmented by a catalogue of Statehouse paintings and artifacts.

Two quarterly magazines keep Vermonters informed about their past and present. *Vermont History*, the proceedings of the Vermont Historical Society, contains scholarly articles and reviews and is issued by the society in Montpelier. *Vermont Life* magazine, published by the Vermont Department of Development and Community Affairs, features photo-essays and other popular articles about the state.

Since Vermont is an experience to live as well as a state to live in, its spirit has been conveyed in poetry by several able writers of verse. William D. Mundell in *Hill Journey* (Brattleboro, Vt.: Stephen Greene Press, 1970) depicts the Vermont countryside around his native town of Newfane, and Walter Rice Hard conveys dry humor and the Vermont idiom in the character sketches he has collected in *Vermont Valley* (New York: Harcourt, Brace and Co., 1939), *A Mountain Township* (New York: Stephen Daye Press, 1963), and eight other books of verse. Not to be overlooked is Robert Frost, Vermont's poet laureate and America's most acclaimed poet of the twentieth century. *The Poetry of Robert Frost*, ed. Edward Connery Lathem (New York: Holt, Rinehart and Winston, 1969), deserves space on any Vermont bookshelf.

Index

Printed in the United States
85587LV00002B/25/A

9 780393 302233

Made in United States
North Haven, CT
24 November 2022